BUSINESS OR BLOOD

PETER EDWARDS & ANTONIO NICASO

BUSINESS

OR BLOOD

MAFIA BOSS
VITO RIZZUTO'S
LAST WAR

RANDOM HOUSE CANADA

PUBLISHED BY RANDOM HOUSE CANADA

www.penguinrandomhouse.ca

Random House Canada and colophon are registered trademarks.

Library and Archives Canada Cataloguing in Publication

Edwards, Peter, 1956–, author
Business or blood : Mafia boss Vito Rizzuto's last war /
Peter Edwards and Antonio Nicaso.

Includes bibliographical references and index.
Issued in print and electronic formats.

ISBN 978-0-345-81376-3
eBook ISBN 978-0-345-81378-7

1. Rizzuto, Vito. 2. Bonanno family. 3. Mafia—Québec
(Province)—Montréal—History. 4. Mafia—New York (State)—
New York—History. 5. Mafiosi—Canada—Biography.
I. Nicaso, Antonio, author II. Title.

HV6453.C32Q8 2015   364.1092   C2014-905934-5

Book design by Five Seventeen

Cover images: (police car) © Reuters / Christinne Muschi;
(mugshot) © Metropolitan Correctional Center, New York

Printed and bound in the United States of America

2 4 6 8 9 7 5 3 1

Penguin
Random House
RANDOM HOUSE CANADA

Contents

The hottest places in Hell are reserved for those who in time of moral crisis preserve their neutrality.

AMERICAN PRESIDENT JOHN F. KENNEDY,
interpreting Dante Alighieri's *The Divine Comedy*

Men of honour are neither evil nor schizophrenic. They are people like us. The tendency of the Western world . . . is to exorcise the evil by projecting on ethnic groups and behaviours that seem different from ours.

But if we are to effectively combat the Mafia, we should not turn it into a monster nor think it's an octopus or a cancer.

We must recognize that the Mafia resembles us.

JUDGE GIOVANNI FALCONE
Murdered by the Mafia in 1992

CHRONOLOGY

OCTOBER 16, 1828: Attorney General's office in village of Cattolica Eraclea in Agrigento province, Sicily, notes presence of criminal organization with more than one hundred members, bound by oath of secrecy that calls for death of anyone who even divulges its existence.

APRIL 12, 1901: Vito Rizzuto's grandfather, Vito Rizzuto Sr., born in Cattolica Eraclea to Nicola and Giuseppa Marra.

JUNE 23, 1921: Vito Rizzuto Sr. sentenced by a military tribunal to two months in jail for theft.

MARCH 9, 1923: Vito Rizzuto Sr. marries Maria Renda of his hometown. She's the daughter of Paolo Renda Sr. and Grazia Spinella.

FEBRUARY 18, 1924: Nicolò Rizzuto born to Vito Rizzuto Sr. and Maria Renda in Cattolica Eraclea.

DECEMBER 1924: Nicolò Rizzuto is just ten months old when his father departs for North America with a forged passport, leaving his young family behind.

AUGUST 1933: Vito Rizzuto Sr. buried in pauper's grave in Patterson, NY, after his body found hidden in a nearby swamp.

MARCH 20, 1945: Nicolò Rizzuto marries Libertina Manno, daughter of Antonino (Don Nino), Mafia boss of Cattolica Eraclea. Nicolò is twenty-one and Libertina eighteen.

APRIL 22, 1946: Vito Rizzuto baptized in Cattolica Eraclea. His paternal grandmother, Maria Renda, stands up for him in place of his late paternal grandfather, Vito Rizzuto Sr.

FEBRUARY 21, 1954: Vito Rizzuto arrives in Canada at Pier 21 in Halifax on his eighth birthday, with his parents Nicolò and Libertina, and his six-year-old sister, Maria. Nicolò lists his occupation as "farmer" and declares he has just thirty dollars. Vito doesn't speak English or French. He's to be educated in English, considered the language of business.

FEBRUARY 1956: Nicolò Rizzuto declares that he is a "cement contractor" as he buys a fourplex on Montreal's De Lorimier Avenue.

SEPTEMBER 11, 1964: Nicolò Rizzuto's father-in-law, Antonino (Don Nino) Manno, immigrates to Canada.

SUMMER 1967: Nicolò Rizzuto is now a partner in four construction-related firms and works on Expo 67 world's fair. His mob counterparts Paolo Violi and Vic (The Egg) Cotroni are also involved at Expo, supplying hot dogs made from tainted meat.

LATE 1972: Nicolò Rizzuto learns there are plans afoot to murder him that were put in motion by Violi. He relocates to Venezuela, getting farther from Violi and closer to South American drug-smuggling routes. The move also puts distance between him and a public inquiry into organized crime under way in Montreal. By this time, Nicolò Rizzuto is a partner in five construction-related companies in the city.

JANUARY 22, 1978: A shotgun blast kills Violi as he play cards with supposed friends at the Reggio Bar at 5880 Jean-Talon East in Montreal. His murder clears the way for Nicolò Rizzuto to return from Venezuela and assume the top spot in the Montreal underworld.

OCTOBER 1, 1980: Nicolò Rizzuto's father-in-law, Antonino Manno, dies of natural causes at the age of seventy-six. He had sponsored many immigrants to Canada. He is entombed in a mausoleum crypt in Montreal alongside his wife, Giuseppa Cammalleri Manno. Beside them is the body of their daughter Giuseppina Manno, younger sister of Libertina and Domenico Manno.

MAY 5, 1981: Nicolò Rizzuto's son, Vito, is among the gunmen slaughtering three mob captains in a Brooklyn social club. The crime secures Vito's status in the Bonanno crime family of New York, which considers Montreal its turf. The slain captains were disloyal to acting family boss Joe (Big Joey) Massino.

AUGUST 2, 1988: Nicolò Rizzuto and four others arrested and imprisoned for cocaine trafficking in Venezuela.

MAY 23, 1993: Nicolò Rizzuto greeted by thirty friends and family as he returns to Montreal, a few months after he is finally freed from Venezuelan prison.

OCTOBER 24, 1994: Québécois mobster Raynald Desjardins hit with a fifteen-year prison term for massive marijuana-smuggling conspiracy. While boss Vito Rizzuto is strongly suspected in the operation, Desjardins takes the fall.

MARCH 1999: Vito Rizzuto's friend George (George from Canada) Sciascia murdered in New York City by Gambino crime family, with no reaction from Vito's bosses in Bonanno crime family.

JANUARY 19, 2004: Montreal strip club owner and former Rizzuto friend Paolo Gervasi shot dead. He was a mentor for several local mobsters, including Giuseppe (Ponytail) De Vito, who was once also considered part of the Rizzuto group.

JANUARY 20, 2004: Vito Rizzuto arrested at his Montreal mansion and told he faces deportation to New York in relation to the 1981 Three Captains Murders. He immediately begins prolonged legal battle to stay in Canada.

APRIL 21, 2004: Louise Russo, a forty-five-year-old mother of three, paralyzed by a stray bullet while standing at the counter of a California Sandwiches shop in North York, Toronto. The intended target of the hit team, mobster Michele (Mike, The American) Modica, escapes unscathed. Also in the sandwich shop and uninjured were Michael Marrese, convicted of mortgage fraud, Modica's bodyguard Andrea Fortunato Carbone and mobster Pietro Scaduto. Modica, Scaduto and Carbone are later deported from Canada to Sicily.

JUNE 2, 2004: Raynald Desjardins freed from prison on statutory release.

JULY 30, 2004: Joseph Massino of the Bonanno crime family quietly becomes first New York mob boss ever to work as a police agent. His switch immediately follows his conviction for murdering George Sciascia of Montreal. Massino secretly begins wearing a listening device while in custody.

FEBRUARY 11, 2005: Italian police allege Vito Rizzuto planned to launder money in a multi-billion-dollar project to build a bridge across the Strait of Messina, connecting Sicily to mainland Italy. Italian authorities accuse Vito of engineering the plot while in custody, fighting extradition to the United States.

MARCH 10, 2005: Rizzuto family enforcer Mike Lapolla shot dead in upscale Moomba nightclub in bar fight with Thierry Beaubrun of the 67's street gang. Beaubrun shot dead trying to flee.

2005: Brothers Salvatore, Giuseppe and Antonio Coluccio quietly arrive in Woodbridge, north of Toronto. They're immediately treated with great respect by the region's 'Ndrangheta, or Calabrian Mafia.

MAY 25, 2005: Frank Martorana, a luxury car dealer connected to Vito and Nicolò Rizzuto, abducted from barbershop by four men. He is released after several days but refuses to co-operate with police.

AUGUST 11, 2005: Giovanni (Johnny) Bertolo, a construction union representative close to Raynald Desjardins, shot dead while leaving a Montreal gym.

AUGUST 17, 2006: Vito Rizzuto finally extradited to USA to answer charges for Three Captains Murders.

AUGUST 30, 2006: Rizzuto soldier Domenico Macri killed in Montreal. Within weeks, Rizzuto crime family members begin to buy armoured cars and underboss Francesco (*Compare* Frank) Arcadi takes an extended European vacation.

NOVEMBER 22, 2006: Police hit Rizzuto crime family with eighty-two arrests at culmination of Project Colisée. Top-level members taken into custody include Paolo Renda, Rocco (Sauce) Sollecito, Lorenzo (Skunk) Giordano, Francesco Arcadi and Nicolò Rizzuto

AUGUST 15, 2007: Six men murdered in German town of Duisburg in latest stage of 'Ndrangheta feud that began in Calabria two decades earlier over an egg-throwing incident. The murders put an international spotlight on the 'Ndrangheta, which is particularly strong in Greater Toronto Area (GTA) and dominates the European cocaine market. Despite its low profile, the 'Ndrangheta is now considered Italy's most dangerous Mafia group.

AUGUST 2008: Giuseppe Coluccio arrested in GTA. Italian authorities say he heads powerful 'Ndrangheta family.

AUGUST 11, 2008: Antonio (Tony) Magi, a former associate of Vito Rizzuto's son Nicolò (The Ritz) Rizzuto Jr., survives murder attempt.

JANUARY 16, 2009: Gunman murders Sam Fasulo, a close associate of imprisoned Rizzuto leader Francesco Arcadi.

APRIL 2009: Salvatore (Sal the Ironworker, The Bambino Boss) Montagna, head of the Bonanno crime family, quietly moves from New York to Quebec.

MAY 3, 2009: Former GTA resident Salvatore Coluccio arrested in a bunker in Calabrian town of Roccella Ionica, on the Ionian Sea. Italian authorities say he's one of country's thirty most dangerous fugitives.

AUGUST 21, 2009: Rizzuto close family friend Federico (Freddy) Del Peschio shot dead.

SEPTEMBER 17, 2009: Member of powerful Commisso crime family from GTA flies to Montreal and meets with Vittorio (Victor) Mirarchi, the son of a deceased underworld figure.

OCTOBER 7, 2009: Meeting held in Woodbridge, Ontario, home for members of *camera di controllo*, ruling body of the GTA 'Ndrangheta.

DECEMBER 15, 2009: Antonio Coluccio of Richmond Hill, Ontario, told he is inadmissible to live in Canada because close family members are considered members of the 'Ndrangheta.

DECEMBER 28, 2009: Nicolò Rizzuto Jr., forty-two, shot to death in broad daylight. His murder is considered Montreal's most audacious gangland slaying since the killing of Paolo Violi thirty-one years earlier.

MARCH 19, 2010: Street-gang leader Ducarme Joseph escapes murder attempt in Old Montreal. He had been suspected in murder of Nicolò Rizzuto Jr. Joseph's bodyguard, Peter Christopoulos, killed. Move comes as street gangs push for old Rizzuto turf in wake of Vito's incarceration.

MAY 19, 2010: Rizzuto family *consigliere* Paolo Renda abducted near his home on Vito Rizzuto's street and never seen again.

JUNE 29, 2010: Long-time Rizzuto family loyalist Agostino (The Seigneur of Saint-Léonard) Cuntrera and his bodyguard, Liborio Sciascia, murdered at midday walking from Cuntrera's Montreal business. At the time, Cuntrera is in charge of Rizzuto family's day-to-day operations.

JULY 13, 2010: Italian authorities charge 304 people—including some GTA residents—at culmination of two-year probe code-named Operazione Crimine, which targeted 'Ndrangheta. Organization begins shuffling GTA leadership in response.

NOVEMBER 2010: Antonio Coluccio returns to North America from United Kingdom. He travels first to New York City, then Niagara Falls, NY. Canadians travel to United States to see him, including a former moneyman for Vito Rizzuto.

NOVEMBER 10, 2010: Nicolò Rizzuto murdered in his home by sniper in front of his wife and daughter. The killing bears startling similarities to murder of Rizzuto enemy Rocco Violi three decades earlier.

FEBRUARY 1, 2011: Stockpile of weapons seized in Montreal warehouse tied to Vito Rizzuto, who remains in Colorado prison.

APRIL 13, 2011: Bonanno crime family boss Joseph Massino appears in Federal District Court in Brooklyn, becomes first boss of a New York crime family to take witness stand against a former confederate.

SEPTEMBER 16, 2011: Former Vito Rizzuto ally Raynald Desjardins survives murder attempt outside his home. Would-be assassin escapes on a Sea-Doo.

OCTOBER 4, 2011: Police in Reggio Calabria, Italy, seize 'Ndrangheta property and business assets. The seizure comes amidst an ongoing offensive against the Aquino clan. The clan retains deep roots in the GTA.

OCTOBER 24, 2011: Vito Rizzuto's neighbour turned enemy Salvatore (Larry) Lo Presti, forty, shot dead when he steps out to smoke a cigarette on balcony of his Saint-Laurent condo.

NOVEMBER 24, 2011: Salvatore Montagna, head of the Bonanno crime family of New York, murdered near Montreal.

DECEMBER 13, 2011: Vito Rizzuto's ally turned rival Antonio (Tony Suzuki) Pietrantonio shot but not killed.

DECEMBER 20, 2011: Raynald Desjardins and wealthy café owner Vittorio (Victor) Mirarchi among six men arrested for Montagna murder.

MARCH 1, 2012: Former Vito Rizzuto ally Giuseppe (Closure) Colapelle murdered. He had spied on Montagna and followers for Raynald Desjardins and was considered close to Giuseppe (Ponytail) De Vito.

MAY 4, 2012: Giuseppe (Joe) Renda from the Montagna camp disappears after going to a business meeting. He had once been close to Vito Rizzuto.

SEPTEMBER 2012: Charbonneau Commission begins hearings on corruption in Quebec construction industry.

OCTOBER 5, 2012: Vito Rizzuto released from Colorado prison. Flies to Toronto and immediately drops out of public view.

NOVEMBER 5, 2012: Giuseppe (Joe) Di Maulo, a key figure in consortium that challenged Rizzuto's dominance in Montreal during Vito's imprisonment, murdered outside his home. Di Maulo was Desjardins's brother-in-law.

NOVEMBER 17, 2012: Mohamed Awada killed. He had earlier been implicated in kidnapping of Rizzuto soldier.

DECEMBER 8, 2012: Former Rizzuto ally Emilio Cordeleone killed in Montreal.

JANUARY 22, 2013: Gaétan Gosselin murdered outside his Montreal home. Gosselin was involved in construction industry and close to Raynald Desjardins.

JANUARY 31, 2013: Anti-Vito mobster Vincenzo Scuderi murdered outside his home in Montreal.

FEBRUARY 1, 2013: Anti-Vito residential building contractor Tonino (Tony) Callocchia survives gun attack in Montreal.

MAY 8, 2013: Burned, bullet-riddled bodies of former Toronto residents Juan Ramon (Joe Bravo) Fernandez and Fernando Pimentel found in Casteldaccia, just outside Sicilian capital of Palermo. Fernandez had tried to sit on the fence and not take sides in Rizzuto–Desjardins war.

JULY 8, 2013: Giuseppe (Ponytail) De Vito found dead of cyanide poisoning in his cell in Donnacona, Quebec, penitentiary. Less than a month before his death, his wife was convicted of murdering their two daughters while he was on the run from police.

JULY 10, 2013: Big Joey Massino, Vito Rizzuto's former boss in the Bonanno crime family, enters witness protection program after lengthy crime career that included taking part in at least eight murders.

JULY 12, 2013: Toronto hit man Salvatore (Sam) Calautti shot dead with his long-time associate James Tusek while leaving stag for bookie in Woodbridge, Ontario. Calautti had been suspect in murders of at least five men, including Nicolò Rizzuto and Vito Rizzuto's Toronto lieutenant Gaetano (Guy) Panepinto.

SEPTEMBER 2013: Vito Rizzuto golfs in Dominican Republic, where his associates include London, Ontario, Hells Angel with extensive Internet gambling interests.

NOVEMBER 10, 2013: Former Vito ally Moreno Gallo murdered in Acapulco pizzeria, on three-year anniversary of Nicolò Rizzuto's murder.

DECEMBER 18, 2013: Roger Valiquette shot dead in broad daylight in Laval. He had once been close to Joe Di Maulo and Moreno Gallo. At time of his death, he was working as mortgage broker and was close to Tonino (Tony) Callocchia.

DECEMBER 23, 2013: Vito Rizzuto dies of apparent natural causes in Montreal hospital. A quick decision is made not to hold an autopsy.

JANUARY, FEBRUARY, MARCH 2014: Middle-aged man with no criminal record taken to Vito Rizzuto's old Mafia haunts by long-time member. Newcomer rumoured to be assuming top spot in Rizzuto crime family.

APRIL 24, 2014: Carmine Verduci of the GTA 'Ndrangheta shot dead in mid-afternoon outside a café in Vaughan, Ontario.

AUGUST 1, 2014: Bullet-riddled body of gang leader Ducarme Joseph found dead in middle of street in the Saint-Michel neighbourhood of Montreal.

To Barbara, Sarah and James
P.E.

To Antonella, Massimo and Emily
A.N.

ONTARIO-QUEBEC-NEW YORK: VITO'S TURF

ONTARIO

Barrie

Kings

York Region
King City
Richmond Hill
Vaughan
Woodbridge
Brampton **Toronto**
Mississauga

Lake Ontario

Hamilton

NEW YORK

Niagara Falls
Buffalo

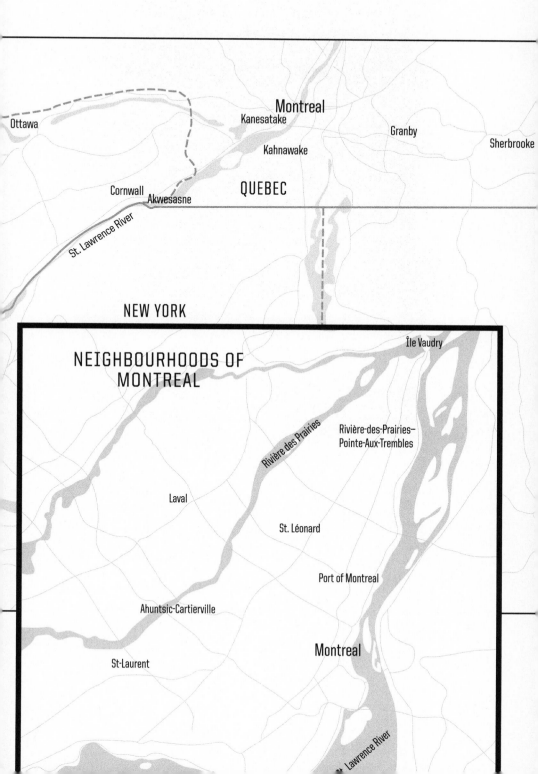

Ottawa

Kanesatake

Montreal

Kahnawake

Granby

Sherbrooke

Cornwall
Akwesasne

QUEBEC

St. Lawrence River

NEW YORK

Île Vaudry

**NEIGHBOURHOODS OF
MONTREAL**

Rivière des Prairies

Rivière-des-Prairies–
Pointe-Aux-Trembles

Laval

St. Léonard

Port of Montreal

Ahuntsic-Cartierville

Montreal

St-Laurent

St. Lawrence River

INTRODUCTION

"I entered along the deep and savage road."

The Divine Comedy, Inferno, Canto II
DANTE ALIGHIERI

T his is the story of Vito Rizzuto, the most powerful leader in the history of the Canadian Mafia, during the period of his life that would define his legacy. His father and his eldest son were slain while he sat helplessly in an American prison, and their deaths cried out for revenge. His myriad businesses—both criminal and outwardly legitimate—were under siege. A stampede of gangsters, politicians, crooked cops and business people were deserting or exposing him. A lifetime of schooling in the Mafia hardly seemed enough training for the challenges awaiting Vito when he finally walked free in October 2012.

By telling the story of this crucial time at the end of one man's life, we aim to give an account of the Mafia that goes beyond just one corner of one country. During the writing of this book, central characters kept falling dead. There were gangland hits in Acapulco, Mexico, and Casteldaccia, Sicily, as well as several assassinations in and around Montreal and Toronto, some with serious repercussions for the old Mafia families of New York City.

The violence isn't surprising. It was thanks to their refinement of violence and intimidation that Mafia groups first became wealthy in southern Italy and then moved on to the rich economies of North America; we will tell a few stories from this era in the chapters to

1

come. And regardless of where people are, when they stand in the way of the Mafia's profit-taking, there's a good chance murder will follow—much is shadowy in the Mafia's world, but that can be stated as an absolute truth. Another bankable truth is that the ultimate goal of the Mafia is not money but power. Money is simply a tried-and-true way of attaining the power and influence that makes a family respected for generations.

Not only do members of our cast die in several corners of the world, they come from many corners of it as well. In fact, the diversity of characters in the pages that follow offers proof that the Mafia is not a backward-minded, genetic or racial problem strictly related to Italians. Characters in this book who are equally powerful within the global and Canadian underworld of organized crime—in a few cases, even within the traditional Italian Mafia itself—speak half a dozen languages and come from even more cultures. Defining this criminal world as simply an Italian problem isn't just bigoted, it's also inadequate. That kind of narrow thinking is largely responsible for the delay with which Canada and other countries have come to understand the essence of the Mafia and its relationship with power.

Vito Rizzuto was made to order for his role as a paragon of Mafia values. In a time of financial globalization, he personified the character of the global criminal, possessing an innate understanding of the nexus between the underworld and the world of state and mainstream economic power. He had only completed the ninth grade when he left school to work for his father, but Vito carried himself like an Ivy League–schooled CEO (although his expensive tailored suits were sometimes a little shinier than might be found on Toronto's Bay Street). He could be polite and affable and speak knowledgeably and calmly about law, business or politics, in English, Italian, Spanish and French. This impressive ability to communicate helps explain why his story is at the heart of Mafia expansion at the turn of this century.

Vito's preferred out-of-office activity was golf, the international pastime of business. Mafiosi like Vito may be specialists in violence, but they are also experts in social and economic relationships. There's a joke that when the economy got tough for Vito and his father, they laid off judges, politicians and CEOs. He enjoyed reading about great civilizations such as ancient Greece and the Roman Empire. Of particular interest was the life of Julius Caesar, who, like Vito, was born into power, expanded his territory beyond the shores of his homeland, and endured a time of exile, banishment and, ultimately, betrayal. When Caesar was gone, the republic collapsed. Well steeped in the lessons of history, Vito had no plans to step aside or let his rivals sink a dagger into his back.

As we worked on this book, Quebec's Charbonneau Commission into corruption within that province's construction industry was diving deep into the industry's particularly murky waters, underscoring in daily headlines how Mafia violence is inextricably linked to political and economic interests. We were nearly finished writing when Vito Rizzuto died in circumstances that were never made clear. Many people predicted his death, of course, but few thought it would be the result of natural causes, as was quickly and widely accepted by authorities and the press.

News of Vito's sudden passing brought relief in some powerful circles, criminal and otherwise. By the time of his death, he had actually become bad for business. Revenge was more important to him than making money, and every day brought news of fresh bloodletting among men known to be his enemies. Exactly what killed Vito himself will most likely remain a mystery, but even in his absence the Mafia tradition he embodied will thrive and evolve—growth that Vito's last war may have ensured will continue for another generation to come.

CHAPTER 1

Blow to the heart

Vito Rizzuto was agonizingly far from his Montreal home when he learned of the murder. Violent death was a fact of life in his world, no more out of place than the slaughter of chickens and cattle on a farm. Murder had been necessary for Vito's family to rise to power in Montreal's underworld, and murder helped them expand that power and make money beyond his ancestors' wildest dreams. And murder—three, in fact, that Vito had a hand in twenty-eight years earlier—explained why he was stuck in a prison cell in the dusty former cowboy boom town of Florence, Colorado, about an hour and a half south of Denver. That said, no murder that the mobster had ordered, witnessed or committed in his sixty-three years of life readied him for what the prison chaplain had come to tell him: this time, the bullet-scarred corpse was that of his own eldest child, Nick Rizzuto Jr.

A prison guard that day—three days after Christmas 2009—witnessed something that people who knew Vito well could not imagine: the face of Canada's top Mafia don contorted with pain and shock. Life as a perpetrator didn't mean Vito knew how to assume the role of a victim. Blindsided by the news, he didn't cry. No one ever talked of Vito crying. But Vito was stunned and hurt and desperately needed to plan his next move. Vito always had a next move.

First, he should go to the funeral. That meant he needed to approach authorities— the same people he had spent his life deceiving—and ask for permission to leave the prison and cross the border. The prospect of asking anyone's permission for anything served as another reminder of how far he had fallen.

If permission were granted, Vito would have to travel with guards and he would most likely be handcuffed. Maybe he would be required to wear a bulletproof vest, too, like he had worn during his extradition to the United States. He would also have to pay his own travel costs, but that was no problem. Vito could afford to buy a fleet of jet craft and hire an army of guards.

In the days following the news, Vito phoned his wife, Giovanna, every chance he could. Many times, Vito had come home in the early hours of the morning smelling of wine and the perfume of a mistress, but there was never talk of their marriage ending. They had been man and wife for forty-three years, and Nick Jr. had shared in that life together for forty-two of them. Giovanna knew life was often hard, even for the powerful; she was the daughter of Leonardo Cammalleri, himself a Mafia killer who emigrated from the Sicilian province of Agrigento to Canada, in part to evade murder charges. But with Vito behind bars, Giovanna needed sedatives to sleep at night. And now things had got worse, as she undertook the worst task a mother can imagine: preparing the funeral of her child.

Vito also spoke with his mother, Libertina, whom some thought was the true guiding force in the family. In times of enormous stress and emotion, Zia (Aunt) Libertina betrayed the emotion of a sphinx. Vito's father, Nicolò (Zio Cola, "Uncle Nick") Rizzuto Sr., had moved up considerably in their world when he gained her hand in marriage over sixty years earlier. In fact, former Sicilian Mafia boss Tommaso Buscetta suspected that Nicolò was admitted to the Mafia out of respect for Libertina's father, Antonino (Don Nino) Manno, one of those old Sicilian Mafia dons who managed to appeared all-powerful and yet humble at the same time.

Zia Libertina's name translated roughly to "Liberty," and she certainly felt free to speak her mind. She and Nicolò raised Vito to be mindful that he was their only son and carried their expectations upon him, wherever he went and as long as he lived. Vito grew up in a culture where a dutiful son takes every action to salve his mother's pain, even if it means breaking the most serious laws in the Criminal Code. In Vito's birthplace of Sicily, men might be the ones with their fingers on the triggers, but often it was the women who dictated the rhythms of a war, calling out for revenge for the deaths of their boys, husbands, fathers and brothers. There is no greater blow to a mob boss's dignity than to sit at dinner and hear the family matriarch moan, "Noi mangiamo al tavolo e mio figlio mangia terra" ("We eat at the table and my son eats the earth").

Vito also spoke repeatedly on the prison phone with his sister, Maria, and his two surviving children, both of whom worked as lawyers. Vito told each of them that he wanted to convince the warden to let him attend Nick Jr.'s funeral. They all came back strongly against this. It would be undignified, even dangerous. His presence would attract more media coverage. He would have to wear handcuffs. "There will be a guard with you."

Helplessness was a fresh emotion for Vito. Although for decades he had been on the radar of more police projects than anyone could remember, this was his first prison stint. Vito was generally the one causing the tears and the funerals, and his underlings were the ones who got locked up. Just a few years before, the only thing in Montreal it seemed he didn't control was the city's nasty winters, and he routinely fled those for warm Caribbean climes, where he mingled business with pleasure on manicured golf courses with city bureaucrats, union and business bosses, Hells Angels and other Mafiosi. Vito was gliding through life at the top of a multi-million-dollar international empire of large-scale construction fraud, drug trafficking, extortion, bribery, stock manipulation, loansharking and money laundering.

For all of Vito's life, the ways of the underworld had been the natural order of things for him, with its cycles of murder and revenge. There had never been room for pacifists at the top level of the underworld, and no one doubted that Vito intended to please his mother and return to the upper echelon of what Montrealers called the *milieu*. Had he been free, an attack on Nick Jr. would have been unthinkable.

Vito's father was a product of west Sicily, but he was himself a Canadian hybrid. A large part of his skill was the ability to pull together disparate North American groups who otherwise might have ignored or plotted against each other, such as rival Haitian street gangs, Hispanic cocaine traffickers, Montreal's Irish West End Gang, rival bikers in the Hells Angels and Rock Machine, and factions from the Sicilian Mafia, Calabrian-based 'Ndrangheta and American La Cosa Nostra. What Vito created was something wholly modern and New World and businesslike: a consortium. Under his leadership these criminal factions could pursue shared business interests, with Vito convincing them that there was enough cake for everyone to eat.

Just a few weeks before his January 2004 arrest, Vito had described his role in this *milieu* of multicultural criminals to Michel Auger, Quebec's best-known crime reporter: "I'm a mediator. People come to me to solve disputes because they believe in me. They have respect in me." That description was wholly true, although deliberately lacking in details. Vito preferred to speak with his intense brown eyes, expressive face and loaded body language. His very few words, such as what he uttered to Auger, were as accurate as a bullet from one of his hit men. Preferring to see himself as a gentleman and a man of destiny, he didn't need to raise his voice or lose his temper to make life-altering— or -ending—decisions. His demeanour was that of someone born into royalty, playing out a role that had been determined long before his conception. It was as though he were from the House of Rizzuto, not the Rizzuto crime family. And if survival for himself and his house meant killing others, then that was his destiny too.

Vito's conversation with Auger took place in a hallway of a Montreal courtroom, not long after a Canadian government lawyer described him as "the godfather of the Italian Mafia in Montreal" in a court document. Vito scoffed at such a pronouncement, telling Paul Cherry of the Montreal *Gazette* that he played a more folksy role: "I'm the jack of all trades."

Whatever his title, it had been an honour in the *milieu* to kill for Vito. The ultimate honour, however, was to share a round of golf with him at top country clubs in Montreal, Toronto and the Caribbean. Inside the prison doors at Florence, however, confined to a cell the size of one of his old walk-in closets, Vito was just US Federal Inmate 04307-748, stripped of all his personal possessions save his wedding ring. Visits were restricted to office hours between Monday and Friday, but it didn't matter much: so far from Montreal, no one was coming to see him.

The power Vito had wielded in Montreal meant virtually nothing to his fellow prisoners. Other inmates in Florence had included American domestic terrorist Timothy McVeigh, before his execution by lethal injection, and numerous 9/11 al Qaeda terrorists, as well as a nasty grab bag of white supremacists and Mexican-American gangs, such as the Nuestra Familia street gang. McVeigh and some of the prisoners within the concrete and steel walls of the neighbouring supermax facility were guilty of attempts to change American history in a profoundly bad way. For all the blood on his hands, Vito had taken pains to confine his violence to the underworld. When one gangster pulled the trigger on another in Vito's *milieu*, police routinely joked it was urban renewal or the street equivalent of a self-cleaning oven.

If some of Vito's fellow prisoners knew anything about him, they had most likely heard that he was a triggerman back in 1981 in the Brooklyn murders of three upstart captains of the Bonanno crime family. That event was hard to ignore, since it had been re-enacted, with dramatic embellishments, in *Donnie Brasco*, the blockbuster 1997 movie starring Johnny Depp and Al Pacino.

Other inmates in Florence certainly would have paid more attention to Vito had they known of his lynchpin role in the importation of narcotics into North America. Getting close to Vito meant the opportunity to quickly become a millionaire. The Port of Montreal is one of a few vital entry points for drugs bound for the United States, and Vito had more control over it than anyone else. Once the drugs reached Montreal, Vito's people had to worry about little more than speed limits as they drove the narcotics through back roads and into New York City, the world's top market for cocaine.

Another key entry point for American-bound drugs is the border at Ciudad Juárez, Mexico, which sits across the Rio Grande from El Paso, Texas. Vito's rivals in the Calabrian 'Ndrangheta worked with Mexican cartels to control Juárez, considered one of the world's most dangerous cities. El Paso sits on Highway 10, which connects the desert city directly to the continent's major drug markets. Most enticing are the profits awaiting in New York City, just 3,315 kilometres (2,060 miles) of open road ahead. Despite the southern competition for Vito, leaders at both ends of the continent were still growing rich.

But none of the old competition mattered after Vito got the news about his son. Aside from trying to arrange his trip to the funeral, there was little Vito could do. How could he soothe his family from so far away? And how could his family comfort him? He lusted for revenge, but he didn't even know whom to blame. Was his family under attack from outlaw bikers, the Irish or Italian Mafias, Haitian street gangs, francophone criminals or some combination of the above?

For the time being, all Vito could do was grieve alone in his cell, rising before 6 a.m. for breakfast, building wooden office chairs for $1.10 per hour and plotting against an invisible enemy.

CHAPTER 2

Nick Jr. and Nicolò

L ife should have been easier for Nick Jr. than for his father or name-sake grandfather, if running an empire based on lies and murder can ever be called easy. Nick Jr. had the same probing eyes, aquiline nose and slicked-back Gordon Gekko hair as his father, and probably one day he would have become stooped and bald, like his grandfather, who sometimes resembled a grinning turtle. Nick Jr. was squatter and more powerfully built than his father, with a neck like a boxer and the occasional flash of a don't-fuck-with-me expression. He also had enough of a temper to be kicked out of his private school as a teenager. Friends had nicknamed him "The Ritz," lightly mocking his cushy upbringing and his to-the-manor-born confidence.

Nick Jr. had some troubles with drinking and driving, a problem he shared with his father and grandfather. When he was twenty-two years old, he blew almost double the legal limit on a Breathalyzer test. He walked when the police officer who performed the test conveniently didn't appear in court. He also walked from an assault charge when a witness's memory suddenly went bad. Despite those strokes of legal good fortune, Nick Jr. was twice convicted of drinking and driving. The first time cost him his licence for six months and a laughable $600 fine. In October 1990, shortly after he got his licence back, he blew more than twice the legal limit after a police officer spotted his grey Porsche drifting across Highway 15 in Laval just before 3 a.m. That cost him his licence for a year and got him slapped with an $800 fine, plus $151 in court costs.

That was the extent of the criminal record accrued for Nick Rizzuto Jr., heir apparent to the largest criminal empire in his country's history. His record didn't account for all the illegal activity he'd been up to, but Nick Jr. clearly had not been involved in real down-and-dirty mob activity such as debt collection or drug distribution. And many doubted he would ever have fully matured into his father's or grandfather's role. Perhaps he wouldn't have needed to. He could have made a nice living simply by investing family money into legitimate and safer things than the drug trade. And yet someone had seen the need to kill him. There were always reasons to kill in the *milieu* . . . but why bother with Nick Jr., unless getting rid of Nick Jr. was never really the point?

When he learned of his son's murder, Vito may have thought back to Nick Jr.'s wedding day on June 3, 1995. The family rejoiced as Nick Jr. swore his vows to Eleonora Ragusa, daughter of Emanuele Ragusa of Saint-Léonard, one of Vito's trusted long-time associates. The history of the Mafia is a history of relationships, and that day RCMP and Laval police photographers got fresh shots of the interactions of mob invitees, including Rizzuto family street boss Francesco (*Compare* Frank) Arcadi and Agostino (The Seigneur of Saint-Léonard) Cuntrera. Also among the six hundred guests at the wedding were Vito's bull-necked uncle Domenic Manno, a serious criminal in his own right; millionaire drug trafficker Oreste Pagano, who attended with Alfonso Caruana and his wife; and Salvatore Scotto, a representative of the Bono Mafia family of Sicily. Pagano later told authorities that Caruana pointed out to him representatives of the major underworld families of New York in attendance, as well as interesting guests from Italy. "Caruana told me . . . that the same Scotto was a fugitive wanted for the murder of a policeman and his pregnant wife."

On that happy day, Nick Jr. married down, but just slightly. In the Canadian underworld there was really no one for a Rizzuto to marry up to. Ragusa, the proud father of the bride, looked like a humble shopkeeper, which is exactly what he once told the parole board he wanted to be. At a parole hearing, a prison psychologist described him as "a burn-out in a sense that the *milieu* and activities don't attract you anymore."

Like many of those who attended the wedding, when pressed to explain his income, Ragusa had told authorities he ran a construction firm. In reality, Ragusa was a top lieutenant in Vito's world. Crusading Italian anti-Mafia judge Giovanni Falcone had called him a major player in Canadian organized crime, before Falcone was murdered by a Mafia hit man.

Ragusa had been a fixture on the Montreal Mafia scene since the early 1970s, when he worked under Vic (The Egg) Cotroni and Paolo Violi. On the day of Nick Jr.'s wedding, Ragusa was on bail awaiting trial for a massive cocaine-trafficking plot, for which he would later receive a twelve-year sentence. He complained at a 2003 parole hearing that there was something stressful and anti-family about his release conditions. How could he attend family functions, such as the christening of his grandson, when he was barred from associating with known criminals?

At the same hearing, Ragusa portrayed the Mafia as something as benign as the Shriners: "In Italy, I think the Mafia is an organization, a good organization. Anyone can call themselves *mafioso*. It comes from Sicily. Here are farmers (*paesani*) came from the same village, maybe fifteen to twenty people." That sounded far softer than his tone on a police wiretap, when he was trying to retrieve an associate who had been kidnapped by Colombian cocaine traffickers for non-payment of a bill. In that tape, Ragusa betrayed a combination of fear and awe of what would befall him if he ever angered his own organization: "The Mafia, you see, Earth will never be large enough to hide me."

Although Nick Jr. wasn't a major power like the two Rizzuto men before him or their closer associates, he still moved in dangerous circles. Police watched him share a table in a Montreal restaurant late in the summer of 1999 with Louis (Melou) Roy, not long before the founding member of Montreal's Hells Angels Nomads chapter mysteriously disappeared. Police looked on from a distance when Nick Jr. met on

April 10, 2004, with Maurice (Mom) Boucher—another Hells Angel Nomad—before Boucher went to prison for ordering the murder of two jail guards. Police also noted with interest that Nick Jr. had run a mob mini-casino on the sixth floor of an office building on Montreal's Jean-Talon Street East, outfitting it with tinted windows and security cameras. The casino had lasted a year before police shut it down in November 2006. Of more interest to those now concerned with solving his murder were Nick Jr.'s connections in the construction industry, which ran the gambit from Haitian street-gang debt collectors to bureaucrats and politicians at City Hall.

Nick Jr. did have energy and he did try. He was also absolutely loyal to his family, and they were the same way towards him. Such trust was rare and went a long way. After the arrest of his father in 2004, Nick Jr. did his best to fill the void. He regularly met his father's old contacts and stepped up Vito's investment in condo development. He was also in the illegal gaming machine business, sharing the space set aside for the machines in bars, cafés, stores and restaurants with others in the underworld. Extortion was another avenue for cash, and one developer said that Nick Jr. unsuccessfully tried to get him to pay $40,000 for the privilege of working on renovations at Montreal's City Hall. It wasn't groundbreaking stuff, but it was a step above his usual activities. Nick Jr. only had to maintain the family business for a few years, until his father was out of prison again. He didn't have to expand the empire, just help keep it from being ripped away.

Business aside, Nick Jr. gave Vito two grandchildren. Something magical happened whenever Vito was around them. He didn't look weighed down by expectations. He didn't look as if he was being watched and probed and judged. There were zero expectations on Vito the grandfather, and no need for him to play the boss or dutiful son. The mask was removed, and what was left was undiluted joy. Those grandchildren would be feeling pure anguish now and needing their *nonno*.

Nick Jr.'s funeral was scheduled for Saturday, January 2. As Vito's family prepared for it, it was natural to wonder if this was the opening phase of an offensive against his family and their allies. His surviving son and daughter seemed unlikely targets. Vito appeared happy that the two lawyers had stayed out of the family business. Still, a prolonged war against Vito threatened not just grubby drug dealers and the mobsters who directed them, but also many ambitious business people and politicians. How could he not fear for the rest of his family too?

As a mortician prepared Nick Jr. for burial in the Rizzuto-run Complexe Funéraire Loreto in the Montreal neighbourhood of Saint-Léonard, Vito's family kept telling him over the phone that he should rethink his plans to attend. Even if he did come for the funeral, he would have no time alone with his father. Both would have police escorts, as Nicolò was on probation after being scooped up in Montreal in 2006 on gangsterism-related charges. Nicolò's arrest was the centrepiece of the massive RCMP-led Project Colisée—the reference to the crumbling Coliseum of Rome being a little jab at Old Nick himself. One of the eighty-five-year-old's tight parole conditions was that he must refrain from associating with criminals. On this saddest of days, father and son would need special permission just to talk.

The church ceremony threatened to become a media circus, with photographers vying for the best angles and reporters trying to sneak into the ceremony posing as mourners. Vito's nature made it torturous for him to do nothing, but his family wouldn't relent: he was Vito Rizzuto, not some zoo animal to be gawked at and photographed by strangers. Finally Vito acquiesced. He would not serve up a spectacle for the public. He didn't need the indignity of being photographed in handcuffs. He would stay in his cell and suffer the day alone.

Vito could deal with his enemies later, one by one, on his own terms.

CHAPTER 3

El Padrino

Nicolò Rizzuto was a semi-literate, one-time South American chicken farmer who had managed to create a government within a government in Montreal. He had pulled himself up from a relatively humble birth in Sicily through hard scheming, contacts, travel, innovation, good fortune, risk taking, marriage and murder. Despite running several construction-related companies, and even more politicians and police officers, Nicolò retained a certain common touch. When he collected money in a backroom of the Consenza Social Club in Saint-Léonard, he sometimes tucked a wad of cash into a sock for safekeeping. There, between a cheese shop and a tanning salon, mobsters sipped espresso, settled disputes, and accepted tributes from associates in the underworld and the world of ostensibly legitimate business. Nicknamed "the house of problems" by his son-in-law, Paolo Renda, "the Cos" sat in a nondescript strip mall at 4891 Jarry Street East, a few minutes from the site of the late Paolo Violi's old Reggio Bar.

Even when things got rough, Nicolò maintained his ability to wink at the world, as though everything was under control. He courted the image of Mafia don, and was seldom seen in public without a sweeping Hollywood-style fedora on his bald head. When he fled to Venezuela for a time in the 1970s, he opened a restaurant in Caracas called El Padrino, Spanish for "The Godfather."

The old man was stuffing money into his socks well into his ninth decade of life because he had the survival instincts of a feral cat. In the dirty, chaotic *milieu*, Nicolò was also known for his catlike mania for cleanliness and order. Friends became rich and enemies became corpses, fueling the dual engines of greed and revenge that powered his world. Through it all, Nicolò's family remained true to each other, if not towards the rest of the world.

The only pronounced difference between Nicolò and his son was Vito's notorious womanizing. Mistresses are a constant in North American mob life, but Nicolò continued to conduct himself like a resident of semi-rural Cattolica Eraclea in Agrigento province, where sexual indiscretious are hard to hide and often end in death. This was particularly true in his case; Nicolò never wavered in his fidelity to Libertina. Only a foolhardy man would brook the ire of the formidable woman and her father, Antonino (Don Nino) Manno.

Libertina was just eighteen and Nicolò twenty-one when they pledged their devotion to each other on March 20, 1945, in Cattolica Eraclea. There was no doubt that Nicolò was the one marrying up. His union with Libertina gave him strength and status, as he rose from *campiere*—an enforcer for local landowners—to the manager of a flour mill and a black market wheat vendor in Sicily.

Nicolò was thirty years old when he and Libertina brought their young family to North America. He declared that he had just thirty dollars on him when they arrived in Canada on February 1, 1954, at Pier 21 in Halifax. It was Vito's eighth birthday. In a photo taken around this time, Vito looks a bit grim, perhaps even scared. Standing up straight, he is a head taller than his sister, Maria, who is only six years old. Vito's hair is neatly trimmed and combed back well out of his eyes. Both children wear carefully chosen clothes: Vito is in shorts, which would have been cold in the Canadian winter, a matching jacket, and light-coloured shoes; Maria, a party dress and white patent-leather shoes. The little white purse in her hands matches the ribbons in her hair. Neither child had any grasp of either of Canada's official languages, but the camera captures something defiant in the young pair's gaze. They give the impression of submitting to their parents' photo out of obligation, and they do not feign joy. Vito's left arm is around his little sister and he also holds her with his right hand in a protective gesture.

By 1956, Montreal city records list Nicolò's occupation as "cement contractor." He evidently became a successful one soon after setting foot in Canada. By 1958, he was a player in Montreal's construction world, with a scent of collusion and corruption already around his tangled and profitable dealings. He ran his own firm yet somehow borrowed $1,777.50 from a rival contractor, and he won a municipal contract despite not being the low bidder. His company, Grand Royal Asphalt Paving, was involved in bidding with the City of Montreal, winning a contract in January 1962 to make over Parc Masson. His paving firm also worked for the municipalities of Laval, Pierrefonds and Saint-Léonard. The City of Jacques-Cartier (now part of Longueuil, on the south shore) was considered particularly corrupt, and Nicolò made money there too.

The early 1960s was a time of mass migration out of Sicily's Agrigento province. In Montreal, Nicolò was soon reacquainted with members of the Cuntrera–Caruana clan, who were originally from Siculiana, just twenty-four kilometres from Cattolica Eraclea. The Cuntrera–Caruanas, who were also known to police as the Siculiana crime family, had existed for generations in Agrigento. They graduated from working as guards for a local land baron to being powers in the twentieth-century drug trade, with a firm grip over local politics. It was an accepted truth in their home region that people got hurt when things didn't go their way. Pasquale Cuntrera and his brother-in-law Leonardo Caruana were each acquitted in 1953 of double murder, cattle theft and arson before heading abroad. In the early 1960s, Pasquale Cuntrera, the head of the Siculiana Mafia family in Agrigento, moved to Caracas, Venezuela, as the family gained international scope. A key to their success in the illegal drug trade was their flexibility: they worked with anyone who could help them but steadfastly refused to align themselves exclusively to any of Sicily's feuding Mafia families. As they gained power and connections, the Cuntrera–Caruana men developed their own look. They differed from old-school fedora-wearing mobsters and staid, buttoned-down, pinstriped international financiers. Instead, they tended to resemble mildly successful Florida used-car dealers, with an affinity for white shoes, eye-popping gold watches and poorly dyed jet-black hair.

On September 11, 1964, Nicolò's father-in-law, Antonino Manno, immigrated to Canada as well. Like several of the Cuntrera–Caruanas, Don Nino had been forced to serve a period of court-imposed internal exile in Italy. The sentence was called a *soggiorno obbligato*, and for its duration a mobster was banished from living near his hometown or criminal associates. Such a record might have been an impediment if Canadian authorities had been more vigilant.

In 1967, Canada was marking the one hundredth anniversary of its arrival as a nation with year-long Centennial festivities. There was plenty for Nicolò Rizzuto to celebrate in his new home. He was now a partner in four construction-related firms and had secured construction work on the Expo 67 world's fair in Montreal. His mob counterparts Paolo Violi and Vic (The Egg) Cotroni were also involved in the Expo fun, supplying the international showcase with hot dogs made from tainted meat. Opportunity found Nicolò's son, Vito, as well. After he had dropped out of high school, there was work running the New Cheetah nightclub at the corner of Beaubien Street and Saint-Laurent Boulevard.

Nicolò Rizzuto was sponsoring many Agrigento residents to move to his new city, expanding the Cuntrera–Caruanas' Canadian base, and expanding the clan's financial base too, bringing heroin to Montreal by boat and then transporting it to New York by car. For three months in late 1969, they hosted Tommaso Buscetta, the hound-faced senior member of the Porta Nuova Mafia family in Palermo, Sicily. Buscetta would become a key figure in the history of the Sicilian Mafia, as the network's first major informer. At the time of his arrival in Montreal, his mob credentials were still intact and impressive, as he had helped set up the Sicilian Mafia Commission, which ruled upon disputes between members. His acquaintances included top-level New York mob figures Charles (Lucky) Luciano and Joe Bonanno.

Buscetta's Montreal visit was at least his second trip to Canada. He had been in Toronto in the fall of 1964, travelling under the name Manuel Lopez Cadena and trying to gain a visa under this false identity to enter the United States. While in Toronto, Buscetta stayed at the home of Antonino (Nino) Cammalleri, the uncle of Vito Rizzuto's future wife. Decades later, Buscetta would remember playing cards at the Il Gatto Nero café.

When Buscetta returned to Canada in 1969, staying in Montreal from October until just after Christmas, he did so for medical reasons. He sought treatment for a genital infection, long rumoured to be a venereal disease. He feared he actually had cancer, although he would later claim to have learned he suffered from an African fly bite.

Twenty-three-year-old Alfonso Caruana chauffeured Buscetta around Montreal during those three months, as the visitor met with Nicolò Rizzuto, Pasquale Cuntrera and other local Mafiosi. Buscetta picked up on tensions between Paolo Violi and Nicolò. Violi struck Buscetta as a jealous man. Relationships were complex and sometimes crossed ethnic lines. He noted, for instance, that the Calabrian Violi was a close associate of the Sicilian Leonardo Caruana (in 1981, Caruana would be deported from Canada and murdered in front of his Palermo home, on the day of his son's wedding, in a gesture of operatic cruelty), and although Nicolò wasn't a member of the Siculiana crime family, he did work closely with them.

Despite his standing in the Sicilian Mafia, Buscetta—in the guise of Manuel Lopez Cadena—remained under the radar of Canadian police until long after his departure from Montreal. He later recalled an odd incident that occurred toward the end of that visit. He was standing outside his Montreal motel when police moved in and blocked his exit. He must have feared that his cover had been blown. Then police began grilling him about a bank robbery. Unbeknownst to Buscetta, he had been standing near a bank-robbery team's getaway car, and police mistakenly thought he was part of the gang. Once they were convinced he was innocent of that crime, he was freed to go and made his way to Pasquale Cuntrera's home for Christmas dinner.

A few days after Christmas, Buscetta left Montreal. He was reunited with his friend Nicolò in Caracas in 1972. Buscetta was in South America on his honeymoon with what was believed to be his third wife. Nicolò told Buscetta that he had left Montreal for a far less happy reason. He had been "called for an appointment" of the Montreal *décina*, a branch of the Bonanno crime family, headed by Vic Cotroni and Paolo Violi. Nicolò was certain he knew the agenda for the meeting: he was to be murdered.

CHAPTER 4

Going to war

T he murder of Nick Jr. got people talking again about Nicolò's private war two generations earlier with Paolo Violi. Nicolò and Violi had been rivals in the old *décina* of Vic (The Egg) Cotroni, back when Vic the Egg was the Canadian branch plant manager for the Bonanno family of New York. Nicolò could barely stomach being under Vic Cotroni in the Montreal mob pecking order, and when Cotroni promoted his fellow Calabrian Violi above Rizzuto, Nicolò responded with a haughty grandeur. The prospect of being under two Calabrians was too much to countenance. He didn't just disobey Violi; he refused even to acknowledge his existence. Tensions were so high between Paolo Violi and Nicolò that Giuseppe Settecasi, head of the Agrigento crime family, travelled to Montreal in 1972 to mediate, with no success.

Later that year, when Violi could stand Nicolò's insolence no longer, he asked the Bonannos for permission to kill him. The Bonannos initially balked, then relented. Wise to the conversation happening behind his back, Nicolò slipped away to Venezuela, where he could bide his time and extend his contacts.

Like many bitter enemies, Nicolò and Violi had much in common. Violi had also married into power. His father-in-law was Giacomo (Jack) Luppino of Hamilton, an 'Ndrangheta boss and lieutenant of Stefano (The Undertaker) Magaddino of Buffalo. Luppino was said to carry the leathery ear of a rival in his wallet, like a treasure that could never be deposited in a bank. In November 1967, police listened in on Luppino through microphones hidden among his tomato plants and elsewhere around his red brick house on Ottawa Street North in east end Hamilton. They heard him explain how horrible things should be done to a man who was disloyal to his wife. Paolo Violi shared his father-in-law's rigid sense of morality. That kind of talk was never heard from Vito or his father when police listened in on their conversations, even though Nicolò was of a similar if less punishing mind about marital infidelity.

Police also overheard Luppino talking about a wedding in New York at which he'd crossed paths with his boss, Stefano Magaddino. The highlight of Luppino's evening came when Magaddino deigned to spend twenty minutes with him.

Magaddino was in an angry mood that evening. He complained that he had also invited Paolo Violi and Vic Cotroni to the wedding, but neither of them showed up. Violi had a credible excuse, as he explained that he was always under police surveillance and he didn't want to bring that heat to New York. That was a permissible, even courteous response. But Cotroni? Vic the Egg had said only that he was too busy, as he had matters before the court. Such insolence rendered Magaddino livid, or, in the words of Luppino, he "turned mad like a beast."

Magaddino said Violi and Cotroni had a choice: they could side with his cousin Giuseppe (Joe) Bonanno of New York City or with himself. They couldn't be loyal to both. Bonanno and Magaddino might be related, but they couldn't stand each other. Magaddino's anger peaked as he told Luppino about a November 1966 meeting in Montreal between Bonanno's son Salvatore (Bill) and Cotroni. Cotroni didn't bother to tell Magaddino before attending the meeting, which also included half a dozen men from the New York Mafia. Magaddino heard that Bill Bonanno told Cotroni at the meeting that Montreal belonged to his father, Joe Bonanno. Vic the Egg's response? He just sheepishly listened to Bonanno's arrogance.

It was bad enough that Bonanno would say something so stupid, but for Cotroni to say nothing in Magaddino's defence was unacceptable.

How could Magaddino remain calm when he heard of such a slur? And why hadn't Cotroni told him beforehand about the meeting? Had Bonanno and the visiting New Yorkers not been arrested shortly afterwards, Magaddino could have started a small war over the slight. In Don Stefano's eyes, Montreal was his territory and Cotroni commited nothing less than an act of treason by meeting with the Americans there without his permission. How he came to the conclusion that Quebec was his turf was anyone's guess, but he considered this to be an absolute truth. And in his mind, he must know anything of significance that happened there. As Luppino recalled his words: "I don't care what others do, all I want to know is what is done in my house."

To rectify the damage Cotroni had done, Magaddino wanted Luppino to move to Montreal to assert control on the Buffalo boss's behalf. However, Luppino preferred life in Hamilton, amidst his tomato plants. Ambitious people had a way of getting shot in Montreal, and Luppino had a good life in the Ontario steel town, with his family, his respect and his tomatoes. As Luppino put his refusal, "Stefano Magaddino is the biggest man in the world, but not even he can lead me by the arm and tell me what to do."

Nicolò realized that his rival Paolo Violi had connections to more than just Luppino and Magaddino. Violi's reach also stretched back to the emerging 'Ndrangheta in his native Calabria, including the heroin and cocaine trafficker Saverio (The Playboy) Mammoliti of Castellace di Oppido Mamertina in the province of Reggio Calabria, the 'Ndrangheta heartland. Mammoliti was best known for his role in the 1973 kidnapping of sixteen-year-old John Paul Getty III, bohemian grandson of oil tycoon Jean Paul Getty, the world's richest man. Even the mobsters must have been startled by the coldness of Getty Sr.'s initial response, when he refused to cough up a cent: "If I pay one penny now, I'll have fourteen kidnapped grandchildren." Eventually, the old man grudgingly agreed to a payment. Some of the estimated $2.2 million in ransom money, paid after the youth's ear was hacked off, was tracked down by police in an investigation that led them to Montreal streets.

Paolo Violi cultivated the image of an old-school boss, the kind of mobster who stayed out of the nasty emerging business of drugs. Word on the street suggested he was actually elbow deep in it. When two American undercover drug agents of Italian descent told Mammoliti in 1973 they wanted to make a major drug deal, they were instructed that if they wanted heroin, they needed to get in touch with "his friend Paolo Violi" in Canada.

After Nicolò moved to Venezuela at the end of 1972 (alternately reported as early 1973), he settled into the drug trafficking business with the Cuntrera–Caruanas. His old associates had worked their way into the country's economic and political life, to the point that American Drug Enforcement Administration intelligence noted that president Carlos Andrés Pérez attended the wedding of a Cuntrera–Caruana clan member.

It wasn't the product but the profit that mattered, and they also smuggled powdered milk into Venezuela. Importing powdered milk was illegal and profitable, and they seized the opportunity to make extra money. Tommaso Buscetta also spent much time with Nicolò in Venezuela throughout the 1970s. Police believed the pair were involved together in a business called Brasil Italian Import, which was a front for narcotics trafficking.

Perhaps Nicolò's most lucrative business at the time was a cattle breeding ranch called Granaderia Rio Zapa in the Venezuelan state of Barinas, near the Colombian border. His partners there included Salvatore (Cicchiteddu) Greco, head of the Commission of the Sicilian Cosa Nostra and a close associate of senior members of the Gambino crime family of New York City. Conveniently—especially for a cattle ranch—Granaderia Rio Zapa had its own private airstrip.

It was in Caracas, Venezuela, in 1977 that Gennaro Scaletta of Montreal first met with the Rizzuto clan: Nicolò, Libertina, Maria, Vito and Giovanna and their children Nick Jr., Libertina (Bettina) and Leonardo, who looked remarkably like a young Vito. There was also Vito's brother-in-law/cousin Paolo Renda, who was also Nick Jr.'s godfather. It seemed to Scaletta that everyone in this one bar was from

Italy. Soon, he was associating with transplanted Mafia clans from all over Italy without leaving Caracas.

Scaletta said that Nicolò kept his family in Venezuela for six months and a day at a time, which he thought was just long enough to exclude him from having to pay taxes to Canada for the money he earned outside the country. In South America, Scaletta learned quickly that power and influence in the Rizzuto family wasn't always in the hands of the obvious person.

"The Rizzutos were under Cuntrera and Caruana at that time," Scaletta later said. "They were like actors in the sense that everyone should know what they were, they advertise . . . and at that time to be part of the Mafia was something important . . . they showed off their affiliation with the Mafia." The person who seemed to impress Scaletta the most was the matriarch, Libertina. "Who commanded more in the Rizzuto family was the wife [Libertina] . . . because she was the daughter of a mafioso, a Mafia boss, in the town of origin, which is Cattolica Eraclea. The wife's name is Manno. Her father was the Mafia boss in that area, all the people from Cattolica who went to Canada were funded by Manno. He advanced money for the airfare, airline tickets. . . .

"Then I gradually discovered that almost everyone trafficked in drugs, with the difference that the Rizzutos moved out money from Canada in the suitcases. . . . The laundered money returned to Canada because Nicolò had a fake document from the Venezuelan Ministry of Finance showing that he had earned the money honestly, and they returned [the money] to Canada. . . . Once I carried in a suitcase $300,000. . . . The Rizzutos told me that I had to bring this money into Canada, but I did not know if it was legal or not."

The Rizzutos also had the ability to obtain documents from Aruba that stated their money had been legally won in a casino there. Aruba was a popular spot for the Mafia, as it was close to the northern shores of Colombia and Venezuela. It also attracted thousands of tourists, which made it easy to get lost in the crowds and profitable to set up businesses such as hotels and casinos to grab the money visitors were all too happy to throw away.

———

The slaying of Nick Jr. was Canada's most audacious Mafia murder in a generation. Montrealers expected mobsters to be murdered, and so there was seldom real shock when the guns came out. The last time a gangland hit had generated such attention from the public or within the *milieu* was on January 22, 1978, the evening one of Nicolò's men put a shotgun to the back of Paolo Violi's head. That murder came at 7:32 p.m., a time marked with a floral tribute at Violi's funeral. That pull of the trigger, as Violi sat playing cards with supposed friends at the Reggio Bar at 5880 Jean-in Saint-Léonard, marked the culmination of the Violis' feud with Nicolò and the beginning of the Rizzuto family's era at the top level of Canadian organized crime.

Violi had been cautioned by police well in advance that his life was in danger. Neither Nicolò nor Vito had been in Canada when it happened, but they were still central players in the crime. They also were out of the country when someone turned a shotgun on Violi's *consigliere* Pietro (Zio Petrino, "Uncle Pete") Sciara, as he walked with his wife from a Montreal theatre playing *The Godfather* in Italian on Valentine's Day 1976. The Rizzutos were still in Venezuela a year later when Violi's brother Francesco was shot dead in the office of his Montreal import-export business.

The last gasp of the war between the Rizzutos and the Violis came in 1980, with the sniper slaying of Rocco Violi as he sat at the kitchen table of his home on Houel Street in Saint-Léonard. Authorities speculated that the assassin was perched on the roof of a nearby building, waiting for a clear shot with his .308 rifle. There had been some twenty murders to that point in the one-sided Mafia war, but no one considered Rocco Violi a mobster. His murder resulted from an abundance of caution by Nicolò. Ever the one for tidiness, Nicolò wasn't taking the chance that Rocco might pursue a vendetta to avenge his two murdered brothers. There was no way of knowing then that the final hit that brought the Rizzutos to power would come back to haunt them when they fell from grace three decades later.

With his figurative housecleaning finished in preparation for his return to Montreal, Nicolò commissioned an actual house, a custom-built mansion on Antoine-Berthelet Avenue in the Ahuntsic–Cartierville borough, on a tiny cul-de-sac alongside new homes for Vito and other trusted relatives. Their previous Montreal home had been one in a string of cramped semis on Des Vannes Street, Saint-Léonard, near Jean-Talon East and Lacordaire Boulevard. Now, on Antoine-Berthelet, only families who were close to the Rizzutos would live close to the Rizzutos. Vito lived two doors down from Nicolò, with his house registered in the name of his wife, Giovanna Cammalleri. Between the father and son was the home of Vito's sister, Maria, and her husband, Paolo Renda. Soon the little street was called "Mafia Row" by everyone but its residents.

During the summer of 1982, Nicolò, who was still living in Venezuela, was visiting Milan on a business trip with Giuseppe Bono. Bono was boss of the Bolognetta family near Palermo, but lived in New York City at the time. The Rizzutos were setting up their new homes on Antoine-Berthelet, and Nicolò arranged for the shipment of two or three containers of furniture from Italy to Montreal. When the containers landed in North America, initially in New Jersey, a drug detection dog reacted as if there were drugs inside. Police searched the containers but couldn't find the suspected stash.

In 1984, Nicolò left Venezuela and the family's transition back to Montreal was complete. Trusted associate Raynald Desjardins settled into a luxury home in nearby Rivière des Prairies. Desjardins and Mafia Row residents such as Vito and Nicolò didn't bother to erect fences with security gates. They knew that no one would dare take the short walk from the street to their front doors to attack them.

For a quarter century, that confidence seemed enough to keep them safe. The slaying of Nick Jr. changed that. Who might come knocking now was anyone's guess.

CHAPTER 5

Invisible enemy

The hundreds of mourners who filed into Notre-Dame-de-la-Défense church at Henri-Julien Avenue and Dante Street on the morning of Nick Rizzuto Jr.'s funeral passed by a statue that commemorates "victims of all wars" and under a fresco of Il Duce, Italian dictator Benito Mussolini, surrounded by fascist dignitaries, saints and angels. It seemed that anyone who was anyone in the Montreal mob was buried out of that ninety-year-old church in Little Italy, beneath the image of a dictator hell-bent on destroying the Mafia tradition. Even the services for the Rizzutos' avowed enemies and victims, the Violi brothers, were held under that idealized portrayal of Italian power from a generation before.

Nick Jr.'s widow and two children sat in the front pews, along with his mother and surviving siblings, Bettina and Leonardo. Nicolò and Libertina sat with their daughter, Maria Rizzuto Renda, and the family's lawyer, Loris Cavaliere. Nicolò's parole conditions were relaxed for the funeral of his namesake grandson; for this day he would not be forbidden from associating with known criminals. Pews filled quickly and many mourners stood in the aisles. Muscular men in trench coats and black gloves acted as security guards, briskly escorting two outsiders from the church. Police filmed those who came and left while hundreds of others took in the spectacle from the sidewalk.

The most notable mourner on the day that Nick Jr. was laid to rest in his gold-coloured casket was the one who didn't attend: his father.

The service was said in Italian, and when it was over, police and mobsters retired to their respective quarters to hone their theories about who was behind the first killing of a Montreal Rizzuto during their entire thirty years in power. Then it would be a race to see who could get to the suspected killers first—for an arrest or another funeral.

Not so long ago, a leaf couldn't rustle in the *milieu* without Vito knowing about it. Now his people were scrambling for any particle of information that might give them a clue to solving his son's death. There was precious little real information to glean from press reports: the killing was precise, as the assassin apparently waited near Nick Jr.'s Mercedes for him to emerge from a building. Witnesses reported a volley of four shots, like fireworks, a pause, and then the final two. Next came the sound of screeching tires, and the killer was gone. The murder weapon was discovered near the scene of the crime. The handgun didn't yield any clues, but none were expected from it. The fact that a black man was seen running away from Nick Jr.'s body didn't mean much, even if he was the killer. Almost all crime groups contracted their killings. The key was to learn who had ordered the hit, not who carried it out.

The murder underlined how little control Vito and his family had left on the streets. Immediately after Vito's arrest in 2004, the man left to sort things out in the crime family's day-to-day affairs was Francesco (*Compare* Frank) Arcadi. He quickly alienated the black street gangs with whom Vito had worked so hard to nurture relationships. Arcadi was then scooped up during the 2006 Colisée raids and remained behind bars, leaving the family's leadership even thinner—though even before Arcadi's arrest some believed leadership in the family to be weaker than it looked.

Doubts had been surfacing in Vito's group about *Compare* Frank's loyalty. Arcadi was Calabrian and the Rizzutos were Sicilian. He was supposed to be the Rizzutos' ambassador to the Calabrian 'Ndrangheta in Ontario, but some worried that he'd become too chummy with the other side. Perhaps, while awaiting extradition in a Montreal jail, Vito had heard about a weekend in the winter of 2005 before *Compare* Frank's arrest, when he met in Hamilton with members of the Violi family. Even two decades after the Rizzutos' slaughter of their rivals, they and the Violis remained the Canadian mob version of the Hatfields and the McCoys, or the Capulets and the Montagues. So the question naturally arose: what possible reason could *Compare* Frank have for sitting down with Vito's avowed enemies on their home turf? And why would Vito have to learn about it from others and not from *Compare* Frank himself?

With Arcadi locked up, millionaire baker Moreno Gallo might still be on Vito's side and willing to lead the family's operations, but, like Arcadi, Gallo was Calabrian. He was born in Rovito, Calabria, and he had, a generation ago, been close to Paolo Violi. Since then, Gallo had been particularly close to Joe Di Maulo of the Montreal mob's Calabrian wing. And even if Gallo could prove true to Vito's side, after his conviction for murdering a man in the 1970s, his parole conditions made it difficult for him to help in a war, as in typical fashion they forbade him from associating with known criminals.

Nicolò could try to step up his role in the family's leadership, but he was old and tired and preferred his grappa to the hurly-burly of the streets. *Consigliere* Paolo Renda was behind bars for the next few years thanks to Project Colisée. So was adviser Rocco (Sauce) Sollecito, who was a trusted friend, even though he wasn't from Sicily either, but from the southern mainland region of Apulia. The crime family's prospects for filling its leadership vacuum were looking grim.

In the absence of real evidence, plenty of theories emerged about who killed Nick Jr. It certainly felt as though an insider was responsible: someone who knew Nick Jr.'s routines would have expected to see him park his black Mercedes in that area of Notre-Dame-de-Grâce (NDG), near the corner of Upper Lachine Road and Wilson Avenue. It was close to both the home of Nick Jr.'s mistress and the office of FTM Construction, owned by Nick Jr.'s business associate in land development, Antonio (Tony) Magi. Magi had invisible enemies of his own, having survived an ambush the previous year in another section of NDG. The corner was also near a controversial housing development built by one of Magi's companies that had links to the Rizzutos. The development had raised eyebrows for what appeared to be a series of irregularities between the builders and city officials.

Was the hit arranged because of a business deal gone sour? Perhaps Nick Jr. had grown impatient over money he felt was owed to him and squeezed someone a little too hard, which was not his specialty. A more frightening theory was that somewhere behind the killer stood the 'Ndrangheta. The Ontario 'Ndrangheta bosses were trouble enough for Vito's group, but since its inception decades earlier the Calabrian Mafia had grown to a global breadth the Montreal clan could never match, with interests ranging from drug trafficking, construction, extortion and loansharking to environmental waste disposal scams, weapons trafficking and prostitution. Besides Italy and Canada, the 'Ndrangheta had become strong in Australia, Germany, Holland, Belgium, France, the United Kingdom, the United States, Colombia, Venezuela, Argentina and Brazil. Law enforcement estimated the group was bringing in 44 billion euros worldwide a year.

Despite its extraordinary reach, the sprawling 'Ndrangheta felt more like a ghost haunting Vito's world, a potent force that was often felt but almost never seen. If Nick Jr. was dead at the hands of the 'Ndrangheta, or someone operating with its support, Vito and his family members could expect life to get far worse—and perhaps also shorter.

Locked up in Colorado, Vito would have been keenly aware that a great deal was happening that he wasn't hearing about, though he was no doubt hearing enough to keep him worried. For instance, on September 17, 2009, a man connected to the powerful Commisso crime family of the Greater Toronto Area (GTA) had flown to Montreal to meet with wealthy café owner Vittorio (Victor) Mirarchi, among others. Mirarchi was barely thirty years old but reputedly a force, although a quiet and mysterious one who had never been convicted of a crime. Born in Montreal on October 10, 1977, he traced his family roots to Isca sullo Ionio in the province of Catanzaro in southern Italy. That part of Calabria was considered another 'Ndrangheta hotbed.

His father, Antonio Mirarchi, had been a friend of Vito's old ally Raynald Desjardins, and also had close ties to the Quebec Hells Angels. In the summer of 2001, Antonio Mirarchi knew his ailing heart wouldn't last much longer and he asked Desjardins to look out for his boy. Desjardins agreed. As anticipated, Antonio Mirarchi died young, at age fifty-one. Desjardins honoured his promise and took the younger man under his wing.

There was a time when Vito would have looked to Desjardins for help in a time of crisis. Now he considered him with suspicion, perhaps even fear. They had known each other since the early 1970s, and within a decade Desjardins was like a younger brother to Vito, much as Vittorio Mirarchi now seemed like a younger sibling to Desjardins. Back then, Vito and Desjardins brought in literally tonnes of hashish from Lebanon and Spain through Newfoundland and then washed the profits in Swiss banks. For at least a decade, the terms "loyal" and "right-hand man" precisely described Desjardins's relationship to Vito.

Now the former cabaret waiter was a force in his own right and possibly also a deadly enemy. Desjardins had maintained a close relationship with charismatic bar owner Giuseppe (Joe) Di Maulo since the early 1970s, a man whose confidence and charisma rivalled Vito's own, which helped explain why he and Vito were the *milieu*'s two great mediators.

Di Maulo had managed to stay out of jail since beating three murder charges at age twenty-eight, cultivating friendships and charming potential enemies as he rose to become a mainstay of the city's Calabrian faction of the mob. In November 1973, Desjardins drove Di Maulo to New York City so Di Maulo could attend a leadership meeting of the Bonanno crime family, at which Phil (Rusty) Rastelli was installed as acting boss.

Di Maulo was also tight with Paolo Violi at the time Violi sought permission from the Bonanno family to have Nicolò Rizzuto assassinated. Di Maulo and Violi travelled together to New York in 1974 to a Bonanno meeting, when Violi was acting head of the Cotroni crime family. After Violi's murder in 1978, Di Maulo made a decision to go on living and reached a détente with the new masters of the Montreal underworld, coexisting with Nicolò and Vito. With time, he even became an amiable member of Vito's golf foursomes. It made good business sense for Vito to tolerate the former Violi associate, but could he ever really trust him?

For his part, Desjardins had helped Vito forge ties with the Hells Angels Motorcycle Club and French-Canadian gangs. He ran a vending machine business in the 1980s with Di Maulo and Nicodemo Cotroni, the son of Vic the Egg's younger brother, Frank (The Big Guy) Cotroni. The mob had made considerable money in jukeboxes in the 1960s, followed by vending machines and then online games. They were all easy businesses to run, once the competition was scared away, and since they were cash driven, income was easy to hide from Revenue Canada.

Vito and Desjardins clicked on a business level. In 1984 they were seen together in Milan, organizing the importation of 3.5 tonnes of hash. Their schemes only got bigger. In 1987 police believed the pair were organizing a 30-tonne shipment. Later that year, Desjardins and Vito were charged with smuggling 16 tonnes of hashish via a small island off Newfoundland. Charges were dropped when the RCMP was caught hiding an unauthorized recording device in a lamp at a restaurant table frequented by the two men's lawyer.

As a team, Vito and Desjardins flooded the country with drugs by air as well as by water. In May 1989, they were behind the flying in of five hundred kilos of cocaine from Colombia. Their ongoing relationship was clearly a profitable one. Despite his humble beginnings in the service industry, Desjardins began to collect vintage automobiles and cruised the St. Lawrence in a forty-foot yacht. Sometimes he made his way up the river to Château Montebello, the opulent log hotel where Winston Churchill and other Allied leaders met during World War II. Desjardins was the highest-ranking Québécois in the Montreal mob, but he still remained an outsider of sorts in the world of the Italian Mafia. For all his trappings of success, Desjardins also remained a junior partner to Vito. In contrast, the growing link between Desjardins and Di Maulo transcended business and friendship to become one of family when Di Maulo married Desjardins's sister. Together, they ran a disco bar that was almost always empty of real customers but provided a comfortable venue for criminals to meet.

Then Desjardins was the fall guy in the massive cocaine-smuggling plot that sent him to prison for more than a decade while Vito enjoyed golf, cafés and southern vacations. Vito simply carried on with a string of new right-hand men, including his childhood friend Valentino Morielli and lawyer Joseph Lagana. Like Desjardins, they eventually went to prison for their dealings with Vito, while Vito kept gliding along. Soon the media was calling Vito "The Teflon Don," a moniker first used for John Gotti, boss of New York's Gambino crime family, back when he seemed impossible to convict.

The press repeatedly made the mistake of calling Di Maulo a Calabrian, when in fact he was from the province of Campobasso on the Italian mainland near Rome, far north of Calabria. This lent him a position in the Montreal underworld that Desjardins could sympathize with to a degree—that of an outsider. But at least in Di Maulo's case, being Italian, his neutral origins along with his affable nature made him a natural mediator particularly in disputes between Sicilians and Calabrians. Such talks often took place at a downtown restaurant on Sherbrooke Street or in a buffet in Saint-Léonard.

Di Maulo was never comfortable around drugs, despite the enormous profits to be had, while at the time of Nick Jr.'s murder police suspected Desjardins was moving seven hundred to nine hundred kilograms of marijuana a week into New York, and also transporting Venezuelan cocaine through California into Montreal. Perhaps thanks to his bitter years in prison, Desjardins had learned he could function just fine without Di Maulo or Vito.

His new right-hand man, young Vittorio Mirarchi, was reaping the benefits of his mentor's independence. In just his early thirties, Mirarchi purchased a fortified house in Sainte-Adèle in the Laurentian Mountains and a condo in the bunker-like development at 1000 de la Commune Street in Montreal's Old Port. He could often be found at his business, Café Luna, which was considered a popular meeting spot for Raynald Desjardins's allies. Sometimes Mirarchi travelled in a sport-utility vehicle owned by the Hells Angels, and seldom did he travel alone. There were trips to Ontario, where the young man sat down with well-established 'Ndrangheta members. If Desjardins was looking to overtake his former friend Vito, using his protege to reach out to the Ontario Calabrians was one way of doing it. No one was going to confront Vito head-on. Far better to forge a strategic alliance with the low-profile 'Ndrangheta and keep his quiet manoeuvring in a corner where prying eyes seldom got a good look.

As he sat in his Colorado prison cell, Vito must have wondered about possible links between Desjardins and Mirarchi and the Ontario 'Ndrangheta. He would have been curious to hear details of a daytime meeting in a yellow brick home on a gently winding street in Woodbridge, just north of Toronto, on Wednesday, October 7, 2009. The host of the meeting was Carmine Verduci, considered a loyal member of the 'Ndrangheta by Canadian and Italian police, with ties to senior members of the Coluccio-Aquino crime family in Canada and Italy. At the time of the meeting, Verduci had been making frequent forays onto Vito's turf in Montreal.

Pear-shaped but physically powerful, at six feet and 265 pounds, Verduci was known on the streets as "The Animal." His criminal record included assault with a weapon and weapons possession, but he was believed by police to be guilty of far more serious things, including murder.

He ostensibly leased cars for a living, but he also directed a street crew that worked in the GTA and Hamilton. Police believed he graduated from street-level heroin dealing to arranging heroin shipments from Mexico and multi-kilo shipments of cocaine that travelled from Mexico to BC to Toronto. He was also believed to be smuggling AK-47 assault rifles into Toronto from the States through the Akwesasne First Nations reserve. Moreoever, his reach extended to Toronto Albanian mobsters and the Gambino crime family in New York.

Some friends called Verduci "Ciccio Formaggio," referring to his love of homemade cheese, bread, grappa and wine. Aside from his Woodbridge home, he also owned a sprawling farm in Caledon, with a farmhouse, barn, tractor-trailers and several large dogs. He enjoyed hunting with a shotgun and working the hobby farm, where the phone was set up to not accept incoming calls.

Verduci was a Canadian citizen but had been born in Oppido Mamertina in Reggio Calabria province. Italian police noted he had recently attended high-level 'Ndrangheta dinner meetings in Reggio Calabria. At one of these meetings, in September 2009, he learned that a boss based in Milan wanted to run his own independent group. A month later, that upstart boss was murdered.

That year, Verduci also attended the annual 'Ndrangheta world summit in the Calabrian sanctuary of Polsi. At one summit, his voice was captured by a police interception device saying he was concerned about a brother who was in jail. He was reassured that "the jail never bites anyone who's a good Christian." The declaration of faith was code: everything would be okay as long as his brother kept his mouth shut. Verduci was known to detest publicity, which made him a logical host for the 'Ndrangheta gathering.

The eight or so men who gathered at Verduci's home that afternoon wouldn't have struck the public as particularly threatening, more like members of a seniors' gardening club than criminal conspirators. Despite their benign appearance, the police who were filming them knew these men wielded considerable clout in the underworld; according to police, they were members of the GTA *camera di controllo*, a network that moderated disputes between the nine Toronto-area 'Ndrangheta clans. Like Verduci, his visitors habitually drew minimal attention to themselves.

It wasn't the full board of the *camera* in attendance, but it was a strong cross-section and included members who were active in gambling, drugs and stock manipulation. Easily the most senior member of the group that afternoon was Cosimo Stalteri, whose door was opened and closed for him as he climbed in and out of a Toyota SUV, a show of respect for the octogenarian Mafioso.

The *camera* members were all well aware that the ground beneath their feet was in the midst of a seismic shift. The underworld abhors a vacuum as much as nature does, and the hole left by Vito's departure to the Colorado prison was being filled by a new alliance. Desjardins and Mirarchi now seemed in sync with some members of the Toronto area 'Ndrangheta and some heavy-duty Quebec Hells Angels.

Police witnessed two senior members in an animated argument on the street before they climbed into their cars and drove away. The reason for their sharp words remained a mystery, as police had no listening devices inside or outside Verduci's house. What was clear was that Vito's crime family appeared ripe for attack. There is never a clear announcement when a mob war begins or ends. It just happens. And it was starting to look as if it was happening now.

CHAPTER 6

Dangerous new associates

I t was tempting to wonder if the answer to Nick Jr.'s murder lay behind the walls of the Gibralter-like condominium development near the Jacques-Cartier Bridge. Prestigious, posh and secure, 1000 de la Commune Street was home to millionaire hockey players, socialites and also some mobsters. Owning condos there were Vittorio Mirarchi; Haitian street-gang veteran and convicted pimp Vick Sévère Paul; Hells Angels Normand (Casper) Ouimet and Salvatore Cazzetta; and Ducarme Joseph, co-founder of the 67's street gang and the Blue gang alliance.

Nick Jr. had been involved in turning the old refrigerated warehouse into the massive complex it is now. The location was inviting: it had a prime view of the St. Lawrence River, and sat close to the earthy thrills of the Main (Saint-Laurent Boulevard) and the boutiques of Old Montreal. The condo project had originally been headed by Montreal developer Tony Magi. When it seemed to be teetering near financial collapse in 2002, some of its investors turned to Vito for help. They didn't seek Vito's money. Vito had moved beyond simply pumping money into a project to launder his drug proceeds. It was his arbitration skills among investors and contractors that were needed to keep the project moving. For Vito, it was an obvious opportunity. A police wiretap picked up his reply to a businessman complaining about the financial direction of the project.

"If we get somebody who can help him out either by finance, private finance or finding finance for him to continue the project, he's willing to give us half of the project," Vito says. "You get it?"

Vito was a man who could get others to do things on a deadline, with a minimum of haggling. Plumbing, electrical, hardwood flooring and other work could be farmed out to firms with whom he had a friendly relationship. Naturally, he expected that work done at a considerable discount.

Vito displayed his knack for mediation shortly after midnight on May 29, 2003. Someone stole the Cadillac Escalade SUV of one of the project's investors, who had left it near a Dorval restaurant. A police wiretap picked up the investor's call to Vito. He told Vito that the Escalade was less than two weeks old, but he didn't really care about the vehicle.

"Is there any way of tracking, or knowing what happened?" the investor asks Rizzuto. "It's the briefcase inside it. It's killing me."

Vito immediately phones Frank Arcadi.

"They stole a friend of mine's truck—a Jewish guy," Vito tells his street boss. "See what you can do to find this truck. He is not interested in the truck; the bag is what interests him."

The Cadillac was located before noon of that day and the thief was given $3,500 for his co-operation. Who was Vito to punish someone for committing a crime? The vehicle, with the briefcase intact, was returned promptly to the investor. The thief had an easy sale, albeit at a low price, and a grateful, powerful contact, while the investor was duly impressed.

For his efforts as a silent, controlling partner of the condo development, Vito charged 6 percent of monies paid in deals he negotiated. He was also allowed to buy five units there for a combined total of one dollar. Those condos, which had cost just twenty cents each, were then sold for $1.7 million. After taxes, Vito netted $1.6 million, a tidy profit even by his standards.

The condo project wasn't the only time Magi talked business with Vito. RCMP bugs at the Consenza Social Club picked up a call between Vito and Magi in August 2003. They are discussing a deal for a patch of land at Décarie Boulevard and Chemin de la Côte-Saint-Luc. Magi tells Vito that he is standing with a Montreal city councillor and then tells the councillor that he is on the phone with "my partner Mike Sully."

Magi refers to the municipal politician, telling Vito: "He'll help us with his support, what he can do is he's gonna help us get the zoning."

"Yeah," Vito replies.

"Okay," Magi continues. "I just want to give you, to give you an update, what's going on and, you know, I told him we have the money ready to close, we just don't wanna close and get stuck with the piece of land, you know."

At this point, Vito closes things down, switching to Italian. Even with the bogus name "Mike Sully," he knows it's foolish to be speaking so openly. "Yeah," Vito says. "Ma questo no lo devi dire più al telefono, Tony," which translates to, "But this, you can't say it anymore on the phone, Tony."

The Montreal newspaper *La Presse* reported that Nick Jr. was "placed" in various construction projects to monitor their progress for his father. The condo development was one of them. However, Magi once told the Montreal *Gazette* that the name Rizzuto had actually worked against Nick Jr. as Vito's eldest son tried to make his way in the development world.

"We had bought a piece of land together which we are developing," Magi told the newspaper. "He's studied law and he's a smart kid. He's smart in real estate. The poor guy. He tries to do something in his life and, because of his family's past history, every time he turns around, he gets hit with something."

Whatever law Nick Jr. had studied was outside of law school. Magi's remarks seemed more than a little disingenuous, considering the mob's python-like grip on construction projects in Montreal. It was a bit like saying that being a member of the Rothschild family hindered a man in the world of nineteenth-century European banking.

Whatever the case, Magi had troubles of his own. The year before Nick Jr.'s murder, he had barely escaped an attempt on his life by a gunman who opened fire on his Range Rover at a red light. The shooting left him in a coma and it was six months before he could leave the hospital. After that, he travelled with a bodyguard in an armour-plated car.

If the condo development didn't hold the secret to Nick Jr.'s murder, perhaps the answer lay in recent firebombings of a dozen north and east Montreal Italian-run cafés and bars. With Vito in prison, café owners no longer knew who was receiving their extortion money. In 2008 and 2009, black street gangs from the east end of Montreal flexed their muscles and pushed into territories usually controlled by the Rizzutos, along Saint-Laurent Boulevard and in Rivière des Prairies. Throughout the course of 2008, someone lobbed Molotov cocktails into twenty-four Italian bars and cafés, and the number rose to twenty-eight in 2009. Not so long before, Vito and the street gangs had got along so well that there was only one protection payment necessary for café owners.

With Vito gone, that co-operation had been replaced by confusion and hatred. One member of Vito's group reportedly referred to the black gang members as "animals and monkeys that grow like mush-rooms." Frank Arcadi had particularly venomous relations with them. Arcadi was so crude and thoughtless, many believed the rumours that he couldn't read or write.

Lorenzo (Skunk) Giordano was one exception in Vito's group. The gangster—who took his nickname from a prematurely white swath of hair on his head—had enjoyed a positive relationship with the Syndicate, a largely Haitian street gang run by Gregory Wooley, who also guided the Rockers, a Hells Angels support club. Giordano was a fit man with a tough reputation. That reputation was forever linked to an incident in a Saint-Laurent Boulevard bar, when a heroin dealer disrespected him. Skunk opened fire on the man's groin and left him so terrified he didn't co-operate with police or seek revenge. On another occasion, in a Peel Street restaurant, Giordano was so offended by a man—a man with links to the Hells Angels, no less—that he went outside and pumped a bullet into the man's Porsche. The man was likely relieved that Skunk didn't blast him in the groin too.

In a January 1, 2005, conversation intercepted by police, Skunk Giordano was overheard bragging to Arcadi and rising mob soldier

Domenico Macri about the rush he got administering a sound beating on an unidentified man: "We gave it good. . . . And boom, boom, boom. I made his face like this and he couldn't even stay in the bar. We cleaned up his face and brought him in his car. . . . Then he called and he says give me two weeks and I'll give you the money." Unfortunately for Vito's crime family, Skunk Giordano was out of commission for the foreseeable future, after being pinched in November 2006 for Colisée-related charges.

At the time of Nick Jr.'s murder, almost all of the remaining leadership of the family was behind bars because of the RCMP bugs and tiny cameras hidden in the walls of the Consenza Social Club during Project Colisée. While Vito's Mafia group remained atop the national crime pyramid, those bugs had it sitting upon a dangerously teetering perch. Street gangs had more members than any other class of criminal organization in Quebec, including bikers and the mob. Where street gangs in other provinces were often made up of listless kids with guns and lousy aim, in Montreal the gangs included members in their forties and fifties. The gangs also had far less structure than the bikers or the Mafia, who met regularly and had clear-cut divisions of power. To understand the gangs, you had to understand the idiosyncrasies of key personalities, and toss aside any notion of predictability.

In the absence of Arcadi and Giordano, there was talk that the Mafia offered to share turf with the Bloods street gang but that the Bloods balked. The unprecedented attacks on the north Montreal cafés escalated. Unless something happened soon to stem the tide of disrespect, it was easy to wonder how long it would be until the city's Mafiosi were reduced to glorified street-gang members themselves.

CHAPTER 7

Gangs

Amidst all the chaos and killing in Vito's world, street-gang boss Ducarme Joseph set out to sell some high-end women's clothing. He owned a boutique at 240 Saint-Jacques Street in Old Montreal called Flawnego, short for "Flawlessness Never Goes." The pillars of century-old banks around Flawnego called to mind the classical architecture of ancient Greece. Less than five minutes up Saint-Jacques was the Palais de Justice courthouse, another classically inspired place all too familiar to Joseph, who was out on $50,000 bail for assault charges related to a beating at the Buona Notte nightclub on Saint-Laurent Boulevard and for possessing a firearm silencer.

Joseph had come a long way to the world of haute couture since the mid-1980s, when he first appeared on the police radar, and the path to the Flawnego was rumoured to include the murder of Nick Rizzuto Jr. Joseph and Guyanese newcomer Richard Ogilvie (Ritchie Rich) Goodridge had co-founded a street gang called the 67's, named for the bus route in their Saint-Michel neighbourhood. The 67's fell upon internal strife, marked by murder attempts, and somewhere along the line Goodridge and Joseph morphed into businessmen and mortal enemies.

Two decades later, Goodridge and his Blue/Crips street-gang members sometimes sported silver chains with a six-pointed Star of David. There was no great symbolism to the star; it just looked cool. For his

44

part, Joseph wore a T-shirt with a one percent symbol to show his connection to the Hells Angels' Montreal Nomads chapter. The Hells Angels didn't allow black members, but there were no such restrictions for its support clubs such as the Rockers or the Scorpions. The fact that Goodridge and Greg Wooley could belong to both the Rockers and a black street gang at the same time just showed how much more complicated things were becoming in the organized crime world.

Goodridge wasn't a huge man, at 175 pounds and standing five foot ten, but he was solid as a linebacker and someone to be taken seriously as he cruised about in his Hummer H2, Range Rover or Mercedes sedan. His clout extended into Ontario, both to the streets of Toronto and to the well-travelled drug-smuggling channel of the Akwesasne reserve on the St. Lawrence River, where Goodridge successfully collected gambling debts. He had been the target of an attempted hit in the Toronto suburb of Scarborough shortly after noon on November 10, 2004, when a black Maxima pulled up beside his silver Mercedes and someone inside opened fire, tearing off part of Goodridge's finger. Asked by police what had just happened, he dismissed the shootout as a random attack by a stranger who coveted his jewellery.

Life wasn't any calmer for Goodridge's friends. On March 10, 2005, Rizzuto family enforcer Mike (Big Mike) Lapolla dropped by the Moomba Supper Club in Laval's Chomedey district, a Latin nightspot that prided itself on "sober and chic décor, voluptuous forms and pure lines" and "a zen environment without pretension." Also there after midnight for some zen-inspired socializing was Goodridge's associate Thierry Beaubrun of the 67's.

There had been tensions between Lapolla and Beaubrun a few nights earlier at another club, and both men carried tough reputations and serious firepower. Lapolla ran a transport company from his home, but his real money came from the Rizzutos. He had been convicted of cocaine trafficking and was considered muscle for the mob family. Beaubrun, a regular at downtown clubs and strip bars, was facing armed robbery and assault charges.

It was about two-thirty in the morning when the shooting started. Big Mike fell bleeding on the dance floor as Beaubrun and some two hundred patrons rushed to safety. In the stampede, someone in the parking lot opened fire on Beaubrun, making him the night's second fatality.

The next day, hidden police microphones at the Consenza caught Rizzuto family bosses trying to divine what had happened. Rocco (Sauce) Sollecito hoped the violence was an isolated incident. His son, Giuseppe (Joe), wasn't so optimistic, saying the black street-gang members were "not people you can sit down and reason with . . . they are animals."

Skunk Giordano, who had been present at the Moomba the night of the shootings, told the Consenza crowd that Big Mike "had no chance." Paolo Renda cautioned Giordano to be careful of overdrinking and to avoid shootouts that might "attract attention." It was clear that things would get worse before they got any better. "There will be blood," Giuseppe Sollecito said (two years before the Paul Thomas Anderson movie *There Will Be Blood*, starring Daniel Day-Lewis, made the expression a part of popular culture).

Attacks on the Rizzutos' crime family escalated. On May 25, 2005, luxury car dealer Frank Martorana was dragged from a Saint-Léonard barbershop on Jean-Talon Street East in broad daylight by four men, pistol-whipped and forced into a sport-utility vehicle. The barbershop was a place where Martorana should have felt secure, as it was just a few minutes' drive from the Consenza Social Club. Martorana was clearly a Rizzuto man, although not a high-ranking one. He had once pleaded guilty to taking part in a luxury auto theft ring that lifted high-end cars in Montreal, and his record included convictions for rolling back the odometers of used cars for sale. His tastes for the finer things in criminal life also ran to art, and he had another criminal conviction for taking part in the theft of fifteen paintings from a Montreal art gallery.

It wasn't the first time someone had targeted the car salesman to make a point with the Rizzutos. In July 2001, Vito's former drug-smuggling partner Christian Deschênes and an accomplice were arrested by police as they approached the Consenza Social Club, attempting to collect what Deschênes felt was a $2-million debt owed to him by

Martorana and Arcadi. Deschênes had learned to weld in prison, and police later learned that he'd put those skills to use constructing zoo-like cages for the two Rizzuto associates. Secretly recorded conversations revealed that Deschênes was even willing to escalate the violence to Vito: "You know, I'm telling you this, you know, even Vito, he could get involved in this." All of this was well known in the *milieu,* and so an attack on Martorana was a symbolic attack on Vito himself.

When Martorana reappeared six days after his May 2005 kidnapping, he had nothing to say to police, beyond declaring himself safe and sound. Vito's people would take care of things on their own, without police interference, but it wasn't going to be easy.

The two masked gunmen would have walked past the stylized red LOVE sculpture in front of the neighbouring L'Hôtel around 1:45 p.m. on Thursday, March 18, 2010. The sound of ever-present construction workers creating new condo units on the grand old street may have briefly disguised the noise of the fifty bullets they sprayed into Flawnego, but afternoon shoppers and tourists were quickly sprinting for cover. Falling dead amidst the designer dresses were 27-year-old Peter Christopoulos, one of Ducarme Joseph's many bodyguards, and sixty-year-old store manager Jean Gaston, Ducarme's uncle. One of Joseph's friends and an electrician's apprentice survived, despite injuries. In the confusion, Joseph escaped out the back door. The attack marked at least the fourth time he had escaped a murder attempt.

The assassins bolted down the cobblestone streets of the old quarter. They had doffed their masks and slowed down by the time they passed the nearby Intercontinental and Westin hotels, perhaps not realizing their movements were captured by video surveillance cameras as they continued on towards Saint-Antoine Street. Video cameras also recorded images of the black Dodge Caravan van in which they drove off.

Within ninety minutes, Joseph was huddling with trusted associates—including a reputed assassin nicknamed "Gunman." The meeting alone gave police enough to arrest Joseph; like so many of his

peers in the *milieu*, he was out on bail conditions that forbade any association with gang members. In his pockets, police found what they
considered to be a to-do list and some voodoo prayers. A priority task
on the list was finding photos of the men Joseph believed were trying
to kill him.

Jean-Claude Gauthier, a Montreal police street-gang specialist, told
Joseph's bail hearing that Joseph was suspected of a quarter century of
misdeeds that included attempted murder, arson, assault, sexual assault,
obstruction of justice, identity theft and inciting prostitution. Joseph
only smiled when asked if he was worried for his life, replying "It's part
of life and there's nothing I can do about that."

Police speculated that the attempted hit on Joseph was some sort of
Rizzuto-sponsored payback for the murder of Nick Jr. There were
some holes in that theory—which presumed that Joseph had either
masterminded the hit on Nick Jr. or co-operated with the killers—but
it was plausible. Hit men working for the Rizzutos were generally
more efficient, economical shots than whoever sprayed Joseph's
Montreal boutique. Shoddy marksmanship was more of a Toronto
street-gang thing. Also, Joseph had plenty of problems of his own that
didn't necessarily involve Vito and which made him eminently killable
in the eyes of many others in the *milieu* who had little or nothing to do
with the imprisoned godfather.

Chatter emerged that Agostino Cuntrera would step in and try to
calm things down. The Cuntreras had the reputation of being great
moneymakers but not so good at the muscle end of crime. Sixty-six-
year-old Cuntrera understandably preferred his mansion's massive
wine cellar to the chaos of playing street boss amidst the volatile
likes of Joseph and Goodridge. The last time the public had seen him,
he was a disco-age mobster, appearing in court wearing an Edwardian
suit with an open shirt and a white man's Afro, pleading guilty to
conspiring to murder Paolo Violi. He was a tired senior citizen now,
but someone had to stand up for Vito. Perhaps Cuntrera could at
least gather some useful information and staunch the bleeding. In a
world where information was power, Vito and his family were flying
in the dark.

CHAPTER 8

Blood trail

When Raynald Desjardins finally walked free on statutory release in June 2004 after a decade in prison for drug trafficking, he grandly announced to the press that he was no longer a criminal. From this point onwards, he was a "construction entrepreneur." How he had mastered the building trades while behind bars was left unsaid, but there was no question that the former waiter had the money to launch a new career.

By that time, Vito was already behind bars in Quebec, fighting extradition to the United States. Many years had passed since their golden days in Italy's fashion capital of Milan, when the two men arranged multi-tonne drug deals for eye-popping sums of money. Desjardins and Vito had been like brothers, but now they didn't even speak.

Also walking free that summer was Desjardins's old associate Salvatore Cazzetta, one of the few outlaw bikers without a nickname. Cazzetta was a founder of the Rock Machine Motorcycle Club, along with his younger brother Giovanni. Even with his greying ponytail and ZZ Top–style goatee, Salvatore Cazzetta had a keen business sense and natural leadership ability. He also had very few enemies for an outlaw biker leader, especially one whose club had waged a bloody, prolonged war with the Hells Angels in the late 1990s and early 2000s for control of the downtown Montreal cocaine trade. He had spent most of the war behind bars in Florida, meaning he hadn't been trying to kill Hells Angels and Hells Angels hadn't been trying to kill him.

Cazzetta had been close to Quebec Hells Angels leader Maurice (Mom) Boucher in the early 1980s. Back then, both were members of the SS, a small outlaw biker gang that cast a big shadow in the east end of the island of Montreal. Boucher moved on to the Hells Angels, and *les Hells* would have been happy to give Cazzetta one of their winged skull "death head" patches as well, but he declined. Cazzetta may have been dissuaded by a dispute between the Lennoxville and Laval charters of the club. The Lennoxville Angels suspected the Laval bikers of partying hard with drugs that were meant for sale. So Lennoxville invited members of Laval to a party—and then beat them to death with ball-peen hammers. Two months later, the decomposing bodies of five Laval Angels surfaced in the St. Lawrence River, wrapped in sleeping bags. Cazzetta reportedly considered the slaughter of fellow members to be an unforgivable breach of the biker code of brotherhood. To his mind, biker brotherhood was a forever thing, and his Rock Machine wore rings bearing their motto, À La Vie À La Mort, roughly translating to, "As We Live, So We Shall Die."

As Cazzetta returned to the *milieu*, Boucher—who had never lost his respect for Cazzetta—was gone and Vito was leaving. Cazzetta had a lot in common with Vito. He had strength, charisma and contacts. He had the diplomatic skills to find consensus between groups that gladly killed over trivial differences. And most of all, Cazzetta thought big when it came to money-making.

The bust that kept him out of the Quebec biker wars in the nineties stemmed from his role in a ring that tried to import 4,900 kilograms of cocaine into Canada through the States at a rate of 998 kilograms a month. A member of Cazzetta's ring turned police agent and introduced the biker to an undercover drug enforcement officer in Florida, who posed as an intermediary for Colombian cocaine traffickers. The undercover officer arranged to show Cazzetta and his confederates 1,000 kilos of cocaine, which he offered for $10,000 per kilo. Even on Florida's drug-washed streets, that was a first. Never before had so much cocaine been shown to suspects in a sting. Such a tactic would have been considered entrapment, and illegal, in Canada.

When the arrest warrants were drawn up, Cazzetta was nowhere to be found. He remained that way for fourteen months, before police finally caught up with him in May 1994 at a pit-bull farm in Fort Erie, Ontario, along the American border near Buffalo. Police actually had him in their grasp a month earlier, when he was pulled over in the Niagara Region for suspected drunk driving. It wasn't until police later checked his fingerprints that they realized who had just slipped through their grasp.

Cazzetta was transferred back to Quebec from Florida in 2002. When he was deposited at Archambault penitentiary, he quickly got involved in the drug trade, although, to his credit, he didn't use intimidation or threats. His prison file stated that he wasn't a particularly impulsive or aggressive person, but displayed anti-social traits such as narcissism and passive-aggression. In a description that could apply equally to many of us, his prison file also said he valued personal gratification over the greater social good. All of this made him a strong candidate to reoffend.

In June 2004, Cazzetta was up for automatic release from prison. It must have felt good, since Florida authorities had sought a life term for him less than a decade before. On his way out the door, he told the parole board that he wasn't a violent man and that his Rock Machine wasn't intended to be a criminal organization, but simply a group of entrepreneurs who sold clothing and biker accessories in boutiques. He vaguely told the board that he now intended to go into business, and blamed his involvement in the drug trade on his own personal chemical problems, when he took "a little of everything and alcohol. . . . I wanted to get rich quick. That's what got me into trouble."

In June 2005, another of Desjardins's associates was released from prison after a decade behind bars for his own cocaine-smuggling plot. That month, Desjardins attended a party at the Jaguar bar for Giovanni (Johnny) Bertolo. Like Cazzetta, he had proven solid in the face of serious prison time. Before his cocaine bust, Bertolo had worked with Desjardins's brother Jacques as a loan shark, putting out money on the street with 10 percent weekly interest to struggling business people and degenerate gamblers. He didn't soften after he was the target of a murder plot in the 1990s, and his would-be killer was arrested before he could do the job. When Bertolo felt the cold steel of handcuffs on his wrists two days before Christmas 1992—busted for a scheme to import fifty-eight kilograms of cocaine—he could have pointed a finger at men whom police would much rather have had in their net: Raynald Desjardins and other higher-ups in the Rizzuto food chain, Vito included. Instead, Bertolo quietly took the fall, as a solid guy does.

Upon his release, Bertolo was shocked to learn that his old drug turf was gone. Frank Arcadi had handed it over to someone else in Vito's organization. That was understandable. Business had to continue. Addicts want their drugs. Mobsters want their profits. What shocked Bertolo was the news that he wouldn't be getting it back. So much for loyalty. So much for keeping his mouth shut and protecting Vito. Compounding the insult, Arcadi made no accommodation to give him something else in return. No one said life in the underworld was fair, but sometimes it sucked more than others.

Bertolo's criminal record didn't stop him from finding work as a union representative for a district council within the Fédération des travailleurs et travailleuses du Québec (FTQ). A cynic might quip that the nasty criminal record looked good on his curriculum vitae in the building trades. (Quebec is hardly a distinct society in terms of corruption, though it might be unique in Canada in its willingness to expose corruption and use anti-gang legislation to fight it.) Bertolo's new job involved dropping in on construction sites to make sure collective agreements were being respected. By all reports, he was good at the job and put in long hours. Still, the feeling that he had been cheated festered inside him, and soon there was word that Bertolo was moonlighting by moving drugs on his old turf, in defiance of Arcadi.

On August 11, 2006, Bertolo was leaving a gym on Henri-Bourassa Boulevard East in Rivière des Prairies. The forty-six-year-old had plans to fly to Italy with his son later that day. Before he could step into his black BMW X5 SUV, a hail of bullets ended his life. The hit was clearly a professional job, carried out by three men who fled in a stolen Mazda

Protegé. It was abandoned on Marc-Aurèle-Fortin Boulevard, torched in typical Montreal gangland style.

There was some talk that Bertolo's murder had been ordered by Vito's group but carried out by Colombians. It did have a certain Colombian signature, with a spray of bullets to the legs followed by fatal shots in the chest and throat. The Colombians were freer with their lead distribution than old-school Montreal mobsters, who often did their deadly jobs with three shots or fewer. Shortly after Bertolo's death, a representative of the New York Bonanno family arrived in Montreal. Whatever that meant, it was hard not to see the hand of Vito's organization in Bertolo's hit, as the body wasn't handled by the Complexe Funéraire Loreto funeral home, as befitted a good soldier for the family.

News of the murder enraged Desjardins, who considered Bertolo a personal friend. It was also an ear-popping wake-up call. If this was the treatment a once-solid soldier could expect from Vito's group, what sort of man wouldn't fight back?

CHAPTER 9

Unravelling

Vito had been in custody awaiting extradition for only a few months when things started to go horribly wrong in Toronto. As if being locked up in a Montreal jail wasn't trouble enough, he was about to endure more grief, and much of it would arrive through the misbehaviour of Sicilian mobster Michele (The American) Modica and Toronto restaurateur Salvatore (Sam) Calautti.

Wherever he landed, Modica proved to be a big money-earner and a consummate management challenge. In the 1980s, he worked for the Gambino family while living illegally in the USA, until he was pinched for drug trafficking. He faced deportation in 2000 after his prison stint and the Gambinos tried hard to find a way to keep him in their ranks. Some men can quietly hide, but Modica was too loud, well known and abrasive to fade into the background. So the Gambinos worked out an arrangement with the Sicilian mob in Toronto and Modica headed north, where he would live for a year under the names Carlo Martoni and Antonio Reta. Vito's associate, blue-eyed Peter Scarcella of York Region, just north of Toronto, took him under his wing and floated him $300,000. The idea was for Modica to put the money out on the street for loans, and things would have gone swimmingly had Modica simply stuck to the plan. Instead of pumping his grubstake into loan-sharking, which promised a stable monthly return of $30,000, Modica invested in the drug trade, with potentially much higher rewards but equally higher risks.

Eventually Modica had screwed over Scarcella and most of his other Canadian hosts, as was his way. Bit by bit, he muscled his way into debt collection, drug trafficking and running illegal gambling machines, and seemed to think it was his birthright to rip off and even slap some small-time local mobsters.

Understandably, few tears were shed across the GTA underworld when Modica's Canadian adventure went sour. On June 19, 2001, police charged him with possession of stolen property. He volunteered to go back to Italy at his own expense in return for a stay in proceedings of the outstanding charges.

To all concerned, Modica's compromise seemed too good to be true. It was. In April 2003, he snuck back into Canada using a forged passport and quickly re-established himself with Michael Marrese, a round-faced, avuncular-looking man who specialized in stealing people's homes through mortgage fraud. Modica also felt a bond with Sam Calautti, and the feeling was mutual. Calautti had a split personality of sorts. Diners at his Italian restaurant on Dufferin Street in west-end Toronto would have been shaken to learn that the same soft-spoken man who gloried in serving them such tasty comfort food was also a hit man who revelled in inflicting extreme pain on the streets.

Calautti's big weakness was gambling, and whatever he won, he quickly lost. Some of his bigger losses came online through Platinum SportsBook, a Canadian-run, multi-million-dollar sports betting enterprise that linked Vito's group, York Region mobsters, independent criminals and some London, Ontario, Hells Angels. Platinum SB had an offshore server in Costa Rica, but local thugs collected its debts. Often, it was other thugs who were running into debt problems. In fact, Calautti owed Platinum about $200,000. He dealt with it like his friend Modica would: Calautti told his creditors to go fuck themselves.

Calautti sat beneath Modica in the mob pecking order, meaning that Modica bore ultimate responsibility for the lesser's conduct and debts. It wasn't just that Calautti was taking Platinum SB's money; his refusal to pay up was making all the organizations involved in running it, and

Vito himself, look as if they couldn't handle him. If Calautti wasn't made to pay up, others could be expected to shrug off their debts too. A string of meetings followed, in which senior mobsters resembled harried schoolteachers trying to decide what to do with a particularly troublesome student. Gambinos from New York City came up to York Region for some of the meetings, including one on April 9, 2004, that drew some thirty men to the Marriott Courtyard Hotel in Woodbridge. Modica arrived with two mobsters from New York and another from Ottawa. He proposed at the meeting that Calautti just pay the principal on the gambling debt and not the interest. But Calautti argued that he had already covered this and refused to pay anything more. Suspicions emerged in the room that Calautti was telling the truth, and that in fact Modica had taken Calautti's money and pumped it into a drug deal, screwing over both Calautti and his creditors.

The mob diplomats made every effort to reason with Modica, but in the end it was futile. Scarcella, who had been asked to loan out even more since the original $300,000, stepped away from the man he had once hosted and sponsored. Marrese's driver, Raffaele Delle Donne, later said he heard about what had gone on from attendees at the hotel summit: "Scarcella [was not] told the whole truth . . . and Mike Modica asked Scarcella to help him out . . . and at that point Scarcella is saying at the hotel that he washed his hands . . . basically that he wanted nothing to do with Mike Modica." According to Delle Donne, "Uh, after the meeting was over, this is what . . . I didn't see it but I heard that uh, [Platinum official] Mark [Peretz] . . . and uh, his bodyguard [Paris Christoforou of the Hells Angels] I guess . . . kicked [Modica] in the face and put a . . . gun in his mouth." Delle Donne said that Modica responded with threats of killing Scarcella, Peretz, Christoforou and others in their circle, with the ungodly phrase "clean house."

Later that month, Modica was out looking for an evening snack and stopped in at a shop called California Sandwiches in north Toronto. With him were Michael Marrese and Sicilian bodyguards Andrea Fortunato Carbone and Pietro Scaduto. These guys were serious protection befitting a tense time. Carbone was eluding Italian charges for shooting a police officer in Sicily, while Scaduto was the son of a murdered mob boss whose name still carried weight in Bagheria, nineteen kilometres outside Palermo.

A van cruised by the sandwich shop and three dozen bullets were fired inside. Modica, Carbone and Scaduto each drew nine-millimetre handguns but fled out the restaurant's back door without firing a shot in return. When the shooting stopped, Louise Russo, a forty-five-year-old mother of three, lay on the floor paralyzed.

Up to that point in Toronto, the Mafia had thrived in large measure because it didn't draw attention. Great pains had been taken to avoid blood on the streets, as this invariably brought headlines and pressure on police and authorities to crack down on crime groups. Far better to allow politicians to pretend the Mafia didn't exist.

At the time of the California Sandwiches shooting, the Ontario Hells Angels had also been making a massive effort to distance themselves from the bloody, warlike image of their Quebec brothers. They had even taken out a billboard overlooking Toronto's heavily travelled Don Valley Parkway, likening themselves to war veterans and guardians of liberty. All of that public relations work was ruined in a matter of seconds with a hail of thirty bullets.

Modica knew his would-be killers wouldn't stop at a single botched attempt. When strangers approached him near Queens Quay at the Toronto lakeshore, he dropped to the sidewalk and clutched his chest. When they told Modica that he was under arrest and not about to be murdered, his apparent heart problems abated and he got up on his feet.

On May 21, 2004, Modica was deported once again to Italy. Distance didn't cool his fury or his lust for revenge on Scarcella, his one-time sponsor. For all his own lying and cheating, Modica believed that he was the victim. Delle Donne later told police that he'd heard Modica wanted revenge on Scarcella, Peretz and Calautti. One plan was to kill Scarcella, an avid soccer fan, when he attended the Euro 2004 soccer championships in Portugal. It didn't jell, but there would be other chances. In Modica's world, a vendetta need not be rushed.

It came as no surprise that such spasms of underworld tension increased when Vito went behind bars. This situation called to mind comments made decades earlier by Palmina Puliafito, sister of mobster brothers Vic (The Egg), Frank (The Big Guy) and Giuseppe (Pep) Cotroni, to journalist Joe Marrazzo on the May 4, 1980, edition of Italian national television's *Dossier* program. She spoke proudly of relative peace when Vic the Egg was on the streets. "When my brother was in jail, someone was shot here every day," the Egg's sister said. "My brother was not here and they all felt they were the boss. When he's around, he always puts peace ahead."

Her words had a prophetic ring midway through 2005, as Vito's world felt ready to explode. Mobsters from Granby, Quebec, a small city east of Montreal, felt ripped off by Vito's group after an $11-million marijuana-smuggling operation was derailed. At the centre of the hostilities was an enigmatic strip club operator named Sergio (Grizzly, Big Guy) Piccirilli. Once a gunsmith in the Canadian Forces, he had returned to Saint-Léonard to work as a driver and muscle in the Rizzuto group. There was a story that he had fallen afoul of some of Vito's people when he refused to kill a woman and a child over a drug debt, and that he then shifted over to the Granby mob. Grizzly Piccirilli was neither a biker nor a Mafioso, but he did have connections in both camps, including Salvatore Cazzetta and relatives of Paolo Violi in Hamilton.

Some of Piccirilli's influence came from his girlfriend. Her name was Sharon Simon, but the press loved to call her "the Queen of Kanesatake" or "Smuggling Queen-pin"—she'd been previously convicted for cannabis production and smuggling tobacco and cigars, among other things—and she was the focus of a massive police operation named, in her honour, Project Cleopatra. Simon lived in a luxury home/bunker with a three-car garage on Simon Street in the Kanesatake Mohawk community fifty kilometres west of Montreal. Neighbours sometimes heard popping sounds from her backyard, as the Queen-pin undertook target practice on tin cans with an AK-47 assault rifle.

In a male-dominated milieu, Simon's connections were formidable, including links to the Sherbrooke and Trois-Rivières Hells Angels and former members of the Magog municipal police. In the world of marijuana trafficking, she was a bulk distributor, moving some forty-five kilograms of Quebec-grown marijuana to the United States per week, mostly by truck at crossings between Coaticook, in Quebec's Eastern

Townships, and Cornwall, Ontario. When Piccirilli told her he'd heard that Vito's group had a contract out on him, she grabbed him an AK-47 out of her car.

On February 4, 2005, Piccirilli drove to Hamilton, Ontario, where he met with relatives of the late Paolo Violi. By this time, Vito had been in custody for more than a year and it wasn't looking as if he would be back any time soon. Rumours circulated that Piccirilli now planned to kill Nicolò Rizzuto, even though the former soldier had shown nothing but respect for the aging Mafioso while in his employ. He scoped out the Consenza. He also secured the right guns for the job. Like the former military man he was, he watched rooftops in case a sniper was drawing a bead on him.

A last-ditch attempt at negotiations in August 2005 failed miserably, and the *milieu* appeared on the verge of open warfare. Arcadi may have been talking about Piccirilli when he said that a "biker" in Granby desired "to cut off his head." The Arcadi forces went on the offensive in a dramatic way, renting a helicopter, flying to Granby and opening fire on the home of one of the Granby mob with machine gun. It didn't cause any real damage, but it did serve notice that Arcadi was prepared to bring war literally to the homes of his enemies.

Such was the chaos that Vito heard about while fighting extradition in Sainte-Anne-des-Plaines, often in long and intense talks with his sister, Maria. When his battle to remain in Canada was finally lost, and he was being driven on August 17, 2006, to the airport, Vito lost his composure. Did no one see that he was necessary for keeping things from going even more crazy? Vito began lecturing Montreal police officers Nicodemo Milano and Franc Guimond that he was the only one who could keep relative peace among the city's criminal organizations. "You should go after the street gangs," Vito told them. "Not me. They are the ones who would create trouble."

Vito must have known that Frank Arcadi didn't have the chops to lead his organization, but *Compare* Frank seemed to be the best they could muster. "You will rue the day that I leave Canada," Vito ranted to the police officers. "You will see what will happen when I leave Canada."

Then Vito's voice softened. With his final words before boarding the government plane, he made an emotionally charged plea to the officers. "Spare my father," he said. "He's an old man. He's a sick man. Spare my father. He's not doing anything wrong."

CHAPTER 10

Undeclared war

It took less than two weeks for Vito's dark prophecy in the police car to start coming true. On August 30, 2006, Domenico Macri, the thirty-five-year-old rising soldier in the Rizzuto mob, was riding in his Cadillac through the intersection of Henri-Bourassa Boulevard and Rodolphe-Forget Boulevard at mid-afternoon when a Japanese motorcycle pulled up alongside carrying two men. Macri was a guiding force in a Rizzuto operation that used corrupt employees at Pierre Elliott Trudeau International Airport in Montreal to help with cocaine smuggling. Macri and his driver would scarcely have had time to notice as the motorcycle's passenger raised a gun and opened fire. When the bullets stopped and traffic flow resumed, Macri's driver was bleeding from his neck. He recovered, but Macri wasn't so lucky.

Macri's murder sent shivers through Vito's crime family. No one was more nervous than Arcadi, who was Macri's uncle. He had been driving just ahead of his nephew in a vehicle that looked almost identical to Macri's Cadillac. Arcadi had run the yellow light while Macri had stopped on the red. That was where the hit team drew alongside Macri and started shooting. It was wholly possible—even probable—that someone got the wrong man.

Not surprisingly, the murder was a huge topic of conversation at Bar Laennec, a coffee dive in a small strip mall on René-Laennec Boulevard in Laval. Bar Laennec was the junior version of the Consenza, where the Rizzuto family underbosses gathered. Like the Consenza, it was bugged by police.

"Yeah, bro, they shot DM, man," Skunk Giordano said.

Francesco Del Balso, who ran gambling for the family, was more expressive: "He's dead! He's dead! What happened? What are we going to do now?"

When the underbosses huddled to talk strategy in the Laennec the next day, Arcadi did his best to sound statesmanlike: "Here we are father, son and holy spirit. I agree that it's things that we have to reason out, things have to be measured, things have to be evaluated, but when it gets to a certain point and we are touched by some stupidities, the discussions have to be short."

Forever the diplomat, Paolo Renda said they should spare no expense on his funeral, calling Macri "a very nice young man." Then the *consigliere* suggested Arcadi go somewhere far away and safe: "See, what you gotta do now, find an island, take your wife and leave."

Skunk Giordano quickly agreed: "Even your wife, come on, I feel bad, *Compare*, all this shit."

"Arrange, *Compare* . . ." Renda continued.

"I have to decide if I go or don't go," replied Arcadi. "Maybe I go to Italy with my brothers."

It didn't take much more convincing to point Arcadi out of town. Before fleeing, though, he attempted to give his fellow mobsters a little pep talk, sounding like an officer on the *Titanic* poised to leap onto a life raft. He also sounded like he knew who he was looking for. "Nobody is going to get rid of me, but . . . we are looking, we are looking for that pig, we are looking for him because he's a sea of problems. What do we do, us, what we do, us, when one of us has been killed? To tell you the truth, we do what we have to do."

Not long after that, *Compare* Frank embarked on a European cruise with his wife. When push came to shove, Vito's new street boss donned casual slacks and played tourist while others inside the crumbling empire braced for more violence.

One of Vito's associates was trolling the Internet and pulled up the website of Streit Manufacturing in Innisfil, Ontario, near Barrie, north of Toronto. Soon, members of Vito's group were ordering armour-plated vehicles, including a Nissan Armada and Toyota 4Runner that could weather AK-47 blasts and bombs. They appreciated the quality of the workmanship provided by Streit, a reputable firm whose customers included the US Defense Department, the Red Cross and the United Nations, as well as Middle Eastern and African heads of state. Business at Streit improved with tough economic times, as executives and business people in the world's danger zones were particularly concerned about kidnapping, carjacking and terrorist attacks. Streit rendered high-end vehicles bomb- and machine-gun-proof with modifications including ten-centimetre-thick windows and metal inserts inside the tires, so the car can keep going even when its wheels have been shot up. Window edges were shielded with bulletproof metal seams to foil even the most knowledgeable of snipers. Rear passenger windows were modified so they wouldn't roll down, to prevent a playful child in the back seat from creating an opening for a sniper attack. Front airbags were often disabled so they wouldn't inflate if a driver was trying to crash his way out of danger. Gun ports were discreetly built into the rear panels, allowing passengers to return fire.

Meanwhile, Giuseppe Fetta and two others in the muscle end of Vito's organization were stockpiling weapons. Fetta was tied to Rizzuto underboss Francesco Del Balso. Fetta was arrested after police filmed him and two other men handling weapons on September 4, 2006, inside a warehouse belonging to Del Balso on Saint-Laurent near Sauriol, close to where he had most recently been shot. Police surveillance recorded the three men checking out a pistol with a silencer and assembling two machine guns. When police finally raided the warehouse, the pistol with the silencer and one machine gun were already out on the streets, but they still were able to seize two AR-15 semi-automatic rifles, a machine gun, a twelve-gauge shotgun, two bulletproof vests and some ammunition. Fetta was released with a suspended sentence after pleading guilty to possession of a prohibited firearm and committing an offence for a criminal organization. The raid was an annoying loss of assets for Vito's group, but nothing that couldn't be quickly replaced.

Del Balso and Giordano always travelled with bodyguards in those weeks between Macri's shooting and the Colisée raids, and much of the conversation overheard by police in Bar Laennec was about weapons.

"What you have?" Del Balso asked bodyguard Ennio Bruni.

"A .38," Bruni replied.

"The old fucking cop [gun]," Del Balso continued.

A few seconds later, there was the sound of a gunshot. One of them was clearly testing the firearm.

"Bro, this is fucking nice one," Bruni said, referring to the pistol's magazine. "Once you place it inside, it loads the gun automatically."

"That's what I want . . ." Del Balso replied.

"The best gun to have is a .22, the long one," Bruni opined.

"Long nose . . ." Del Balso added.

".357, short nose," Bruni continued. "Tha's a power you don't miss. The first shot that you're getting, the first one you're . . . you make him a hole like this."

The hoarding of arms by Del Balso, Fetta, Bruni and others built a fearsome stockpile, but it wasn't one the Rizzuto camp would soon have a chance to use in its defence.

By the time of the massive Colisée raids on November 22, 2006, Vito had already been extradited to stand trial in New York. Perhaps he saw some of the news images of his father, as Nicolò faced the media cameras with a perfectly knotted black tie against his crisp white shirt, along with a 1940s-style fedora that matched his tailored camel-coloured suit. Aside from the plastic handcuffs, Nicolò appeared dressed for a night at the theatre, not a jail cell, and as the old man was led into custody, he appeared to be grinning broadly.

Police drew upon some 1.5 million wiretap intercepts and 1,500 hours of video to arrest eighty-two members of his organization. The four-year, multi-million-dollar RCMP investigation had received assistance from the Sûreté du Québec (SQ), the police services of Montreal and Laval, Canada Border Services Agency and Canada Revenue Agency. Those arrested included such stalwarts as Paolo Renda, Lorenzo (Skunk) Giordano, Francesco (*Compare* Frank) Arcadi and Rocco (Sauce) Sollecito.

At the time, Sollecito was the least known publicly of the group, although his name frequently appeared in confidential police reports and photos. He was picked up on police recording devices receiving bundles of cash eighty-five times between February 2, 2004, and August 31, 2006, at "the Cos," where he was manager. He had garnered little direct attention since the mid-1970s, when he'd served fifteen months in jail for forging a $26,000 cheque.

Sollecito generated few headlines for the Rizzutos but plenty of money. He had been involved with Vito in Toronto stock market scams during the late 1980s, along with family stalwarts Gennaro Scaletta and Dino Messina. Schemes included wash trading, in which Vito's group would establish artificially high prices for stocks they held. Sollecito spent extended periods of time in his native province of Bari in Italy, where he invested heavily in real estate.

By the time Project Colisée had caught Sollecito on tape, he had settled tightly within the inner circle of Vito's management group. He told an Italian visitor at "the Cos" on May 23, 2005, that while Vito was in jail, the Mafia was acting as a committee of sorts: "Whenever they do something, they always bring something and we split it among us, all five—me, Vito, Nicola (Nicolò) and Paolo," Sollecito said. He might also have mentioned Arcadi as among the top level of the family.

Sollecito was also picked up on a cellphone interception in Italy on July 14, 2006. Vito was still fighting extradition and Nicolò was back in charge of the family. Two days earlier, Richard (Rick) Griffin of the West End Gang was gunned down at 2:30 a.m. in front of his home on Terrebonne Street in the Notre-Dame-de-Grâce district. Killers had pumped some forty shots at him from the lawn of the Rosedale–Queen Mary United Church across the street. Griffin had drawn the ire of Nicolò —refered to on the Consenza tapes as "the old man"—after a failed effort to import 1,300 kilograms of cocaine in partnership with the Rizzutos. The Rizzutos wanted their $2-million share of the upfront money back, and Nicolò had grown impatient. Sollecito and his thirty-year-old son Giuseppe (Joe) were apparently talking about the Griffin hit when Sollecito said, "It would be a shame if they arrested someone because of that piece of shit. And they did it in front of his house, eh?"

For Arcadi, the Colisée arrests were a rude welcoming back to Montreal, as he had barely returned from his extended European holiday when police scooped him up. There were a few inescapable ironies to the sweeping Colisée arrests. Investigators had originally targeted Vito, but he was tucked away behind bars for the American triple murders when the secret videotaping and wiretapping began. As the police mapped out their multiple raids, one of the Rizzutos' former workers—Sergio Piccirilli—had just finalized his plot to murder his old boss, Nicolò. The elder Rizzuto was in custody by the time the former soldier was ready to tap his trigger. The four-and-a-half-year, multi-million-dollar operation that was designed to take down the Rizzutos had just saved Nicolò's life and possibly spared Vito a much longer sentence than the one he would serve in Colorado.

What the RCMP didn't know the mobsters had planted a mole deep in their midst. The mole worked out of the RCMP District C headquarters on Dorchester Boulevard in downtown Montreal. Angelo Cecere was an unlikely-looking spy: he was a federal employee with a degenerative eye disease who guided himself about with a dog and a white cane. Cecere drew a government salary for a quarter century as a translator, interpreter and transcriber of wiretapped Italian-language conversations in about a dozen major Mafia cases involving Vito.

The RCMP had an inkling something was wrong, but it took them some time to focus their suspicions on the nearly blind man. After their massive Colisée roundup, the Mounties received a credible tip that one of their employees was feeding information to Vito's group. Cecere was among a small group of workers who had access to such information, so they decided to tempt him with some bait.

The Mounties installed a hidden camera in his office and began monitoring his computer activity. Then, on July 17, 2007, they invited Cecere to a meeting in which they laid out plans for a fictitious investigation, complete with a fake underworld target list. Once the meeting was over, investigators recorded a call in which Cecere instructed his son to come to his home and to "bring your friend."

The Mounties staked out Cecere's home in Saint-Léonard and saw that the "friend" was none other than Nicolas Di Marco, who had managed Nick Rizzuto Jr.'s clandestine casino. Around midnight, officers stopped Di Marco as he left Cecere's home. In his possession was paperwork from two police investigations on which Cecere and another translator had worked. Di Marco was also carrying documents outlining what appeared to be vulnerable legal points in the police translations of Colisée conversations. In those notes, Cecere zeroed in on what he thought was an incorrect translation of Italian regional slang for sexual intercourse. "What kind of qualifications do translators for the RCMP have if they don't even know how to say 'fuck' in Italian?" he'd written.

A search of the translator's home yielded a computer diskette containing a document entitled "Questions lawyers should ask." On the diskette was a discussion of the case against Giuseppe (Ponytail) De Vito, who was currently on the run from Colisée investigators. De Vito had been a major money-maker for a time, smuggling cocaine through the Trudeau airport in Montreal and paying a cut to the Rizzutos. He had friends in the Hells Angels and wasn't afraid to give the likes of Arcadi a piece of his mind if he felt cheated. But De Vito's days of paying a tax to Vito's family were over.

The diskette included mention of how De Vito stopped paying tribute to Vito's organization after the murder of De Vito's boss, Paolo Gervasi, in 2004. De Vito was deeply unimpressed that the city's Mafia bosses had somehow allowed their headquarters to be filmed and audio recorded by police. Information on that diskette noted that De Vito shouldn't turn himself in to police because they were seeking a stiff fourteen-year prison term for his attempt to import more than two hundred kilograms of cocaine into Canada.

Confronted by his employers, the best defence Cecere could manage was that he had purloined the paperwork because he had plans to write a book. Four months after he was sentenced to a year in custody, he wasn't talking about literary aspirations. This time, he told the Quebec parole board that he had wanted to get at least $250,000 from the Mafia in exchange for information. He added that his conduct might have been influenced by his use of antidepressants. The parole board declined to set him free early.

Colisée cost Vito's crime family a half-dozen senior members at a time when leadership was sorely needed. It also exposed the Rizzutos as old and vulnerable, for all their power. The most memorable footage captured by hidden police cameras comes from the backroom of the Consenza Social Club, where Nicolò holds court at a linoleum table under a hanging light, and the top level of the family routinely huddles with construction leaders and others, playing cards. As Nicolò, acting head of the largest criminal empire in the country's history, handles money some seventy-six times and stuffs wads of bills into his socks, there is something doddering, even quaint, about the way he and the others conduct their business.

Quebec's underworld was recoiling from the repeated body blows delivered by police, but Calabrian 'Ndrangheta members in Ontario were glimpsing the promise of a golden future. They made negligible ripples as they tightened up ties with the Gambino and Lucchese families in New York State on drug schemes and boiler room and stock frauds. They already enjoyed strong international drug ties, including ones to the Mexican cartels. Some things were obvious, even from Vito's faraway cell in Colorado. 'Ndrangheta power was on the rise; his family's was not.

CHAPTER 11

Ponytail's nightmare

Giuseppe (Ponytail) De Vito had a tattoo on his arm of the date November 22, 2006. That was the day his world started to crumble and he became a fugitive, a lone escapee from the massive Project Colisée bust. The tattoo would always remind De Vito what a mistake it had been to tie his fortunes to those of Vito Rizzuto.

Working in the Rizzuto organization had started off well for Ponytail. He was still a chubby-faced, grinning young man when he was bought a luxury home in Laval with his high school sweetheart, Adèle Sorella. The couple's first daughter, Amanda, was born in 1999, two years after Giuseppe and Adèle were married. A second child, Sabrina, arrived two years later, premature, and needed special care from the day she was brought home. One evening, Ponytail reeked of cigarettes when he returned from work, which wasn't surprising considering what he did for a living. Aside from running a motorcycle shop, Ponytail also helped Paolo Gervasi manage the Cabaret Castel Tina, a downmarket strip club on Jean-Talon Street East. When Ponytail entered the house, his mother-in-law, who was visiting, told him a doctor had advised that no one should smoke near Sabrina. Giuseppe was quick to jump where his daughter's health was concerned; he immediately went to a bathroom, removed his clothing with the offensive smell and took a shower.

Sabrina also suffered from juvenile rheumatoid arthritis, which caused her persistent joint pain, swelling and stiffness. Ponytail paid roughly twenty thousand dollars for a Vitaeris hyperbaric chamber, which was installed in a spare bedroom. Sabrina was afraid to go inside the chamber alone for pure oxygen treatments, and so Ponytail climbed in with her, reading her stories and soothing her fears. On the streets he was a feared mobster, but inside the walls of their family home he was a devoted dad who wasn't too proud to do what was best for his kids.

Just a few days after the Project Colisée arrests forced Ponytail to go on the run, Adèle tried to kill herself. Adèle's mother moved in with her, and her family made a point of holding regular dinners with her. Unable to help his wife, Ponytail coped with the stress of life as a fugitive by working out hard in a gym. His previously soft face turned lean and the addition of a goatee made Ponytail appear almost like a new man.

He was hardly ever able to see his daughters now, for fear the police might have his house staked out. Like many mobsters, he had a mistress and moved with her into a duplex on De Capri Street in Saint-Léonard. Still, his thoughts often drifted back to his home, his wife and his daughters.

Adèle didn't cry when she learned of her husband's mistress. She couldn't. Her tear ducts had been removed after Sabrina's birth, when a surgeon cut away a tumour from behind her ear that also left her face partially paralyzed. Adèle felt her pain intensely, even if she would never shed tears for it. Two more suicide attempts followed. Her energy was sapped. Everything that mattered was often lost in darkness. Adèle's family dearly loved her, but that just wasn't enough.

Ponytail greatly valued his relationship with bar owner Paolo Gervasi, who was close to Vito, Nicolò and members of the Rock Machine Motorcycle Club. The Rock Machine members felt so comfortable with Gervasi that they had their own reserved table at his Cabaret Castel Tina. Vito and Nicolò liked it there too. Nicolò and Gervasi often sipped grappa together in the downstairs bar while Vito used an upstairs room as his office.

The relationship shifted as Vito began working with Hells Angel Mom Boucher. Together, they sought to maximize profits by jacking up the street price of cocaine. The Rock Machine wouldn't go along with the new pricing, and kept undercutting Vito and Boucher. The Hells Angels didn't appreciate Gervasi's son Salvatore dealing drugs—cheap drugs—with the Rock Machine. They thought Vito, a fellow Italian, would be able to bring him into line.

Three-hundred-pound Salvatore didn't like being told what to do. Vito cautioned him that it wasn't smart to carry on dealing with the Rock Machine. It wasn't a direct threat, but it was a strong caution. *Compare* Frank Arcadi also warned Salvatore that it was a mistake to go on dealing with the club. The younger Gervasi ignored them both and kept on dealing with the Rock Machine—until April 2000, when someone shot him dead, wrapped his body in plastic and canvas, and hoisted him into his Porsche, which was parked in front of his father's house. Paolo Gervasi's once-comfortable world changed forever the day he peered inside that car.

The murder of Gervasi's son left the aging mobster with a haunting suspicion that just wouldn't go away. Gervasi hired a private detective to solve the crime, and drew up a list of a dozen possible suspects. He travelled to Italy on the chance that someone there might help him identify the killer. He offered up a six-figure reward for information leading to the identity of the assassin. In the end, he concluded what had seemed painfully obvious to others in the *milieu* from the beginning: his old friend Vito was to blame.

Business meant nothing now, and when Vito's group offered to buy the Castel Tina from him, Gervasi bulldozed it instead, out of spite. Thoughts of vengeance consumed him. Police warned Vito and Arcadi that they were the targets of a murder plot. Not long after that, someone planted a bomb in Gervasi's car, but it was a clumsy job and he drove away unharmed.

Paolo Gervasi's pain continued until just twelve hours before Vito's arrest in January 2004, when someone shot him several times as he sat behind the wheel of his Jeep Grand Cherokee outside a Saint-Léonard bakery. Gervasi died just a few minutes' drive from the site of his old strip club. His past four years had been so consumed with thoughts of avenging his son's death, his murder seemed almost merciful.

For Ponytail, Gervasi's murder meant the loss of a friend and mentor, and he immediately stopped paying tributes to Vito's organization. Then, on March 31, 2009, he turned on the television. The news that day broadcast that the lifeless bodies of his daughters, Amanda and Sabrina, had been found in their family home. The sisters had been discovered lying side by side in a main-floor playroom, dressed in their elementary school uniforms. Their school bags were nearby and their lunch boxes sat in the kitchen on a marble counter, filled with sandwiches and chocolate chip cookies. The girls' beds were neatly made and one was covered with stuffed animals.

The only sign of violence was a slight bruise on Sabrina's head, and a pathologist concluded it could have happened immediately after her death, if someone had moved her body. There were no signs the sisters were poisoned. It was as though Ponytail's little girls had taken a nap and never woken up.

Ponytail also heard through the media that his daughters were in good spirits on the last night of their lives. They put on a dance show for their uncle, mother and grandparents. Then they badgered their grandfather, as little girls do, to teach them a traditional Italian dance. In the final hours of their lives, the sisters learned the *tarantella*, once believed to cure the poisonous bite of a tarantula.

Ponytail knew that police would have their funeral staked out, waiting for him, so he stayed away. Through the media, he heard that the music that day included "When You Wish Upon a Star" and "Somewhere Over the Rainbow." All he could do was tattoo "S.A.D." on his left bicep for "Sabrina Amanda De Vito," along with the date of their deaths, and watch out for police and underworld enemies. How Ponytail's grief might affect his actions was anyone's guess. Vito didn't need to be told that there are few things more frightening than a man with a grudge and nothing left to lose.

Ponytail De Vito and Raynald Desjardins weren't the only former allies who had drifted far from Vito's camp. Giuseppe (Closure) Colapelle had also stopped paying tributes to the Rizzutos on drug deals. Closure got his nickname for his ability to close deals, which often relied on the application of violence. His tensions with Vito's group could be traced to his history with Frank Arcadi. Those problems had their root in Arcadi's dealings with the D'Amico crime family of Granby. Arcadi's extreme lack of diplomacy helped explain how things soured to a dangerous level between Vito's family and the family of Luigi D'Amico, a former cheesemaker who was born in Italy on December 14, 1948, and immigrated to Canada at the age of eighteen. Aside from running a restaurant, making cheese, and raising goats and chickens, D'Amico trafficked drugs.

Vito had been in custody less than two weeks when, on February 1, 2004, D'Amico telephoned the Consenza Social Club to make an appointment. He wanted to collect nine million dollars that he felt was owed to his family. Arcadi replied by calling him a "damn wanker." D'Amico wasn't rattled, answering: "Don't worry, new Montreal godfather, we'll collect with me, with a gang of wankers." Then a convoy of his men drove to the Consenza to confront *Compare* Frank.

The Granby gunmen marched past Vito's golf trophies, which stood over the bar of the Consenza, and continued on to the backroom. Arcadi was nowhere to be found, but the Granby wanker gang had made their point. It would have been impossible to imagine such a show of bravado in the Consenza if Vito were still at large.

This is where Closure Colapelle comes into it, though only Arcadi could say how. Project Colisée tapes from the Consenza Social Club showed that Arcadi somehow blamed Closure for "tarnishing everyone" with the Granby affair. Clearly, Arcadi wanted to make Colapelle a scapegoat for his own bungling. He ordered Closure brought to the basement of a café for a beating. Exactly why Colapelle was to blame was a mystery, and there was no record of that beating ever taking place. What was certain was that Arcadi had just made yet another dangerous enemy.

At least once after Gervasi's murder, Ponytail met with members of the 'Ndrangheta in a York Region coffee shop near Highway 407 and

Weston Road. He wasn't well known in the Toronto area, but it was clear from the local Calabrians' attentive demeanours that Ponytail represented an important opportunity for his hosts.

The scent of blood in the water grew stronger. In September 2007, the body of fifty-six-year-old Francesco (Frank) Velenosi of the Montreal borough of LaSalle was found stuffed in the trunk of his Volvo. Velenosi had been part of the Arcadi cell of Vito's organization, an association that was clearly no longer a ticket to wealth or security. Apparently neither Velenosi's criminal activity nor the distribution company he ran was doing well, as he had slipped into debt and filed for bankruptcy. He died from multiple stab wounds. In the *milieu*, knives were an uncommonly personal way of killing a man.

There wasn't much time to ponder Velenosi's demise before the *milieu* lost another member. Mario (Skinny) Marabella had been close to Ponytail De Vito back when Ponytail was considered one of Vito's men. Skinny and Ponytail had been convicted together for the armed robbery of a liquor truck back in 1992. After he served his time, Skinny ran a Mafia hangout on Langelier Boulevard while compiling a criminal record that included extortion, loansharking and breaking probation.

Since Vito's arrest, Skinny had shifted away from Vito's man Agostino Cuntrera and towards Giuseppe (Closure) Colapelle and Raynald Desjardins. Skinny was suspected in Montreal's first murder of 2008: the January 7 slaying of Tony Stocola, a former escort agency owner. On December 4, 2008, Skinny Marabella pulled his grey Acura MDX up to a gas station on Highway 440 in Laval's Val des Brises district. Moments after he parked, gunmen forced Skinny into a waiting vehicle. Someone drove his Acura from the gas pumps and it was discovered nearby, torched. Skinny had vanished.

Soon, the killings in Vito's old world adopted a numbing sameness. They were as expected now by the general public as the massive potholes that appear every spring in Montreal streets. Gas stations, intersections, gyms, bars: routines had become dangerous, but human nature often wins out over good sense, even in times of war.

CHAPTER 12

Who's next?

Giuseppe Coluccio knew his time in Canada was up when he tried to drive his black Range Rover out of a suburban Toronto parking lot. His path was blocked by a circle of gun-packing members of the Immigration Task Force. Later, when they checked out his waterfront condo, they found a million dollars hidden in the walls.

Coluccio's arrest was a key part of Project Reckoning, which centred on the links between the 'Ndrangheta and the Los Zetas Mexican drug cartel, with investigations in Canada, the United States, Colombia, Guatemala, Mexico, Panama and Italy. Raids netted authorities more than forty tonnes of illegal drugs, and crusading Italian anti-Mafia prosecutor Nicola Gratteri described Canada as the Coluccio brothers' "second home." The case was so big that US attorney general Michael Mukasey, Italy's defence minister Ignazio La Russa and Canada's public safety minister Stockwell Day all made triumphant announcements, with Italian authorities calling Coluccio nothing less than the "King of International Drug Trafficking." It was a rare day when Ontario generated such headlines with an underworld story, as the 'Ndrangheta preferred to operate in the province's shadows. Somewhere in that darkness, contingency plans were being made.

Back in Montreal, on the afternoon of January 16, 2009, *Compare* Frank Arcadi's associate Sam Fasulo had stopped his Jeep at a red light at the corner of Henri-Bourassa and Langelier. He'd been paroled four years earlier at the end of a police operation playfully called Project Espresso, which targeted crack cocaine and heroin dealing out of Italian cafés and bars in Saint-Léonard and Saint-Michel. Fasulo's National Parole Board decision noted that he headed a drug ring which, according to police estimates, netted $100,000 a week. Aside from drugs, the police who had arrested Fasulo had also seized automatic and semi-automatic firearms.

Project Colisée tapes included a conversation in which Fasulo's boss, Frank Arcadi, counselled the thirty-seven-year-old how to employ threats of violence. After a drug dealer with Mafia connections was roughed up, a police bug captured Arcadi commanding Fasulo to go into a bar and deliver a stern message. "You tell him: 'Don't touch this fellow or I will slit your throat like a goat,'" Arcadi ordered.

That day, as Fasulo waited for the light to change, a sport-utility vehicle pulled up alongside his Jeep and someone inside opened fire, ending his life. Anyone keeping track would have been struck by the chilling similarity between Fasulo's killing and that of Domenico Macri in August 2006. The killer's motives were unclear, but police suspected the standard ones for the *milieu*: drug turf, debt, revenge. Whatever the cause of this latest murder, Vito's crime family was a little weaker by the time the light turned green.

On June 15, 2009, Rizzuto family soldier Dany (Dany Arm) De Gregorio exited a Jarry Street gym in Saint-Léonard into a cloud of bullets. De Gregorio lucked out and survived. There was no such good fortune on August 21, 2009, when old family friend Federico (Freddy) Del Peschio walked from his silver Mercedes in the parking lot of his La Cantina Italian restaurant at the corner of Saint-Laurent Boulevard and Legendre Street. Del Peschio was beginning his work-day and the hit man once again appeared well aware of a Rizzuto associate's habits. It was no great secret where to find Del Peschio; his restaurant was an elegant spot for municipal political fundraisers, and Vito had felt comfortable enough there to use it as a meeting spot for his own business affairs.

Del Peschio had a long and close connection with the Rizzutos. Nicolò, Del Peschio, Montreal discotheque owner Gennaro Scaletta and two others were arrested on August 2, 1988, in Caracas, after authorities found eight hundred grams of cocaine hidden in a belt, much like a tourist's moneybelt. The narcotics were split into five different qualities, and police concluded that Nicolò was about to make a bulk order of several hundred kilograms of cocaine he had selected from the samples. Nicolò had lived in Venezuela on and off since the early 1970s, and it was no secret that he was a major player in the cocaine trade there. What had changed by the late 1980s was the political climate, which explained why he was forced to begin his first prison stint while in his sixties.

Vito paid $500,000 to a Venezuelan lawyer to secure his father's freedom and felt cheated when Nicolò went to prison anyway. When it became clear that his father wasn't getting out any time soon, Vito asked Italian drug trafficker Oreste Pagano to kill the lawyer to gain some level of satisfaction for the family. Pagano ducked out of the request. In his roundabout way of speaking, Pagano later explained to authorities that this meant "avoiding the consequences and reactions from the Rizzutos that I knew could be serious, taking account [of] the fact that a favor requested by him had to be brought to term."

Nicolò and his associates, including Freddy Del Peschio, were finally freed on parole in early 1993. Four months after that, the parole board granted his request that he be allowed to return to Canada to be treated for a prostate condition. An RCMP undercover officer later heard that this consent was greased by an $800,000 bribe Vito paid to Venezuelan officials.

Libertina couldn't wait for her husband's arrival and flew down to Venezuela with two of her friends so they could escort him back to Canada. When he finally landed at Dorval airport at 4 p.m. on May 23, 1993, sixty-nine-year-old Nicolò was greeted by Vito and thirty other friends and relatives, like a returning dignitary. Shortly after the elder Rizzuto's return to Canada, a former mayor of Cattolica Eraclea paid him and Libertina a personal visit, staying at their home on Mafia Row. The politician's house gifts included copies of Nicolò's birth and marriage certificates, as if they were valued artifacts marking the life of a great man.

The prison stay didn't appear to have rattled Nicolò too badly. A part of him still seemed to feed off his notoriety. When he and Libertina celebrated their fiftieth wedding anniversary in 1995 at the Sheraton Centre-Ville among some three hundred guests, the accordionist played "Speak Softly Love," the theme from *The Godfather*.

Del Peschio's killing prompted some familiar questions. As in the murder of Nick Jr., a black man was seen running away from the scene, again leaving police and the Rizzuto family to wonder if someone from a street gang had been contracted to carry out the hit. Attacks continued against Rizzuto-connected Italian cafés and bars in Montreal. Even the Rizzuto family funeral business, the Complexe Funéraire Loreto, was targeted by firebombers. Was this the way it would end for the family? Picked off by assassins, one by one?

It was around the time of Del Pschio's killing in 2009 that wealthy Montreal café owner and Desjardins protege Vittorio Mirarchi quietly made a trip to Woodbridge, Ontario, to attend the opening of a modest eatery in the heart of 'Ndrangheta territory—territory where his was becoming a familiar face as Desjardins's group sought to firm up its Calabrian connections. The York Region restaurant was the business of a relative of Antonio (The Lawyer, The Black One) Commisso, who might have attended the opening himself had he not been extradited to Italy in the summer of 2005. There, he began a ten-year term for allegedly heading a Siderno-based group that an Italian judge described as "a dangerous, bloodthirsty Mafia association which had for long imposed on the town of Siderno the burden of a permanent criminal presence." Their crimes included murder, drug trafficking and robbery. (In May 2014, Antonio Commisso won an appeal on the conviction when six other defendants were convicted instead.)

Vito's old *milieu* was changing by the minute. Helpless to staunch the bleeding on the streets or to secure the straying loyalties of his former soldiers, he began legal proceedings to get himself out of the Florence prison. He wrote Judge Nicholas Garaufis, who had heard his guilty plea in a New York courtroom, and argued he should be transferred from the Federal Correctional Institution in Colorado to a New York State penitentiary, so his family could more easily visit. The judge declined. Then Vito attempted to correct Garaufis's "incorrect calculation" of the length of his prison term. The judge declined to alter the release date.

Next, Vito wrote an appeal to expedite his release. If he failed, he wouldn't be eligible for release until October 2012. He argued to the US Court of Appeals that his sentence conditions should have been those in place in 1981, at the time the crime was committed. That was before laws were toughened, requiring inmates to serve at least 85 percent of their prison terms rather than two-thirds.

There were many who thought Vito was getting off lightly whichever way his sentence was calculated. Less than six years for three contract murders in a death penalty state looked more like an inconvenience than real punishment—a quick prison stint to shrug off responsibility for his murderous past before enjoying the spoils of his and his father's work. But now bodies kept falling in Montreal and Vito kept writing appeals in the Colorado prison. It was at least something to focus on, to keep him from being overwhelmed by the big picture. It was a given that there would be more murders. The only question seemed to be: who would be next?

CHAPTER 13

Foreign shore

It was natural for Vito to also look south in his search for answers.
Americans had considered Montreal their turf since at least 1953,
when cigar-chomping sociopath Carmine (Lillo, The Cigar) Galante
of New York's Bonanno crime family headed north and laid claim to
the city's underworld. The short, stocky, ultra-intense mobster wasn't
a particularly bright man—his IQ was assessed in prison to be 90—but
he brought a stupid man's single-minded zeal to his job. Where others
might have used finesse, Lillo set a new standard for brutality. The
diminutive mobster was a suspect in some one hundred murders in the
USA and Canada, and once reportedly amused himself at a nightspot by
making a barefoot busboy dance on cut glass. Galante's immediate goal
was to ramp up gambling enterprises and protection rackets for restaurants and nightclubs. He did that quickly, forging an alliance with local
Calabrian mobster Vic (The Egg) Cotroni and Sicilian-born Luigi
Greco. More importantly, he tightened up the French Connection
heroin-trafficking route from Marseilles to Montreal to the United
States, making use of Montreal's natural harbour as a gateway to the
New York drug market. In effect, he established a Canadian branch
plant for the Bonanno family that endured until Vito's days.

The Rizzutos had a particularly unhappy connection to the United
States that predated Lillo Galante's rise to power. Vito's paternal

grandfather, Vito Rizzuto Sr., was the first of the clan to take a run at the opportunities promised by life in North America. Vito Sr. was born on April 12, 1901, in dusty Cattolica Eraclea to Nicola and Giuseppa Marra. The paper trail he left behind suggests early and frequent troubles with authority, long before his move to America. On June 23, 1921, Vito Sr. was sentenced by a military tribunal to two months in jail for theft and spent the summer sleeping in a sparse military jail cell with no more than a plank for a bed.

On March 9, 1923, Vito Sr. married Maria Renda from his hometown. This was a step up in the world for him, although Maria did have baggage. At age twenty-six, she was five years his senior, a widow and the mother of a five-year-old son, Liborio. She had been just sixteen when she married her first husband, Francesco Milioto, on April 9, 1913. At thirty-three, he had been more than double her age. The young bride became a young widow when Milioto was shot dead in San Giorgio, a rural area in Cattolica Eraclea municipality, while trying to steal produce from another farmer.

At the time of her marriage to Vito Sr., Maria was a woman of some status in the area. Her brother was Calogero Renda, an established *campiere*. A *campiere* was at the hub of an old and durable system. He was expected to collect some fifty kilos of grain a year from small farmers as protection money, with the understanding that such payments would save them the unpleasant business of someone destroying their crops and fruit trees, or worse. A *campiere* embodied power; he could ride into the centre of town and select, with a nod or a wave, the men who would be given work that day as labourers and those who would shuffle away with nothing.

Vito Sr. and Maria had just one child of their own, a son. Nicolò Rizzuto was born on February 18, 1924, in the family home near Cattolica Eraclea's Madonna Della Mercede church. Even closer to his home than the church was a severe-looking white concrete house on a boulevard in the middle of the street that was the residence of the local Mafia don, Antonino (Don Nino) Manno. Don Nino was seldom seen, but his presence was as real as the winds or the soil. The Mafia that he represented had been a fact of life in the area long before his birth. Back in 1828, local court documents referred to an organization in Cattolica Eraclea of more than a hundred people who shared an oath never to reveal the existence of their group, on pain of death.

Nicolò was just ten months old in December 1924 when his father set off for America with a forged passport. It was common at the time for men to travel to the New World to make their fortunes, and then send for their families. Joining Vito Sr. on the voyage were his brother-in-law Calogero Renda and five others, and most likely it was Renda who supplied Vito Sr. with forged travel documents. Although Renda looked like a fresh-faced schoolboy in his passport photo, he was already experienced in the ways of the underworld.

They sailed second-class aboard the masted steamer SS *Edam* from Boulogne-sur-Mer, France, to Rotterdam, Netherlands, and then on to Havana, Cuba, Tampico, Mexico, and finally New Orleans, arriving on January 19, 1925. Vito Sr.'s travel documents declared that he had a cousin named Pietro Marino in New Orleans. There is no record of a relative with any such name, but the lie smoothed his entry into the United States. He also declared that he was an unmarried labourer.

Vito Sr. quickly moved to the Bronx, a magnet for Italian immigrants seeking work. On February 9, 1928, he filled out a form for the US Department of Labor's naturalization service declaring himself to be a patriot of his new country. He signed his name to the statement: "I am not an anarchist: I am not a polygamist nor a believer in the practice of polygamy: and it is my intention in good faith to become a citizen of the United States of America and to permanently reside therein: SO HELP ME GOD." Vito Sr. was an arsonist, but certainly not a polygamist or an anarchist. He left the Bronx and settled in the hamlet of Oradell, New Jersey, forty-five kilometres (twenty-eight miles) from midtown Manhattan.

This was a time in the early twentieth century when the manufacture, sale and distribution of alcohol were all prohibited, which created a massive growth opportunity for gangs to get into bootlegging. Emerging Mafia groups led by newcomers such as Giuseppe (Joe) Bonanno and Charles (Lucky) Luciano all scrambled for money and power, forming a commission to attempt to regulate disputes among criminals. Although

Vito Sr. would become a minor player in the expanding underworld, his first recorded brush with violence in his new country was of a personal, not professional nature, when he survived a shooting in his home on September 25, 1930. Questioned by police in hospital, Vito Sr. said: "I was shot by my best friend, Jimmy Giudice." He decided not to press charges over the dispute, believed to be the product of an incendiary love triangle.

It was around this time that Vito Sr. hooked up with publisher Max L. Simon, who had a degree in law, a string of newspapers and a deservedly nasty reputation. Syndicated newspaper columnist Westbrook Pegler described him as an "inveterate rogue" who had once taken a severe beating that seemed connected to his rackets. "He has maintained files of delicate personal information on individuals in the community who might serve on grand juries and trial juries," Pegler wrote. Soon, Vito Sr. was involved in a gang with Simon, in a business that thrived during the Great Depression: arson for insurance fraud. Arson was a relatively easy money-maker for mobsters, and decades later in Montreal, Vito Jr. and his brother-in-law/cousin, Paolo Renda, would be arrested for the same offence. Working in Vito Sr.'s gang in New Jersey was Stefano (Steve) Spinella from Cattolica Eraclea, who was related to him through his in-laws, the Rendas.

On October 17, 1931, Vito Sr. and Spinella torched the printing plant of the *Elizabeth Daily Times* in Passaic, New Jersey. The *Daily Times* was one of Simon's newspapers, and he expected a sweet insurance payoff for the fire. He had paid Vito Sr. and Spinella three hundred dollars upfront, with a promise of the rest when the job was done. When Simon reneged on settling the bill, Vito Sr. threatened his life and Simon ran to the police.

It was during this time of tensions with Simon, on November 5, 1931, that Vito Sr. was granted his American citizenship. His address was listed as 94 Ridgewood Road, Oradell, New Jersey, and he now told the truth on his government paperwork and declared that he was married. His citizenship form described him as five foot six and 155 pounds, an average size for the time. He stared directly into the camera for the photo that would become part of his police file, looking prosperous in a fine-fitting suit, dress shirt and tie. His expression was deadly serious, with no trace of a smile.

Rather than immediately follow through with his threat to punish Simon, Vito Sr. chose to move on to Patterson, New York, a rural town upstate in the Hudson Valley. (It's often confused with Paterson, New Jersey, a much larger industrial community that featured in some episodes of the television mob series *The Sopranos*.)

Summertime newcomers like Vito Sr. didn't attract too much attention in Patterson. At the time, the tiny community's population doubled during the summer, as tourists were drawn to its scenic hills and waterways. It was also a destination spot during all seasons for lovers of alcohol. Aside from its natural charms, bucolic out-of-the-way Patterson was home to several speakeasies and stills. In 1931, the smell of hops and malt hung in the air as the Patterson fire department was called to the home of Lillian F. Lloyd, where they found an illegal brewery capable of making five hundred gallons of beer per day. In March 1932, the *New York Times* reported that "women turned out by the hundreds and cheered" as federal agents carted out hundreds of jugs of whiskey and wine, dozens of barrels of cider and countless bottles of beer from restaurants, stores and homes throughout Putnam County, including Patterson.

The few people who noticed the newcomer in the summer of 1933 called him "Vito the Watchman," as he settled in a shanty by a swamp at the Tuckahoe-Patterson Marble Company's limestone quarry, a mile off the main road. Limestone from the area was used in the construction of the Empire State Building, but it wasn't a major industry, which left the shanty sitting in a fairly secluded spot. Vito Sr. lived alone by the quarry for about a month and then vanished. His exit was as quiet as his arrival. Oddly, the door to the shanty was found open and Vito Sr.'s clothes and belongings remained inside, as if he had planned to return. There was also talk of a car with New Jersey plates arriving at the quarry hours before Vito was noticed missing.

Within days of his disappearance, a storm hit the area with such ferocity that it uprooted a tree by the swamp, leaving a large crater in the soil. The rain had subsided by August 12, when the local deputy sherrif was startled by an ungodly stench that wafted from that hole. He also noticed a faint trail through the grass from the foot of the uprooted tree back to the shack. Peering into the hole, the deputy sherrif saw something wrapped in canvas, peeking out of the dirt beneath a foot of water. The canvas turned out to be in the shape of a body, with two ropes around its neck. An autopsy at the Oelkert Cox funeral parlour in nearby Brewster determined that the dead man was Vito Rizzuto Sr. and that he had suffered a fractured skull, four cracked ribs on the right side and a ruptured liver. Cause of death, according to the coroner, was blunt-force blows from a heavy object, meaning murder.

Vito Rizzuto Sr. had come to America from a highly structured world where funeral ceremonies were grand public statements of the deceased's power, status and popularity. That made Vito Sr.'s final send-off particularly sad. No family or friends were in attendance as he was lowered back into the ground at taxpayers' expense in an unmarked public plot at Patterson's county farm. For the time being, the Rizzutos of Cattolica Eraclea were anonymous and defeated in the New World.

Investigators suspected Simon had struck back in answer to Vito Sr.'s threats. Certainly the publisher seemed capable of such a thing. Vito Sr.'s murder also meant one less potential witness against Simon's arson gang. Plenty of others fresh off the boat could be found to fill his place. Vito Sr. had already been ratted out by four of his former partners when police had probed a hotel fire; it was no great leap to believe they later plotted to kill him too.

Vito Sr.'s relative Spinella was a natural suspect, as he was the only man from outside the Patterson area who knew where Vito Sr. lived. He was picked up and taken to Patterson for questioning. In a bizarre piece of policing that was perhaps intended to rattle Rizzuto's former partner in arson, Vito's body was exhumed and shown to Spinella for identification.

Until his arrest, Spinella lived at 231 East 150th Street in the south Bronx, about ten blocks from the newly built Yankee Stadium. That placed him in the centre of the crime turf of Jewish-German gangster Arthur (Dutch Schultz) Flegenheimer, a particularly brutal

Prohibition-era beer runner whose life ended on October 23, 1935, when two gunmen interrupted his dinner at the back of the Palace Chop House and Tavern in New York City. Flegenheimer's murder marked the end of the big-time independent gangs, as Italian-American Mafia groups expanded their reach.

A Putnam County grand jury probing Vito Sr.'s death indicted Spinella (incorrectly spelling his name as "Spinello"), Simon and Rosario Arcuri, also from Cattolica Eraclea, for first-degree murder on November 4, 1933. The indictment stated the three men, with "divers other person or persons," killed Vito Sr. "on or about the 6th day of August, 1933" with an iron bar or other blunt instrument. The indictment stated that Simon didn't commit the crime with his own hands, but declared that he was also guilty because he "aided, counseled, advised and procured" the others.

Arcuri was nowhere to be found when charges were eventually dropped against Simon for what was said to be lack of evidence. That left Spinella alone in the prisoner's dock in century-old Carmel courthouse, which was more cute than imposing. Murder trials were rare here, and neither the prosecutor nor the judge had previously been involved in a death penalty case. Not surprisingly, a crowd packed the courtroom for the rare drama.

Spinella must have had a sinking feeling when he saw undercover officer Anthony Aurizeme from the National Board of Fire Underwriters walk towards the witness stand. Aurizeme had been placed in Spinella's cell in Carmel County Jail as part of an undercover operation. Aurizeme testified that Spinella told him in their cell that Max Simon paid him six hundred dollars to kill Vito Sr., and that Spinella further confessed to clubbing Vito Sr. to death in his sleep with a heavy cement tamper.

Spinella had a wife, two children and a father in Italy. If the jury accepted Aurizeme's testimony, he would never see them again. Instead, he faced the very real possibility of a trip up the Hudson River to Sing Sing penitentiary, where his last sights would include "Old Sparky," the electric chair. To escape death row, Spinella pleaded guilty to manslaughter, for which he was sentenced to a term of between seven and twenty years.

Although authorities had dropped murder charges against Simon for lack of evidence, he still faced arson charges in June 1934, after gang member John Chirichillo turned on him. For this, Simon was sentenced to two to three years in prison and fined two thousand dollars, although he used his skills as a lawyer to string out proceedings with a series of delays and appeals. In the end, Simon served only nine months in the state penitentiary in Trenton. Even that wasn't hard time, as he was allowed to continue editing his newspapers from prison, and had access to steaks and a stove for his dining pleasure.

Arcuri fled the area, hunted by police, insurance investigators and mobsters alike. Perhaps he was thinking of his own childhood in Sicily late on the afternoon of August 20, 1934, as he stood under a tree in the Bronx on Crotona Park North, idly watching children play. Maybe he didn't see the maroon sedan as it pulled up alongside him or the barrel of a twelve-gauge shotgun as it appeared from a window. The last sound he would have heard was its loud blast, which dropped him to the sidewalk and left fifteen pellets in his body.

For Vito Sr., insult was added to fatal injury when an immigration and naturalization officer noted on August 22, 1935, that he had entered New Orleans with a fraudulent visa, supported by bogus documents. As he lay in his pauper's grave, Vito Sr. was subjected to one final indignity: he was posthumously stripped of his American citizenship.

Nicolò was nine years old when his father was murdered in America, and they had lived apart almost all of that time. Nicolò's uncle, Calogero Renda, had provided one strong male influence as the boy grew up. Renda, the *campiere*, had outfitted Vito Sr. with his false documents and travelled with him to America, but returned to Cattolica Eraclea in 1936 after a stopover in Argentina. Once back in Sicily, Renda married Don Nino's sister, Domenica Manno, increasing his status in the community. Renda's son, Paolo, would later marry Vito Jr.'s sister, Maria, and become an important part of the Rizzuto narrative. Nicolò also grew up close to his half-brother, Liborio Milioto, who was seven years older and whose father had also been murdered.

Nicolò matured to become a well-established *campiere* himself at just twenty years of age. He was taller, stronger and smarter than most of his neighbours, and his smile called to mind the discomforting grin of a wolf, quietly confident in its strength and instincts. It was a common sight for a sociable Nicolò to ride up on a donkey, offering a freshly rolled cigarette to a labourer in a gesture of friendship. "Nick was charming and tough at the same time," recalled his former neighbour, Liborio Spagnolo, the son of the village's first Communist mayor. "He was always smiling and trying to convince people with words and not violence."

But sometimes words fail.

CHAPTER 14

Administrative meeting

Big Joey Massino was sometimes called "The Ear" for his rule that members of the Bonanno crime family of New York couldn't mention him by name, even when he wasn't around, in case police were listening. Instead, they were to refer to him by tugging on an earlobe. That kind of vigilance helped Massino stay atop the Bonannos for two decades. Among his credos was "Once a bullet leaves that gun, you never talk about it."

Big Joey got his start running a lunch wagon business catering to factory workers, and then worked his way up in the underworld by doing "pieces of work" for the Bonanno and Gambino crime families. His most notable "piece of work" was organizing the Three Captains Murders in 1981 that eventually put Vito Rizzuto in prison.

The twenty-first century opened badly for the Bonannos, and took a nosedive from there. In 2002, beginning a humiliating string of firsts, Frank Coppa became the first known member of the crime family to talk to police. Not long after that, acting captain Joseph D'Amico became the first made member of the Bonanno crime family to wear a police wire. Underboss Sal (Good Looking Sal) Vitale took things a step further when he became the highest-ranking member of the American mob since Sammy (The Bull) Gravano in the early 1990s to co-operate with the government. James (Big Louie) Tartaglione left his own stain on the family's reputation when he became its first member to record an administrative meeting for investigators.

Things had collapsed in a big way for Big Joey by the time the first decade of the new century was half done. The rat infestation in his group led to his conviction for seven murders, with prosecution pending on an eighth and prosecutors mulling the death penalty on that remaining count.

Faced with the possibility of a lethal injection at Sing Sing, on July 30, 2004, Big Joey flipped. He began wearing a hidden recording device in the federal Metropolitan Detention Center in Brooklyn and agreed to testify for the government in upcoming mob trials, including one against his successor, Vincent (Vinny Gorgeous) Basciano, who once teased and clipped hair for a living at Hello Gorgeous, a hair salon on East Tremont Avenue in the Bronx. Among other things, Big Joey's wire caught Basciano outlining plans to murder a federal prosecutor and Nicholas Garaufis, the same Brooklyn federal judge who handled Vito's case. Ironically, when Big Joey took the stand, he testified about talking with Basciano about killing a suspected informer: "Vinny told me that he had him killed. He said he was a scumbag, a rat."

Things only got worse for Big Joey Massino. His seventy-one-year-old former *consigliere* Anthony (Fat Tony) Rabitto was knocked out of commission with sport-betting charges in June 2005. The *New York Post* dined out on the arrests of Fat Tony and some of his geriatric associates, headlining the story THE GOODFOGEY'S—GRANDPAS BUSTED IN $15M LOAN-SHARK AND GAMBLE RING, with a caption over a photo of Fat Tony that read RIPE BONANNOS.

The ultimate low point came when the public learned of Big Joey Massino's decision to become the first top boss to turn stoolie. The New York *Daily News* dubbed the Bonannos "the Rodney Dangerfields of the city's five mob families." No one gave them respect anymore.

That meant both Massino and Vitale were co-operating with authorities in May 2007 when Vito was finally called before a New York judge to answer for his role as a triggerman in the Three Captains Murders. As Vitale told authorities, Massino and Dominic (Sonny Black) Napolitano invited captains Alphonse (Sonny Red) Indelicato,

Philip (Philly Lucky) Giaccone and Dominick (Big Trin) Trinchera to an "administrative meeting" at a Brooklyn social club. Vito was one of the three designated shooters. With him was another Montrealer named "Emmanuel" and yet another Montrealer who was considerably older, whose name Vitale didn't know.

"Was someone designated as the lead shooter?" a prosecutor asked Vitale.

"Vito and Emmanuel," Vitale replied.

"Was there any discussion where the shooters, why some of the shooters were from Canada?"

"Because of a security issue. It would never leak out. And after the murders, they would go back to Montreal," Vitale replied. He continued: "The minute I walked into the club, in the foyer, Vito, Emmanuel and the old-timer, we were issued the weapons, told to have ski masks that we'd put [on] in a closet in a coatroom and before we come out," Vitale said.

"What was the purpose of the ski masks?" the prosecutor asked.

"I have no idea. I guess so the other captains that were there wouldn't know who the shooters were," Vitale said.

Vito and the two others were given guns and ski masks and sent into a closet, where they were told to crouch and wait for a sign. When they exited the closet, they were told by Massino to first say it was a stickup and then open fire. That would keep any mobsters in the club who weren't part of the plot, and who weren't targets, from suspecting that Big Joey was housecleaning inside his family.

"We entered the closet and left the door open a smidge so we could look out," Vitale testified.

The signal for Vito and the other two gunmen to spring into action came when Montrealer George (George from Canada) Sciascia ran his fingers through his hair.

"I heard Vito say, 'Don't anybody move. This is a holdup,'" Vitale said. "Then shots were fired. I seen Vito shooting. I don't know who he hit. I saw Joe Massino punching Philly Lucky."

Their bloody chore completed, it fell upon a cleanup crew to wrap the bodies in drop cloths and carry them to a van. "It was a mess,"

Vitale said. "There was blood all over the place. There was too much blood. We couldn't clean up. It was impossible to clean up." That's when Massino gave the order to burn the club down, Vitale said.

At the United States Courthouse in Brooklyn, Vito was represented by lawyer John W. Mitchell, whose previous clients included the late John Gotti, former boss of the Gambino crime family. Even though he had been a gunman in three contract murders, Vito only faced the racketeering charge of conspiracy to commit murder for a criminal organization. Had he been an American living in the USA, he likely would have been charged with first-degree murder, which was a death penalty offence in New York State. However, the charge was lowered to conspiracy because American officials feared Canada wouldn't extradite him if there was a possibility of execution.

In his pre-sentence statement to court, Vito stopped short of telling the judge that he actually fired a fatal shot. Yes, he held a gun, and yes, there were three murders, but Vito was saying the bare minimum: "I did participate. . . . My job was to say, 'It's a hold-up,' so everybody would stand still."

At the sentencing, Vito looked like a shell of the exquisitely dressed man who used to strut about Montreal as if he owned it. Vito was only sixty-one, which, considering the family's history of longevity, should have given him every reason to think that when he got out of prison he would be able to resume his life at the top level of the Mafia. His father was then eighty-three and facing twenty-three charges of his own from Project Colisée, including ones for gangsterism and importing and exporting illegal drugs. Mob bosses are often just hitting their stride when they begin gumming their food. Vito had his father's energy and the Mafia had no retirement plan. Despite Vito's alleged ailments, Mitchell said in an interview that during Vito's three and a half years in pretrial custody he hadn't lost a pound, which was also rare after so long on a prison diet.

Vito told the judge that he wasn't well and that he'd received some troubling news after a checkup a few weeks earlier. "They said they found a spot in my lungs, but they haven't said what's up to now yet," Vito said. "They have to give me a CAT scan but will bring me to the hospital, but they haven't," he told court. It's a tried-and-true tactic to fake medical problems when brought before a judge, so Vito's words didn't win him much sympathy. He was sentenced to ten years in custody, which amounted to five and a half years in real time, after he was given credit for pretrial custody in Canada and New York. If he stayed in the United States after his prison time elapsed, there would also be three years of parole. The judge recommended that Vito be held someplace where he could receive further medical testing.

Vito originally expected the deal would also include a provision that he serve his time in a prison close to the Quebec border, so his family could visit. Mitchell expected this would mean the Ray Brook medium-security correctional facility in upper New York State, a pleasant two-hour drive from Montreal. The Ray Brook facility was built in the Adirondack Mountains on the site of the 1980 Lake Placid Olympics. Despite the scenic surroundings, Mitchell dismissed the suggestion that it was a country club prison. "It's a serious place," Mitchell said. "There's a lot of gangs up there. It'll be no walk in the park, but he'll be okay."

Soon after the sentencing, Vito's mood must have darkened considerably. He wasn't being sent to Ray Brook. Instead, his home for the next five and a half years was to be in tiny Florence, Colorado, more than 2,600 kilometres (1,600 miles) from Montreal.

As Vito settled into prison life, the Bonannos' troubles extended beyond the stampede of informants within their own ranks. They and other New York mob families were receiving a serious ass-kicking from emerging Albanian, Russian and Chinatown gangs. The Mafia no longer reigned supreme. In one particularly troubling incident for the city's old-school mob, an Albanian boss reportedly demanded Gotti's old table at a mob restaurant to make it clear he considered himself the new top mobster in the city. Five and a half years wasn't a long sentence for helping to murder three men. Still, it was long enough for Vito to wonder what would be left of his old world when he was finally set free.

CHAPTER 15

Northern aim

A dangerous newcomer quietly arrived in Canada as Vito settled into American prison life. Salvatore (Sal the Ironworker, The Bambino Boss) Montagna went virtually unnoticed when he moved north of Montreal, just outside small-town Saint-Hubert, Quebec (population 77,000), in April 2009. His new home, a solid if unspectacular house on a secluded dirt road, belonged to a cousin and looked like the sort of place where the locals wouldn't know a Mafioso if they saw one.

News of Montagna's arrival would leak out soon enough, and when it did, even the calmest man in Vito's world would feel his heart beat a little faster. Men such as Raynald Desjardins and Joe Di Maulo, who had drifted from Vito's circle, would have to decide whether to view Montagna as a potential ally or a threat. He was the leader of the Bonannos, the oldest Mafia family in New York City. Beleaguered as the family was, when Bonannos appeared in Canada, things generally got exciting in a bad way.

Vito's absence presented Montagna with a once-in-a-generation opportunity to gain control of the all-important Port of Montreal, although he would need to pull together a coalition to do it. A firm grip on the port would vault the troubled Bonannos from laughingstock to powerhouse. Still, despite the riches to be gained, Montagna's move north seemed tentative; his wife and three daughters remained in New York, making only weekend visits.

Montagna had the swagger of a New York City mob guy, with the requisite mistress. She visited on the weekends when his wife stayed home. A gaunt brunette who had been with him for years, she knew the routine that went with being on the arm of a mobster without a ring on her finger. There was no fuss from her when the Canadian Border Services Agency asked her about sixty thousand dollars in cash she brought on one trip north. There is nothing illegal about carrying a large sum of money, so she just replied that she was thinking of buying some things in Canada and left it at that. She also didn't get bent out of joint one weekend when Montagna booked her into a hotel near his home, since his wife was also in town. She knew her place in the grand scheme of things and was far beyond getting easily offended.

Montagna wasn't a total newcomer to Montreal. He was born there in 1971, but his parents moved when he was very young and raised him until the age of fifteen in Castellammare del Golfo, Sicily. The Mediterranean fishing community had a generations-old history of partnering with the American mob. The town—whose name translates to "Castle by the Sea"— was the birthplace of a string of notorious American mobsters, including Salvatore (Don Turiddu) Maranzano (assassinated in 1931), Giuseppe (Joe) Profaci (died of liver cancer in 1962), Carmine (Lillo, The Cigar) Galante (murdered in 1979) and Joe Bonanno, who was a model for the Don Corleone character in Mario Puzo's The Godfather (dead of natural causes at age ninety-seven).

In Montagna's youth, Castellammare del Golfo frequently served as a hideout for Mafiosi fleeing American authorities. It was also a training ground of sorts for younger mobsters heading to America, according to Mafia turncoat Antonio (Nino) Giuffrè from Caccamo in Palermo province. Among those who found refuge in the town at that time was Rosario (Saro, Saruzzo) Naimo, who had tight ties with the Gambino family. Barely known in North America, Naimo was considered the top Sicilian Mafioso in the United States during the 1980s, and was described by Sicilian boss Toto (The Beast) Riina, with more than a little hyperbole, as "more powerful than the President of the

United States." While Riina exaggerated, Naimo was a supremely powerful man in his own milieu, reigning with Riina over an influx of Sicilian mobsters who fled to the USA to escape Italian mob wars and crackdowns. Such men were known as *gli scappati*, "the escapees."

The Sicilian Mafia operated in a lower key in the 1990s, after the crackdowns that followed the 1992 murders of popular judges Giovanni Falcone and Paolo Borsellino. The Beast was replaced by Bernardo Provenzano, who was described by some as a "kindly dictator." He was nicknamed "The Tractor" for his relentless ability to plow his enemies down, but he also understood the value of flexibility and charm.

Such was the environment in which young Salvatore Montagna prepared for his future.

When he was fifteen, Montagna moved with his family to New York City, where he went to high school and graduated into the Bonanno crime family. At that time, Vito was still considered a member of the Bonanno organization. Vito was among the honoured guests on November 16, 1980, attending the wedding of Sicilian mob boss Giuseppe (Pippo) Bono at the elegant Pierre Hotel in Manhattan. Also attending were high-ranking members of the American La Cosa Nostra from the Bonanno, Gambino and Decavalcante families, including Dominick (The Chin) Trinchera, J.B. Indelicato, Alphonse (Sonny Red) Indelicato, Philip (Philly Lucky) Giaccone and Cesare (Tall Guy) Bonventre. The goodwill didn't last long. Giaccone and Trinchera were two of the three mob captains Vito helped kill just a year later, while Bonventre's body ended up in two oil drums, dead at the hands of other attackers.

At a considerably less gaudy wedding a decade later, Montagna married Kellice Gucciardo, who was related to members of the Gambino and Genovese families. They had two children, and he and his wife divorced after one of the children died. Montagna first caught the eye of investigators from the New York office of the FBI when he was seen hanging out with Patrick De Filippo, a Bonanno *capo*. De Filippo had spent time in Toronto and Montreal back in the 1960s and 1970s and was the killer of Vito's friend George (George from Canada) Sciascia in March 1999. Montagna was arrested in 2002 after the Manhattan district attorney's office conducted an investigation into illegal gambling and loansharking. Montagna held true to the old Mafia code by refusing to squeal while before a Manhattan grand jury. "The witness . . . continued to insist that his memory was weak, asserting that he could not even recall the date of his wedding," complained prosecutor Vincent Heintz to a judge. "He then jokingly asked the prosecutor not to share this answer with his wife." Heintz continued: "The witness refused to explain his understanding of the word 'wiseguy.' Instead, he made glib, nonresponsive allusions to *The Sopranos* and *The Godfather.*"

Sal the Ironworker's memory did improve when he was questioned that day about his job at Matrix Steel in Brooklyn, where he said he worked as an estimator for his second wife, Francesca, the company's nominal president. He also was able to recall details about complicated labour contracts and the quality of gelato sold by his Toronto cousins. He just couldn't remember the answers to any of the questions about gambling that the prosecutor really wanted answered. His youthful amnesia on Mafia matters brought him an indictment for criminal contempt, to which he pleaded guilty in 2003. That conviction didn't seem then like a particularly big deal.

Between 2006 and 2008, Montagna became an acting captain in a Bronx-based crew of the Bonannos. He rose up under Big Joey Massino and Vincenzo Basciano, both of whom used Montagna to convey messages to Canadian-based Bonanno members and associates.

He graduated to acting leader of the entire family at age thirty-five, earning himself the nickname "The Bambino Boss." There were good reasons for promoting Montagna within the Bonannos. He was both youthful and a traditionalist, which doubled his appeal in some Bonanno circles. That said, Sal the Ironworker's brains and ambition didn't fully explain his quick rise. There was also a distinct shortage of non-murdered, non-arrested mobsters to compete with him for the job. Thanks to the betrayals of Big Joey Massino, once the most circumspect of New York's Mafia family leaders, and a small host of others who had turned evidence on the family, Montagna had inherited a Bonanno organization in free fall, with no end in sight.

Montagna's ride on the Bonanno runaway train came to a sudden halt when he was charged with being a deportable alien, as the

Canadian-born boss had never taken out American citizenship. Suddenly, his 2003 contempt conviction came back to haunt him, as it was enough to have him removed from the country. He chose to self-deport, which got him briefly out of the Bonanno disaster area. It also meant he could reapply to get back into the United States in a year. In April 2009, he flew to Montreal, watched by US Immigration and Customs Enforcement officials.

Sal the Ironworker was not facing warrants for any crime, so he stepped onto Canadian soil a free man. Perhaps he thought Montreal would provide easy pickings after life in the cauldron of New York City and his formative years in Sicily. How tough could it be? Frank (The Big Guy) Cotroni was dead. Vito was locked away in prison, and even Vito's octogenarian father, Nicolò, was behind bars on his Colisée charges. Hells Angels boss Maurice (Mom) Boucher was also out of the way, serving a life term for two murders. The New York tabloids seemed to think Canada was ripe for the taking. When Montagna headed north, the New York *Daily News* crowed, BONANNO BIG BOOTED BACK TO BOONDOCKS, with the subhead: SEEMS TO BE CHOICE OF BOZOS IN BROOKLYN OR EASY PICKINGS IN MONTREAL.

If Montagna believed the newspapers, there was nothing more to conquering Montreal than setting foot in the city. The American papers hadn't noticed that Canadian mobsters had guns too.

CHAPTER 16

Friends like these

Soon after his move to Canada, Sal Montagna quietly appeared in the Greater Toronto Area and nearby Hamilton, meeting up with members of the *camera di controllo* of the local 'Ndrangheta. Curiously, he didn't seem at all interested in meeting with the local Sicilian mobsters, even though this was the accepted protocol since he was Sicilian himself.

By this time, fifteen Mafia groups had settled in Ontario. Most were families of the Calabrian 'Ndrangheta, the world's most powerful Italian-based organized crime group. Nine of those Mafia groups were 'Ndrangheta families based around Toronto, mostly in York Region. 'Ndrangheta groups are notoriously hard to infiltrate, as membership is based on blood relationships, with sons routinely following in their fathers' footsteps on the path to crime. (It goes without saying that daughters aren't allowed into the mix.) The group's members are screened through a lengthy grooming process before they can be considered one of the *uomini d'onore*, "men of honour." Intermarriage often binds group members even more tightly.

Since the heyday of Giacomo Luppino in Hamilton in the 1960s, the 'Ndrangheta had sunk its roots deep into Ontario's relatively calm political and business environment. Between 1967 and 1983, Toronto police blamed sixteen murders on Italian organized crime. It wasn't a huge number, but police weren't playing it down. "These murders depict the realism of the ceaseless progression of the La Cosa Nostra and 'Ndrangheta in our society," cautioned an Ontario police report from the mid-1980s.

By the time of Montagna's arrival in Ontario, the province was the 'Ndrangheta's unchallenged epicentre in North America. When Italian authorities referred to "America" in regards to the 'Ndrangheta, they meant Ontario. This was especially true for the old families of Hamilton and rich transnational newcomers in suburban York Region. The International Monetary Fund estimated some $225 billion was laundered each year in Canada, most of it ending up in Ontario. It was a cozy climate for investment, as few Ontario residents even knew the crime network existed and fewer still could properly pronounce its name (en-DRANG-gheta).

It wasn't just Canadians who underestimated the strength of the 'Ndrangheta. The crime network wasn't really noticed internationally until August 15, 2007. On that day, a two-man hit squad from the Calabrian town of San Luca shot dead six men who were exiting a pizzeria in the normally peaceful German city of Duisburg. The victims had just attended a birthday party and one of the murdered men was an eighteen-year-old boy. The killings showed the reach and staying power and insane potential of a vendetta, as the escalating feud stemmed from an egg-throwing incident at a carnival almost twenty years earlier. The vendetta had led to more than a dozen tit-for-tat killings before the hit men made their bloody statement in Duisburg, including the slaying of the wife of an 'Ndrangheta boss on Christmas Day 2006.

The Duisburg slaughter brought new attention to the 'Ndrangheta, and recognition that it was the most powerful and toughest to penetrate of the Italian Mafias. It dominated the European cocaine trade and was now pushing for control of the North American market by flooding it with almost pure product, squeezing out competition trying to move lower-grade goods. This strategy had worked in Europe and there appeared to be no reason why it shouldn't also succeed in North America.

Cocaine sales provided seed financing for a range of other activities, including marijuana grow operations, international weapons trafficking, environmental schemes like hazardous waste disposal, and stock market scams. But police experts noted that 'Ndrangheta leaders in Canada sometimes worked regular jobs, from accountants to garden centre operators, and even acted as youth soccer coaches. The legitimate activities would help them forge inroads into ostensibly legitimate businesses and governments, and a cloak of legitimacy that made mobsters appear non-threatening.

Post-9/11 crackdowns on border security and foreign investment benefitted the Canadian 'Ndrangheta, as these new pressures forced money north and into their hands. On a broader global scale, the worldwide economic crisis was a blessing for the 'Ndrangheta. In particular, the European debt crisis created opportunities for loansharks and shady investors, especially in the weakened economies of Spain and Greece.

Billions of dollars of drug money also helped banks ride out the global crisis of 2007–8. In turn, this allowed criminal organizations to wash illegal proceeds and insinuate themselves into the mainstream economy. Top Italian anti-Mafia prosecutor Nicola Gratteri notes that banks sorely needed cash and were able to provide a safe investment environment for massive narco-revenues. "Drug dealers are the only ones with cash, especially in times of crisis," Gratteri said in a 2014 interview. Criminal organizations enjoyed the new €500 bills and made them their unofficial currency, as up to €10 million could be packed into a forty-five-centimetre safety deposit box and the equivalent of a million dollars could be easily carried in a suitcase. In Switzerland, a country where Vito's family had enjoyed stashing much of its fortune in the past, the law was slow to act against organized crime, and it wasn't until 2013 that the banking country had an operational witness protection program. By then, Switzerland had become a favoured spot for the 'Ndrangheta to wash dirty money.

For Montagna, meeting with the 'Ndrangheta in southern Ontario opened up refreshing possibilities for growth after being mired in the chaos of New York City. The 1950s and 1960s, when the 'Ndrangheta was sneeringly referred to as the "lunch-bucket mob," were long over. The network had bases on five continents and sat fourth on the White House list of the world's most dangerous criminal groups, behind only al Qaeda, the PKK (Kurdistan Workers' Party) and Mexican drug cartels.

The calm face of Ontario's 'Ndrangheta stood in dramatic contrast to the bloody activities of their Mexican partners. From the Rio Grande to Central America, there were some ten thousand gunmen in the Los Zetas drug cartel alone, and their cruelty knew no limits as they pushed ahead of established Colombian drug cartels. Former special forces soldiers in their ranks played a major role in the slaughter of some sixty thousand people between 2006 and 2012. In a veritable war zone, some of their victims were burned alive in drums of flaming diesel. Severed heads of others were rolled onto crowded nightclub dance floors or sewn onto soccer balls to intimidate rivals and justice seekers. As Montagna settled into Canada, the town of Ciudad Juárez already belonged to the Mexican cartels and their partners in the 'Ndrangheta, giving them control of the back door to the New York drug market. If Montagna could help them gain control of the Port of Montreal, they would enter North America through the front door as well.

Even though his target was Montreal, Montagna looked to settle in Ontario rather than Quebec. He couldn't speak French and wasn't particularly happy with the pace of life in small-town Saint-Hubert. In affluent Woodbridge, just north of Toronto, he would be closer to family members who had already settled there, as well as to the North American base of the Coluccio 'Ndrangheta cell. A move to Ontario promised to make him more comfortable and prosperous, and likely safer as well. These were people who had tolerated Vito but were only too willing to turn on the temporarily deposed godfather for the promise of a better offer. If all went well, he and his family would settle into a house of their own in the Toronto area in the spring of 2011.

But underworld politics in Ontario were complex. The Cuntrera–Caruana group in the province had been aligned with Vito's group, and theirs was a profitable partnership. They maintained a strong presence in the Toronto area, even after Alfonso Caruana was arrested in 1998 for his part in trafficking 1,500 kilograms of cocaine (worth at least a billion dollars) between Colombia and Canada. Montagna would have to be able to convince them that he could offer something even better to ensure he was treading on safe ground. He wouldn't need to start from scratch, though. Relations were warming up between the Cuntrera–Caruana group and the GTA 'Ndrangheta in Vito's absence. While Vito's group was burning bridges to the United States, the 'Ndrangheta was quietly building alliances and reaching out. Meetings were now held in Cuba, a throwback to the heyday of crime on the island in the 1950s, when Cuban dictator Fulgencio Batista was in power. It wasn't just the great weather or the fact that they could fly from Toronto to Havana non-stop in just over three hours; corruption at Cuban airports made the country a good drug drop-off point with negligible risk of surveillance from Canadian police.

Hanging over all of their heads as they planned was the prospect of Vito's release. He was due out in October 2012, and this raised the spectre of spectacular violence, and not just in Montreal. If Montagna and the other groups were going to consolidate their grip on Vito's turf, they had better do it fast and they had better do it well.

CHAPTER 17

Clearing space

There was a time, before mob hit man Ken Murdock pointed a gun at his head and squeezed the trigger, when it seemed Johnny (Pops) Papalia was as permanent a fixture of Hamilton as the limestone cliffs of the Niagara Escarpment. The son of a Prohibition-era bootlegger, young Pops apprenticed in Montreal under Carmine Galante in the 1950s. In the 1963 report of the US Senate Permanent Subcommittee on Organized Crime and Illicit Traffic, Papalia was named as a key Canadian under the wing of the Buffalo mob. Counsel for that subcommittee was future American attorney general Robert F. Kennedy. Back then, Vito hadn't even dropped out of high school yet and the Rizzutos weren't anyone's idea of a crime family.

Less than two months after Pops's murder on May 31, 1997, his lieutenant Carmen Barillaro was shot dead in the entranceway of his Niagara Falls, Ontario, home on the eve of his fifty-third birthday. Murdock was again the shooter. Neither killing was directly traced to Vito, although his shadow fell over both crimes. Certainly Murdock, a long-time Hamilton rounder, had never met the Montreal godfather. But just as certainly, the murder was orchestrated by forces that supported him.

In the late nineties, Vito was seeking to cut links to the American La Cosa Nostra and create a Canadian-based Mafia that was no longer an appendix of the US organization. On October 22, 1997, four months after the Papalia murder, Vito met with fifteen men he considered loyalists in a Woodbridge restaurant, including Murdock's one-time boss, Pasquale (Pat) Musitano of Hamilton. Also there was Gaetano (Guy) Panepinto of Toronto, the proprietor of a west Toronto gym and a cut-rate casket business with the motto "Do not make an emotional loss a financial loss." His merchandise included free caskets for kids, and a country-styled, denim-covered model called the Tucson (also known as the "Bubba Box").

Musitano and his younger brother Angelo were originally charged with two counts each of first-degree murder for arranging the Papalia and Barillaro hits. Eventually, they pled guilty to one count each of murder conspiracy for Barillaro's death. Vito's name was left out of the court proceedings, although Ontario became a much more agreeable place for him to do business after the deaths. Other inconvenient Ontario bodies that fell conveniently dead included that of Papalia's close friend Enio Mora of Toronto. His remains, with an artificial leg detached, were found stuffed in the trunk of his gold Cadillac just off Highway 400 in Vaughan.

The removal from the scene of Papalia, Barillaro and Mora certainly helped Vito create more space for his own independent crime family in Canada, free from the stumbling Bonanno family of New York. While politicians in Vito's home province talked for generations about separation from English-speaking Canada, Vito was making his own version of Quebec independence a reality, except he wanted to take Ontario with him. And the Bonannos were in no position to resist his inter-provincial power play.

Murdock later told the *Toronto Star* that he was instructed by senior members of the Musitano crime family to pull the trigger on a half-dozen others, almost all of whom were key members of the Ontario 'Ndrangheta. Most were blood relatives and in-laws of his father's old rival, Paolo Violi: Jimmy Luppino and Paolo Violi's two sons, four other family members and in-laws of the late Giacomo Luppino, and also mob enforcer and former professional wrestler Ion (Johnny K-9) Croitoru, who once rode with the Satan's Choice Motorcycle Club. Murdock chose not to carry out those jobs.

In all of the cases, Murdock said that he wasn't explicitly told by his superiors to kill someone. He just heard the mention of someone's name, followed by the comment, "He has to go." It was a no-brainer to fill in the blanks. There had once been talk that Jimmy Luppino had brokered a truce with the Rizzutos in the early 1980s in order to spare the male children of the murdered Violi brothers. Even if that had once been true, it was safe to say that all deals were now off.

Gaetano (Guy) Panepinto remained Vito's point man in Toronto, a position that required street sense, toughness, loyalty and a sense of criminal enterprise. His crew included a man nicknamed "Spiderman," whose mother had an ongoing affair with Vito. Spiderman worked out hard to improve his gymnastic skills so that he could be a better burglar. There was also gym owner Constantine (Big Gus) Alevizos, a former pro football player who stood six foot six, tipped the scales on the portly side of 450 pounds and had "Big Kahuna" tattooed across his back. Panepinto's crew smuggled marijuana, manufactured ecstasy tablets and peddled the date-rape drug gamma-hydroxybutyrate (GHB), anabolic steroids, stolen painkillers and magic mushrooms. They made up bogus credit cards, which they used to buy products for resale on the black market. Common to members of Panepinto's group was an affection for the gym and steroids, and also a closeness to local biker clubs, including the independent Toronto-based Vagabonds.

Panepinto's connection to Vito didn't scare off members of the Ontario 'Ndrangheta, particularly Domenic Napoli, Antonio Oppedisano and Salvatore (Sam) Calautti. Napoli and Oppedisano were both recent arrivals from Siderno, where Napoli had been part of a hit team for boss Cosimo (The Quail) Commisso. For a time in Ontario, Calautti and Napoli were roommates, and even when they found separate places, they remained good friends.

Calautti wasn't a physical presence like Panepinto, but out-of-shape mobsters are sometimes the most dangerous, as they are the most likely to start shooting when threatened or irritated. Despite his pudgy, short frame, Calautti commanded fear. Restaurant suppliers dreaded dealing with him, as he would often simply refuse to pay his accounts. At least once, he put a gun on the table to intimidate. "You don't have to be a juice monkey to be a gangster," said a police officer who knew him. "He loved inflicting pain on people and people knew it."

Calautti fell under suspicion in January 1996 when someone lured Toronto baker Frank Loiero from a Sunday family dinner. Thirty minutes later, passersby found Loiero's bullet-riddled body hanging out of a broken side window of his van, which was parked in the deserted Woodbridge Mall. Loiero had been seated in the back and was shot multiple times at close range with a semi-automatic handgun. On the dead man, police found about $5,000 in cash, a $10,000 ring and a Rolex watch estimated to be worth as much as $25,000. He was also wearing a gold bracelet and necklace. Clearly, this was not a robbery. There were whispers that Loiero, who supplied guns and cars for the mob, had been speaking with police.

Oppedisano and Napoli infuriated Panepinto by cutting into what he considered his video-gambling territory in York Region. In March 2000, the 'Ndrangheta men simply vanished. Rumours circulated that they had been cut up and their remains destroyed in the basement of Panepinto's casket business on St. Clair Avenue West in Toronto's Corso Italia, but the building was too clean for police to pull traces for DNA tests. Meanwhile, Panepinto quietly relocated to Montreal to get away from the heat and closer to Vito.

Within weeks, dour-faced 'Ndrangheta men from southern Italy came calling for Vito in Montreal, asking blunt questions about their missing relatives. Did Vito know anything about them? Had he ordered their murders? The people asking the questions were serious men and they expected satisfaction. Panepinto was now a liability for Vito. When the Calabrians left, Vito summoned him for a meeting, which ended with Vito reassuring Panepinto that it was safe for him to go home. Panepinto apparently trusted his boss with his life, and he returned to Toronto.

Calautti fed off the adrenalin of tough jobs, and the thought of avenging his friend Napoli made the idea of a hit on Panepinto doubly appealing. Aside from the Loiero hit, Calautti was already a suspect in a string of other mob killings and considered a made man in the 'Ndrangheta. He worked for three GTA families, all of whom were considered strongly opposed to Vito's stranglehold on Montreal and recent moves in Ontario. Shortly before 8 p.m. on Tuesday, October 3, 2000, Panepinto was driving his maroon Cadillac on Bloor Street West, just west of Highway 27, when a van pulled alongside with its passenger-side window rolled down. Seconds later, the Cadillac rolled through the intersection with Panepinto slumped over the steering wheel, bleeding from shotgun pellets and six bullets in his shoulder, chest and abdomen. His murder was never officially solved, but it wasn't considered a mystery. Suspicions stopped at Calautti and a close associate.

Vito appeared at the Toronto funeral home to pay his respects, even though he had sent Panepinto to his death. Perhaps he even felt bad, as he didn't have a personal grudge against the dead man, who trusted him until the end. Accompanying Vito from Montreal were Paolo Renda, Frank Arcadi and Rocco Sollecito. The murder marked a rare lapse in Vito's judgment, and a subtle turning point in his fortunes. It would have been far better to take action himself against Panepinto if he needed to sacrifice his lieutenant. By bending to the pressure of the Italian team that visited him, Vito had further legitimized the 'Ndrangheta on the streets and undermined his own security.

CHAPTER 18

Man in the shadows

G uy Panepinto's replacement on the streets of Toronto came in an equally large and powerful package. Juan Ramon Paz Fernandez was alternately known on the streets as James Shaddock, Joey Bravo and Johnny Bravo. He shared Panepinto's affection for the gym and once posed for a photo with wrestler Hulk Hogan, beaming like a schoolboy.

Fernandez had been ushered into Vito's circle in Montreal by Raynald Desjardins a decade earlier. When police investigated Agostino Cuntrera between November 1990 and April 1991 for shaking down pizza parlours, Fernandez showed up on wiretaps as a principal acquaintance of the Sicilian Mafioso.

Like Vito, Fernandez was capable of charm and threats in Italian, Spanish and English. Also like Vito, he had been brought to Canada as a child. Born in the fishing port of Ribeira in Galicia, Spain, Fernandez was just five years old when he first set foot in Canada. He graduated from youthful break-and-enters for jewellery, cash and credit cards to being the driver for mob boss Frank (The Big Guy) Cotroni. Fernandez stood out for his movie-star good looks, volcanic temper and black belt in karate, which let him act out his aggressions in an efficient and deadly manner. His temper put him behind bars when in 1977 he punched his seventeen-year-old stripper girlfriend in the throat so hard that it killed her, after she reportedly refused to have sex with one of his associates. At age twenty-two, he was looking at twelve years in prison for her death. In an odd way, the sentence proved to be a career boost. It was behind bars that he met and impressed Desjardins.

He was back behind bars in 1991 for trafficking three kilos of cocaine, and somehow found the time to become engaged. When Fernandez was married in Archambault prison in Sainte-Anne-des-Plaines on April 10, 1992, Desjardins and his brother Jacques were among the guests. Vito was invited too, but authorities considered him too notorious to allow into the prison.

In 1994, Fernandez was in maximum-security Donnacona penitentiary near Quebec City. Somehow, he was able to arrange for strippers to visit and liven up the cellblocks. It was a telling display of power, although running strippers into prisons was not without precedent. Lawyers have the power to designate legal assistants, meaning they can send in assistants who specialize in removing their briefs rather than drafting legal ones.

While doing his time, Fernandez remained an unrepentant gangster. At Sainte-Anne-des-Plaines maximum-security prison, fifty kilometres northwest of Montreal, he was led into a room with Hells Angels hit man turned informer Serges (Skin) Quesnel by a compliant guard. Quesnel would later tell author Pierre Martineau that he feared for his life, until he learned that Fernandez wasn't after his blood. Instead, Fernandez wanted Quesnel to corrupt another prisoner who was to be a witness in an upcoming Mafia trial for a promise of fifty thousand dollars. The bid failed when Quesnel told authorities. This brought furious words from Fernandez and Quesnel was moved out of his reach.

Fernandez had never taken out Canadian citizenship, remaining a Spanish national. His sentence served, he was ordered deported, but remained in Montreal on appeal, selling high-end vehicles and running a juice bar. Soon police were seeing him in the company of Vito, walking a few steps behind, as a trusted associate but not close to an equal. When finally ordered deported in 1999, Fernandez reportedly boasted: "I'm going to show them how I dance."

He danced around Canadian border security, returning to the country within months. He was deported again in 2001, and this time it took him only two months to sneak back. Now known in the GTA by the cartoonish moniker Johnny Bravo, Fernandez had the confidence and friendship of both Vito and Desjardins. He must have thought that such friendships would make him doubly safe.

In January 2001, Vito called a meeting at a north Toronto restaurant, where invited guests included a broad cross-section of Mafia groups, including members of the 'Ndrangheta, the Gambino crime family, the Buffalo mob and local Sicilian mobsters. Vito recognized a power vacuum in the Toronto area, and he was going to fill it with help from associates. He had clearly broken away from the Bonanno crime family and wanted to go from being a strong player in Ontario to the province's dominant force. It went without saying that no one person at the table had the power to stop him.

Vito pushed into Ontario, setting up an ecstasy ring in the Toronto, Mississauga, Bolton and Barrie areas and a hydroponic marijuana grow operation on a farm outside Barrie. At the same time, Vito oversaw the formation of a high-tech gambling ring that worked through video rental stores, bookies with portable computers and gas stations and took in some two hundred million dollars' worth of sports bets per year in Hamilton, Ottawa, the GTA and Montreal for wagering on professional football, basketball and hockey, US college sports and horse racing.

Vito's point men were Stefano (Steve) Sollecito, a son of his lieutenant Rocco Sollecito, and Joe Renda, who wasn't directly related to Vito's brother-in-law/cousin, Paolo. Fernandez was in and out of the country so much at this point that he could not be counted on to maintain a daily presence in the Toronto area. He also had more of a mind for violence than for business. Joe Renda had recently come up from New York City, where he had been on good terms with Vito's friend Gerlando (George from Canada) Sciascia, a Bonanno member and former Montrealer who acted as an emissary of sorts between the Rizzutos and the New York families. It was Sciascia who ran his hand through his silver hair to signal the start of gunfire in the Three Captains Murders. Then Sciascia ran afoul of John Gotti by criticizing a senior Gambino member for his drug use. The worst part about his criticism was that it was wholly true. That made it embarrassing for the Gambinos, and so Big Joey Massino decided to paper things over by having Sciascia killed. Vito could never forgive Big Joey for that betrayal. He had seethed and held his tongue when Salvatore Vitale travelled up to Montreal after the Sciascia murder and lied that Sciascia was likely murdered because of a drug deal gone wrong. Perhaps Vito already suspected that Vitale had been part of the plot to kill his friend. Maybe it sounded like an insult to Vito when he was offered Sciascia's old post as the Bonannos' Montreal emissary, because when the Americans met with Vito in Montreal, a chair was pointedly left empty in the place where Sciascia would have sat.

One of Vito's Toronto contacts at the time was Carmelo Bruzzese of Maple, in York Region. Bruzzese had no full-time job, although he alternately told authorities that he sold cars, furniture and wood. He had lived on and off in Canada since the early 1960s, but remained an Italian citizen. He became a permanent resident of Canada in May 1974 and married a year later, raising a family of five with his wife. Despite having no discernible income, he lived well in both countries, driving a BMW in Canada that was not his own. Pressed by immigration authorities, Bruzzese said he couldn't immediately identify the car's legal owner because the name was Iraqi and difficult to remember. His medical prescriptions were filled from the health plan of an acquaintance. He had homes in Italy and Canada and plenty of cash, but none of that cash was traceable. Like Vito, Carmelo largely stayed out of the public eye.

Italian authorities concluded Bruzzese held a senior rank in the 'Ndrangheta, although he had no criminal convictions in Canada or Italy. Bruzzese's villa in Italy had a custom-built, remote-controlled hiding spot behind the bar. Pressed about it by immigration officials, he described it as a storage space for valuables, such as wine, money and legal firearms.

Police might not have paid much attention to Bruzzese if not for his son-in-law, Antonio Coluccio, whose brothers Giuseppe and Salvatore were considered major international 'Ndrangheta drug traffickers. Their father, Vincenzo, had been a member of the 'Ndrangheta who was murdered in Italy in a Mafia war when Antonio was less than two years old.

Italian police listened in on Christmas Eve 2004, as Bruzzese took a call from Vito's lieutanant, *Compare* Frank Arcadi, who was about to visit Vito in jail in Montreal shortly after his arrest. Bruzzese asked Rizzuto's lieutenant to send the jailed Mafia leader "my best regards," according to the wiretap transcripts.

Earlier that year, Italian police had intercepted a conversation between Vito and Bruzzese in which Vito had spoken reassuringly to the Calabrian grandfather. Vito spoke confidently of the future, saying, "There is no problem."

CHAPTER 19

Steel bracelets

Juan Ramon Fernandez was stylishly dressed when he appeared in Newmarket court in June 2004, wearing a tailored grey suit and open-collared black shirt. He was a vain man and this was a public appearance. Sitting aloof in the body of the court was his girlfriend, a former table dancer dressed smartly in a sleek, bronze-coloured skirt suit.

His trip to court marked the culmination of the police investigation into the murder of Vito's former Toronto lieutenant Guy Panepinto. The investigation was dubbed Project RIP, a not so subtle allusion to the dead man's discount casket business. Panepinto's killers were never charged, but the investigation provided enough evidence to bring Fernandez to court for conspiring to murder one of Panepinto's crew, Constantin (Big Gus) Alevizos, over a rip-off. That murder plot fell apart when Fernandez contracted a police undercover officer to do the hit. There was also a convincing case from prosecutors that Fernandez had conspired to move a thousand kilos of cocaine with Vito and Woodbridge Hells Angels.

Fernandez didn't flinch that day when Mr. Justice Joseph Kenkel hit him with a twelve-year prison term. However, the mobster became visibly upset when he heard that he might not get back all of his jewellery, including bracelets, a gold chain with a cross and a Rolex watch that was said to be a gift from Vito himself. Fernandez was obviously proud of his connection to Vito, and police bugs picked him up referring to the Montrealer alternately as "V," "the old man" and "my partner."

Federal prosecutor Rosemary Warren told the court that she wanted to be satisfied that none of the jewellery was stolen before it was handed back to him. Fernandez snapped at the insinuation. "It's not just a brace-let," he called out from the Plexiglas-enclosed prisoners' box, his wrists bound now with far less expensive metal.

The outburst contrasted sharply with his show of indifference earlier in the trial when he pleaded guilty to the murder plot, drug-trafficking conspiracy and fraud. Those charges were tough to dispute, even though he availed himself of veteran Toronto lawyer Joseph Blumenthal, counsel of choice for many of the province's top mobsters.

In passing sentence, the judge said that Fernandez exhibited a "level of market sophistication in his criminal activity." His sentence would be more than cut in half, as he received fifty-one months' credit for time spent in pretrial custody. The time he did serve was softened by an affair he had with a female staff member at Toronto's aging Don Jail, where he had a reputation with staff as a perfect gentlemen, once even providing them with Valentine's Day chocolates.

Although Joe Renda was supplying Vito with brains on Toronto-area streets, Fernandez's departure left a void in the muscle end of the family business, and Vito enlisted *Compare* Frank Arcadi to help fill it. Flanked by his bodyguards, *Compare* Frank made frequent trips to Woodbridge for Vito in the early 2000s even before Fernandez was nabbed. It didn't hurt that Arcadi was Calabrian as he attempted to build ties between Vito's group and the GTA 'Ndrangheta.

In the year that followed, as Vito found himself in a Quebec jail await-ing extradition, new faces appeared in the mob-connected social clubs of Woodbridge. First to arrive was Bruzzese's son-in-law Antonio Coluccio, whose Canadian wife sponsored his emigration from his family home of Marina di Gioiosa Ionica in southern Italy in December 2004. Most unsettling among the decorations in his million-dollar

Richmond Hill home was a five-foot-high portrait of his murdered father, Vincenzo.

Antonio's older brothers, Giuseppe (Joe) and Salvatore, soon followed. Both were considered among Italy's thirty most dangerous men and were on the run from charges in 2005 stemming from an Italian police operation dubbed Project Nostromo. The project had pursued money that was initially extorted from tuna fishermen and then invested in a South American drug ring of global scope.

An Italian court eventually sentenced Salvatore *in absentia* to six years and eight months in prison for a string of charges including drug and weapons possession and membership in the 'Ndrangheta. Giuseppe was also sentenced *in absentia* to twelve years for organized crime–related charges, including 'Ndrangheta membership and cocaine trafficking. He already had a criminal record in Canada, and his serious drug conviction from 1993 would have made him ineligible for citizenship even if he wasn't a fugitive.

Not surprisingly, Giuseppe and Salvatore Coluccio both entered Canada using false names and papers. Salvatore chose the new name of Maurizio Logozzo, which appeared on his Ontario driver's licence, health card and Canadian Social Insurance card. Giuseppe chose the new name of Giuseppe Scarfo, using his mother's maiden name as his surname. It appeared on several pieces of false identification, including credit cards, a health card and an Ontario driver's licence. In case life in Canada got too complicated for Giuseppe Scarfo, he had a set of backup fake identification bearing the name Antonio Bertolotti.

The Coluccio brothers were living, breathing proof of the 'Ndrangheta's capacity to continually change and refresh its leadership. They arrived in the Toronto area around the time Antonio (The Lawyer, The Black One) Commisso was facing deportation from Canada for Mafia association. Commisso had lived in Canada for about a year before his deportation was ordered in July 2005. The Coluccio brothers' arrival immediately changed the balance of power in Ontario's underworld. In deference to his international power, Giuseppe was quickly given a seat on the 'Ndrangheta *camera di controllo*.

In the course of his new duties, Giuseppe Coluccio made frequent drives from his downtown Toronto waterfront condo to Woodbridge. Sometimes he travelled in a yellow Ferrari or his silver Maserati. Other times a chauffeur drove him in a Range Rover or a Porsche Cayenne. Salvatore wasn't quite so flashy, but he was certainly active as well.

Surprisingly, Giuseppe Coluccio was spending time in Woodbridge with members of the Cuntrera–Caruana crime family. It was easy to wonder if something major was happening. The Coluccio brothers' group in the 'Ndrangheta looked to be forming an alliance of sorts with the Cuntrera–Caruana group of the Sicilian Mafia, which would amount to a seismic shift in the underworld landscape. Antonio Coluccio was also in contact with a money launderer and fraudster from Vito's group, who had been active in a Toronto-based recycling company. Vito's wish to forge ties with the Calabrians was being fulfilled, but without him. And his supposed allies in the Cuntrera–Caruanas seemed to be leaving him behind.

October 10, 2006, saw a startling arrival at Pearson International Airport, the timing of which would be hard not to connect to the emerging alliance. At sixty-one, the Italian fugitive was a long-time veteran of the Sicilian mob and the suspect in a number of hits for the Sicilian Mafia, as well as a suspected weapons smuggler. Interpol had issued a "Red" notice, which called on its 190 member countries to locate and arrest him on sight. The suspected hit man, who had dual Italian and Belgian citizenship, was detained at the airport by the CBSA under the Immigration and Refugee Protection Act and deported back to Belgium to face extradition to Italy.

Not long after that, Salvatore Coluccio fled Canada for Calabria, where he disappeared into a secret bunker with an electric generator, air conditioning and lots of food. His subterranean hideout was just a few kilometres from the five-star Parco dei Principi hotel in Roccella Ionica on the Ionian Sea, in Calabria. The swank hotel featured Turkish steam baths and a helicopter pad, and was considered by authorities to be the crown jewel of the brothers' Coluccio–Aquino 'Ndrangheta group.

There was a high-level meeting in Woodbridge two months after Vito's August 2006 extradition to the USA. Sitting together at a restaurant were Frank Arcadi, Francesco Del Balso, Skunk Giordano and

Giuseppe Fetta, from Vito's Montreal groups, and Antonio Coluccio. The agenda for the meeting concerned a $200,000 gambling debt owed by hit man/restaurateur Salvatore (Sam) Calautti to Del Balso. It was the same $200,000 debt that had been the focus of the Woodbridge hotel gathering in 2004, and the matter wasn't yet resolved. The debt was assumed by an Ontario-based 'Ndrangheta boss who was wanted in Italy on weapons and Mafia association charges. In return for settling his debt, Calautti owed the 'Ndrangheta boss his services. One way of working it off could be for Calautti to kill someone important. For a killer like Calautti, this would be a means of combining pleasure with business. Two hundred thousand dollars was a large sum of money for a hit, since in his world a life can be ended for the price of a cheap used car.

CHAPTER 20

Lupara bianca

P aolo Renda called home around noon on Thursday, May 20, 2010, to tell his wife, Maria, that he had just finished his round of golf and would be home as soon as he picked up four steaks for a barbecue. Beyond the tumult in Montreal's *milieu*, life was agreeable for the seventy-three-year-old: he was cruising along Gouin Boulevard in his luxury grey Infiniti sedan towards his home in the same enclave in the leafy, well-heeled borough of Ahuntsic–Cartierville as Vito and Nicolò. He was nearing Albert-Prévost Avenue and only a few minutes from home when he saw the flashing lights on the roof of a black Dodge Cobra. It was annoying, but there was no need to argue with police and spoil his dinner plans. He eased on the brakes and slowed to a halt by the curb. Two men got out of the Cobra, ushered Renda out of his Infiniti and into the black car, and drove him away.

When her husband still wasn't home by 3 p.m., Maria telephoned the family butcher. Renda was a man of habits and one of those habits was always to buy his steaks from the same butcher shop. The butcher told his wife that he had come by about ninety minutes earlier. Maria felt a flash of panic. She was Vito Rizzuto's sister and fully aware of the possibilities. Her husband should have arrived home long ago. She called his probation officer, but the officer knew nothing of Renda's whereabouts and called police. At around 6 p.m., officers found his

Infiniti just where he'd left it, on Gouin Boulevard. The steaks were on the front passenger seat and his keys were on the dashboard. The Cobra with the flashing lights on the roof was but a hazy memory for the city workers who had briefly seen it. It didn't take much investigation to know it wasn't a police car.

That was the last anyone heard from Paolo Renda. It was a quiet, tidy exit from the often turbulent *milieu*. It befitted a man who generally worked with numbers, not guns, although police did find a loaded .32 Smith & Wesson pistol inside a hidden compartment of a dresser in his walk-in closet and two rifles in his basement. He could easily have passed for an accountant, which was appropriate since he was the keeper of financial secrets for Vito's family: he knew who was paying what to whom in the lucrative construction industry; he oversaw gambling in family-controlled bars and cafés. On paper, he was also vice-president and administrator of Renda Construction Inc., which helped him explain his posh lifestyle to Revenue Canada.

Paolo Renda was three years from his fiftieth wedding anniversary when he vanished. His disappearance was a major loss to Vito. Even if the exact relationship between these brothers-in-law/first cousins was a challenge to decipher, it did allow for one quick and accurate conclusion: Paolo Renda's abduction and probable murder were a strike deep into the heart of Vito's family.

Renda had immigrated to Canada with his parents in 1954 and became a citizen ten years later. He started his work life as a barber, and in 1972 he was sentenced to four years in prison after attempting to burn down his Boucherville, Quebec, barbershop to collect on an insurance policy. It wasn't a tough crime for police to solve, since he was found near the burning shop, his clothes reeking of smoke. His co-accused in the crime was Vito, who was sentenced to two years in custody. In commiting arson, Vito Jr. was carrying on a family tradition started by his namesake grandfather back in New Jersey in the 1930s, although this would be the last time Vito went behind bars before the Three Captains bust.

Renda had rebounded nicely from his arson arrest, setting up a bistro, a motel and a pair of construction firms. He carried himself with a

Zenlike air of casual success, and often appeared at the Consenza Social Club in a stylish sports jacket and open business shirt, but Renda knew much of the darker side of mob life. He was the Rizzuto crime family's *consigliere*: top adviser and number three man in the organization, behind only Vito and Nicolò

Despite his calm demeanour, Paolo Renda did have serious enemies. His name, together with that of his father, Calogero, was often linked to the 1978 murder of Paolo Violi. This explained why Renda left Montreal for Venezuela in the late 1970s before an arrest warrant could be signed or bullets could be fired in his direction. He didn't return until years later, after he was assured the warrant had been cancelled. By that time, most of the people who wanted to kill him had been murdered, banished to Hamilton or co-opted by Vito's organization.

By the early 2000s, Renda might have preferred to spend more time golfing and barbecuing, but the Colisée crackdown and Vito's imprisonment spoiled those plans. In his own Colisée case, Renda pleaded guilty to gangsterism charges while more serious charges of drug trafficking were dropped. He had been released on parole three months before his disappearance after serving two-thirds of a six-year prison sentence.

Parole had returned Renda to a violent, unstable world. With Vito behind bars, independent drug dealers were comfortable selling their wares in Montreal's downtown—Rizzuto turf. Renda had always preferred to try to defuse tensions on the street. A hidden police bug at the Consenza had once picked up Renda counselling Skunk Giordano not to drink too much or attract attention, after Giordano's unsettling target practice on the testicles of an Iranian-born heroin dealer in a trendy restaurant on Saint-Laurent Boulevard on April 18, 2004.

Renda's parole conditions meant that, until October, he was forbidden from associating with others who were considered criminals or from owning a cellphone, pager or any other portable communications device, or any weapon. He also couldn't go to any Italian cafés or what the parole board described as "European-style cafés," or keep the company of anyone involved in organized crime or the drug culture.

On January 19, 2010, three weeks after the murder of Nick Rizzuto Jr., the parole board added another condition to Renda's freedom. He was told he would be monitored by "members of staff who will be in charge of your care." It sounded so paternal, altruistic. Clearly, though, they weren't monitoring him too closely when he stepped into the black Cobra.

Renda's disappearance gave rise to horrific speculation. Perhaps he had been spirited away somewhere so that the Rizzutos' many secrets could be tortured out of him. It felt like life imitating art. In *The Godfather, consigliere* Tom Hagen is kidnapped at the outset of a mob war. The fictitious Hagen was held for only a few hours, so that he could relay a warning to his family. In Renda's case, there would be no message.

Did Vito's brother-in-law know that he was a dead man the instant he stepped into the fake police car? He would have understood the Sicilian term for such Mafia jobs: *lupara bianca.* It's impossible to translate cleanly, but Renda and Vito knew what it meant. The *lupara* refers to the short shotgun popular with mobsters in Sicily. Its two barrels are stacked one atop the other, making it easier to slide into a pocket. *Bianca* translates to "white," but in the case of *lupara bianca* it means something more like "invisible." *Lupara bianca* is perhaps the cruellest of Mafia murders and was generally saved for spies and traitors, who deserved nothing better than an anonymous end in a ravine, acid barrel or pit, covered in lime. A *lupara bianca* means no ransom notes, no body, no answers, no sense of closure, no funeral or flowers on a grave. Nothing but loss and fear.

The day after Renda's disappearance, Nicolò Rizzuto was scheduled to appear in municipal court on an outstanding impaired driving charge dating back to an incident on December 31, 2005, before his Colisée arrest. That New Year's Eve, he crashed his Mercedes into a fire truck that was en route to an emergency call. Police called to the scene reported he was unsteady on his feet and appeared confused. After Renda's disappearance, the prosecutors and defence lawyers agreed the impaired case could wait. There was too much danger in the air to treat this like just another day in court.

Locked up in Colorado, Vito was shocked to hear the news of Renda's abduction. He appeared nervous. Vito didn't often look that way. Talk increased that the 'Ndrangheta groups and others who had once been his allies and associates were pooling their forces to move against him. Renda's abduction seemed too smooth and too well planned for the thuggish likes of Ducarme Joseph. How could any but the most sophisticated of assailants know when and where the *consigliere* would be travelling that day and how to avoid surveillance cameras on the streets? Only a pro could make Vito's trusted confidant disappear so silently and completely, like a puff of smoke in the breeze.

CHAPTER 21

Home fire

Inmates at Montreal's Bordeaux Prison normally are housed two or three to a cell, but they refused to be placed with Nicolò Rizzuto It wasn't a snub, but rather a show of respect, so that the old man could have some degree of privacy in what could be claustrophic conditions. Nicolò particularly wanted to be kept away from members of black street gangs, whom he didn't understand or like. Hells Angels and mobsters obliged, shielding the old man from any unwelcome contact.

Libertina visited daily. Jailhouse rules barred Nicolò's wife from bringing him gifts or food, but she was allowed to prepare him meals with pasta, onions and tomato paste in a private kitchen area. Such accommodation wasn't without precedent. Indeed, Nicolò had enjoyed a special cooking area when in custody in Venezuela. Mobster Frank (The Big Guy) Cotroni calmed his own nerves and expanded his waistline in the late 1980s at Sainte-Anne-des-Plaines penitentiary by cooking vats of spaghetti for fellow inmates. There, members of the Hells Angels ironed Cotroni's clothes and placed them on his bed every day, like attentive staff members at a quality hotel.

While in custody, Nicolò's high blood pressure and prostate problems meant regular trips to nearby Sacré-Coeur hospital. It wasn't unusual to see inmates being treated there, and the hospital even ran an inmate volunteer program on site. Hospital visits were a welcome social event for Nicolò, who charmed nurses, doctors and other staff. Nonetheless, the old man sometimes appeared disoriented and lost. He was out of his routine and away from his family, and there was plenty for him to worry about, if he let his mind go there.

On October 16, 2008, after two years in custody, Nicolò Rizzuto smiled broadly in court when he heard that he was about to return home. The great-grandfather received a suspended sentence and probation after pleading guilty to possession of goods obtained through criminal gains and possession of proceeds of crime for the benefit of a criminal organization. That marked a massive reduction of charges from what he had originally faced: twenty-three counts ranging from gangsterism to importing and exporting illegal drugs. At the time of his arrest, many thought the octogenarian would spend his remaining years in custody, where the high point of most days would be a good game of cards. Instead, that very night, he would sleep in his own bed on crisp, clean sheets.

The Crown had agreed to a plea bargain before his case went to trial, bolstering the case of those who blamed the Canadian legal system for the strength and diversity of organized crime groups in Canada. In Italy, crusaders like prosecutor Nicola Gratteri put literally thousands of mobsters behind bars. In the United States, the prospect of real life sentences or even the death penalty turned many hardened criminals, like Big Joey Massino of the Bonannos, into rats. In Canada, the founder of the country's most powerful crime group could cut a deal and return home to his mansion without even facing trial.

There were a few minor face-savers for the Crown in Nicolò's case, but one had to look hard to find them. The case marked the first time that the old don had publicly admitted he was part of a criminal organization. This wasn't exactly a revelation; it was akin to Wayne Gretzky divulging that he played hockey or Stephen King saying he writes scary books. It was also the first time Nicolò had been convicted of any crime in Canada since assuming the top spot in the Montreal underworld thirty years before. That last fact worked in his favour during sentencing, as did his advanced age and fragility with prostate and respiratory problems, and some question about whether he was now anything more than a gangster emeritus.

Sharing the good feelings in the spectator section of the court that day were Nick Jr. and other family members—minus Vito, of course. Also basking in the cheerful mood were other crime family members in the prisoners' box, who were about to hear their own good news. During the same hearing, *consigliere* Paolo Renda pleaded guilty to the same two charges, as well as to three weapons offences related to firearms seized from his home on Mafia Row. Long-time family members Frank Arcadi and Rocco Sollecito admitted guilt in conspiracy and gangsterism charges that included cocaine trafficking, extortion, running gaming houses and bookmaking.

Younger family leaders like thirty-eight-year-old Francesco Del Balso and forty-five-year-old Lorenzo (Skunk) Giordano each pleaded guilty that day to conspiracy charges that included extortion. Del Balso further admitted to filing false income tax returns between 2003 and 2006, during which time he had claimed he was a grocery store worker, and to trafficking cocaine with the Hells Angels. He had caught a whiff of something odd in 2004 when Hells Angels were arrested as part of Project Ziplock while he had been left untouched.

In the end, Nicolò, the crime family's founder and currently its top man, had received the lightest sentence of the more than eighty people charged in Project Colisée. The name Colisée had been a pointed jab at Nicolò, a reference to collapsing Italian ruins, but ultimately it was the prosecution's case against him that had crumbled. All the others in the prisoners' box that day smiled upon learning they would be eligible for parole in five and a half years at most. Marc Fortin, an RCMP investigator and member of the Combined Forces Special Enforcement Unit, admitted the obvious to reporters that day after court: Project Colisée didn't mean the end of Vito's crime family. "It was dismantled in part, but it's certain it still exists," he said.

Vito would be free before several of the Colisée prisoners, even though he had been the complex and costly operation's preferred target. And Colisée was just the latest in a long list of ambitious projects since the late 1980s to take aim at Vito, including Neige, Bedside, Cercle,

Battleship, Omerta, Jaggy, Compote, Cicéron/RIP, Calamus, Chili and Cortez. They had failed to deliver a single conviction against him. It was easy to understand why the mobsters smiled that day in court.

On February 11, 2010, Nicolò was back in court to settle up with Revenue Canada in a sixteen-year-old case. He pleaded guilty to two counts of tax evasion and agreed to pay $209,000 in fines—the value of his original taxes plus a 35 percent penalty. Again, the mobster's case was settled with a plea bargain and no trial. That case harkened back to 1994, when the RCMP found millions that the elder Rizzuto had squir-relled away in Swiss banks. In August 1994, his wife was arrested in Lugano, considered the financial core of Italian-speaking Switzerland, along with her restaurateur friend and neighbour Luca Giammarella. Libertina had power of attorney over Nicolò's financial matters, show-ing his absolute trust in her.

Swiss authorities found fourteen bank accounts registered to Nicolò, enough to arouse suspicion even in this country of extreme secrecy. Libertina and her friend were held for six months in preventive deten-tion. The old woman never cracked, following a time-honoured tactic of deny, deny, deny.

Even before the discovery of the secret Swiss bank accounts, there certainly had been plenty to make the taxman suspicious. Nicolò claimed he was a pensioner living on $26,574 worth of Old Age Security and investment income, but somehow he managed to afford $1.8 million in blue-chip stocks, a spacious, pillared mansion, payments of $20,000 a year for a condominium in Milan, and a Jaguar and a Mercedes in his driveway. Not bad for someone who never went to high school.

Nicolò and Libertina had bought the land for their house in 1981, but Libertina purchased his share in 1983, making it tougher to seize as proceeds of crime. Her name also appeared as sole owner of the Jaguar and Mercedes. This was typical for the *milieu*, where men tended to shift their assets over to their wives and daughters to keep them out of government hands.

While many Canadians curse the thought of any contact with Revenue Canada, Nicolò must have held a warm spot in his heart for the tax agency. In September 2013, Radio-Canada reported that he had received a cheque for $381,737 from the tax office in 2007 for reimbursement of taxes. This largesse came while he was still in jail and under investigation for tax evasion, with a $1.5-million lien on his mansion. The news broke a year after the cancellation of Revenue Canada's Special Enforcement Program, which was meant to crack down on organized crime. At the same time, allegations were rife that Revenue Canada's Montreal office was riddled with Rizzuto-friendly employees. After the Radio-Canada revelations, Ottawa admitted that the cheque to Nicolò was undeserved and promised that those responsible would be punished. Then officials went mum, saying they couldn't go into details about the case for privacy reasons. With that, the affair was all but forgotten.

As Nicolò donned his grey fedora and left tax court that day without speaking to spectators, he had just one outstanding legal matter: the impaired driving charge that had been rescheduled because of Renda's disappearance.

On the streets, Montagna kept upping his profile at the expense of Vito's organization. He hadn't yet moved to Toronto, as planned. In Montreal, he tried to shake down construction companies for 5 percent of their profits, which was a couple of percentage points higher than the accepted rate. He also tried to squeeze ten million dollars from the brother-in-law of an extremely wealthy businessman with high-level political and banking connections. His arrogance even extended to Nicolò. Vito would have heard reports of grim meetings between his aging father and the Bonanno boss, where Nicolò was told that his underworld reign was over and it was time to step gracefully aside. Montagna's message was more threat than friendly suggestion. He had made several trips to Toronto and Hamilton, mustering support from the 'Ndrangheta and the old-school Canadian mob. He also had an alliance, however fragile, with Raynald Desjardins, Vittorio

Mirarchi and Joe Di Maulo. Montagna felt poised to take first Montreal then the rest of Canada.

Even in his depleted state, Nicolò considered himself more than a match for any coalition put together by Montagna, refugee leader of the oft-humiliated Bonannos. He made it clear to Montagna, who was less than half his age, that he wasn't going anywhere.

After his release from custody, Nicolò seldom strayed from his home on Mafia Row. Why risk abduction like Paolo Renda or bullets like Nick Jr.? He installed new security cameras on the front of his house to pick up movement on the street. There were worse places to be confined. When Nicolò looked out through the kitchen solarium window, he could see a natural, unspoiled woodland where one of the few man-made things was a statue of the Madonna, her arms outstretched as if offering an embrace. Nicolò had lived to be eighty-six years old in the midst of killers. For now, no place could feel safer than here.

CHAPTER 22

Reluctant mob boss

The clock was ticking. Anyone who wanted to make a move on Vito's family had to act quickly; Vito would be out in October 2012. Until then, Agostino Cuntrera knew that the disappearance of Paolo Renda left him the number two free man in the Rizzuto organization, behind only Nicolò. Cuntrera couldn't have been much surprised when police warned him that his life was in more danger than usual. The aging Mafioso was stockpiling weapons, purchasing an armoured car and travelling close to a bodyguard. These may have been wholly sensible steps during a state of undeclared war, but hyper-vigilance takes a lot out of a man, especially an old one like Agostino Cuntrera. Now, he had to constantly scan the hands of men nearby. Consider their eyes. Check for the nearest exit in case he had to flee. Observe if there was anything threatening or odd about cars pulling alongside. Was a driver following him? It could all become overwhelming, and people close to the tired grandfather worried that he might turn one of his many guns on himself.

Known in the *milieu* as "The Seigneur of Saint-Léonard," Cuntrera must have felt he was being punished for doing exactly what had been expected of him since childhood. He was born in 1944 in Siculiana, close to the Rizzutos' home village of Cattolica Eraclea. Siculiana's population took a dive in the 1950s and 1960s, dropping from twelve thousand to five thousand, with a diaspora spreading to Canada, Belgium, Germany, England, Venezuela and Brazil. Agostino Cuntrera immigrated to Montreal in 1965, joining his cousins Pasquale, Gaspare, Liborio and Paolo. The four brothers later moved to Caracas, Venezuela, where another cousin had established a Mafia base. This move allowed them to sidestep a Mafia war raging in Italy over shares of the worldwide heroin market and the police crackdown that accompanied the hostilities. Venezuela was also a major transit point for Colombian cocaine heading to Europe and the Port of Montreal.

Several of Paolo's relatives later settled around Toronto. Agostino remained in Montreal, establishing a string of food services companies. The family profited from Canada's trusting banking laws, which didn't require suspiciously large transactions to be reported to authorities, as in Italy and the United States. One of Agostino's enterprises was a submarine sandwich restaurant on Pie-IX Boulevard. When a Pizza Hut opened nearby in 1990, the franchise was hit with a wave of fires and bombings. Juan Fernandez was suspected in the attacks but never charged.

Agostino Cuntrera was himself long a suspect in the eyes of police for drug trafficking, but never caught. Police also believed that a business couldn't open in Saint-Léonard without his approval. In 1987, authorities wondered how his tableware company somehow managed to have $1.3 million pass through its accounts between February and August, all of it presumably through selling plates and cutlery. It did help his business that thugs forced restaurant owners to buy supplies from his firm, but that was still a lot of plates to sell in such a short time.

As befitted a modern-day seigneur, he now lived in a 5,214-square-foot, marble-lined château that was more opulent than most hotels or even the homes of Vito and Nicolò It was splashed with hardwood and marble-panelled walls and imported Italian chandeliers. One wall of Cuntrera's wine cellar had room for more than a thousand bottles, with a tasting area that would make any sommelier tingle.

It was far grander than the sturdy home in Lavaltrie on the St. Lawrence outside Montreal that Vic Cotroni had built in 1959, when he reached the pinnacle of the local mob. The Egg's home was also awash in oak and marble, but on a far more modest scale. Like its owner, the exterior of the Egg's house was tidy, solid and unspectacular, while Cuntrera's called to mind a mini Versailles.

Despite the ostentation at home, Cuntrera preferred to travel quietly and stay out of the press. One embarrassing failure to do so followed a police raid on his office. He referred them to his accountant, who turned out to be Liberal member of Parliament Alfonso Gagliano, also born in Siculiana. Gagliano had founded the Siculiana Association of Montreal and Cuntrera had served as one of its directors.

The RCMP also noted with interest that Agostino Cuntrera appeared in downtown Toronto with Vito in April 1995 at the Sutton Place Hotel, at the wedding of the daughter of his cousin Alfonso Caruana, drug smuggler and new head of the Cuntrera–Caruana clan. Also joining the festivities were *Compare* Frank Arcadi and Rocco Sollecito.

Perhaps the Seigneur had once entertained thoughts of heading the Rizzuto crime family, but if those days had ever existed, they were long gone by the time Vito went to prison. By 2010, as he enjoyed the quiet comforts of his kitchen and wine cellar, or sunned himself in the landscaped confines of his backyard pool, Agostino Cuntrera knew perfectly well that ambition brings unwelcome pressures and responsibilities. Haggling on the streets with the brash likes of Ducarme Joseph, Richard Goodridge and Salvatore Montagna couldn't have held much appeal. Many felt he lacked the charisma to be a street-level mob boss anyway.

Cuntrera also knew the risks. There's a Sicilian truism that a man forewarned is a man half saved, but there's also a North American saying that there's no point turning around if you're already halfway across a river. He had got his hands bloody in his younger days as one of the men who helped clear the way for the Rizzutos' rise to power. He did five years in prison for plotting Paolo Violi's murder, and his culpability would never be forgotten or forgiven in certain quarters of Hamilton, York Region and Montreal. Even all these years later, Cuntrera would be a logical and slow-moving target for anyone wanting to exact revenge.

Cuntrera's preference might be for his wine cellar, but his rough trade forced him into an alliance with the likes of Raynald Desjardins and Hells Angels bikers such as Michel (L'Animal) Lajoie and Marvin Normand (Casper) Ouimet. He recognized that Desjardins wasn't the man he had been in the 1980s, when he was like Vito's little brother. The francophone had become his own man, and a frightening man at that, not softened by age or prison. It seemed that no one in Vito's group could reason with Desjardins, save perhaps Vito himself.

The biker Lajoie, also known as Michel Smith, Mike Smith-Lajoie, Michel Lajoie-Smith and Michel Lajoie, had been wanted since 2009 for twenty-two murders as well as gangsterism and drug trafficking. He had strong Central American connections and was known to spend time in Panama. His Hells Angels clubmate Ouimet was no gentler. He was also wanted for twenty-two murders between 1994 and 2002, when the Hells Angels were locked in a war over Quebec drug turf. The Sûreté du Québec also said that Ouimet was now trying to muscle into Quebec's bricklaying industry to launder drug proceeds, and that the biker was once linked to a company involved in renovations on Parliament Hill. Business with such men was enough to make anyone pine for his wine cellar.

Did Cuntrera recognize the face of his assassin on the afternoon of June 30, 2010? Perhaps, for all the old man's attempted vigilance, he didn't even notice him. The gunman moved so quickly that bodyguard Liborio Sciascia could do nothing but absorb a bullet and collapse to the pavement outside the Seigneur's business, Les Distributions John & Dino. A heartbeat later, Cuntrera was cut down too, with a close-range shot to the head, just paces from his armour-plated car. There was so little time between Cuntrera stepping out the door and the bullet crashing into his skull that it was impossible not to think the hit was an inside job, with someone alerting the killer exactly when to strike. How else could one explain why the streetwise bodyguard was caught so clearly off guard or why the killer vanished without being seen?

More than six hundred people filled the Notre-Dame-du-Mont-Carmel church in Saint-Léonard for the Seigneur's funeral. His casket was closed for the service, as even the skills of the family undertaker couldn't disguise the bullet's damage to his head. On the casket was a photo of him, which was wrapped in rosary beads, while white flowers were set about the chapel. The hearse carrying his body was trailed by three limousines with large floral arrangements, the grandest of which was a copy of the Ferrari logo. Another said *Nonno*, "Grandfather." Heavily muscled security men looked on while mourners hugged and attempted to console one another. Attendees and police surveillance alike must have noticed how many members of the Mafia avoided the funeral, at a time when their presence would have been a public show of support for Vito's clan. One of the few with an excuse was Nicolò, whose parole conditions forbade his associating with criminals.

Cuntrera's murder got people talking again about the slaying of Paolo Violi back in 1978, the killing against which all Montreal gangland slayings were measured. It was also difficult not to dust off that hackneyed expression about revenge being a dish best served cold. Like Agostino Cuntrera, Paolo Renda had been one of the suspects in the Paolo Violi murder, and now one of them was dead and the other presumably the victim of *lupara bianca*. In the Mafia there is no statute of limitations for revenge. If Cuntrera and Renda died as the result of a vendetta, then it only made sense that Vito and Nicolò were also targeted for death.

Agostino Cuntrera's murder came six months after the still-unsolved assassination of Nick Rizzuto Jr. and just one month after Paolo Renda's disappearance. Some commentators speculated that this most recent loss marked the end of the Rizzuto family's grip on Canada's underworld. Their pronouncement may have been premature, but the death watch was on.

The Rizzutos lost a little more clout on September 29, 2010, when someone turned a gun on thirty-six-year-old Ennio Bruni outside a café in a small strip mall in Laval. Bruni was also part of Vito's push into Ontario in the early 2000s, and he was just the type of man Vito's group badly needed now. Colisée tapes revealed Bruni as someone who transported money from Rizzuto family gaming houses in Laval and also provided muscle to the clan. Bruni had survived an attempt on his life just ten months earlier, after being shot four times while leaving a Laval restaurant. He refused to provide a statement for police and under Frank Arcadi gamely returned to the streets—and the firing line.

On January 31, 2011, it was time for Antonio Di Salvo to exit the scene. He had been valuable to Arcadi for his work in the drug trade, and perhaps that was why he was dispatched with a bullet to the head in his home on the Rivière des Prairies. Now there was talk that drug traffickers were looking for other outlets to market their product, as Vito's group wasn't as reliable as it had once been. The brief era of the Seigneur of Saint-Léonard's leadership was over. What era would succeed it was anyone's guess.

CHAPTER 23

Home front

The woods behind Nicolò's home offered plenty of cover. It was dark enough at 5:40 p.m. on November 9, 2010, that the intruder was not noticed among the trees and the shadows, close to the statue of the Madonna. So much would depend on the gunman's ability to concentrate over the next few minutes. There was a wind of twenty-six kilometres per hour, which wasn't enough to affect a close-range shot, especially when the power of the rifle was factored in. The gunman held a .300-calibre hunting rifle, capable of bringing down a moose or a bear. It was certainly more than enough firepower for an octogenarian mobster suffering a laundry list of medical complaints.

From a distance, he could see Nicolò as he stepped into the solarium kitchen and gazed outside towards the backyard bushes. He could see Zio Cola move close to his wife, Zia Libertina, and their daughter, Maria. She had lost her husband, Paolo Renda, only a few months earlier and didn't want to eat alone.

The assassin tapped his finger less than half an inch. The bullet dipped slightly as it punctured the solarium glass, catching the old man in the jaw rather than the skull. However, a bullet fragment tore down into his aorta, and that was enough to make the assassin's job a success. Zia Libertina went immediately into shock as her husband of more than six decades collapsed to the kitchen floor at her feet.

The hit harkened back to the death of Paolo Violi's younger brother Rocco in October 1980, when he was struck in the chest by a sniper's bullet as he sat reading a newspaper at his kitchen table. Rocco's death marked the last time anyone could recall that the Canadian mob executed one of its own with a hunting rifle as he sat at home in front of his family. It showed a rare lack of respect for the victim's family. Certainly Zio Cola hadn't been venturing out much recently, but the assassin's choice of location was almost surely meant as a reminder of the morning Rocco Violi slumped over dead. If that murder had secured the beginning of the Rizzuto era, Nicolò's was undeniably intended as an emphatic pronouncement of its end.

Prison authorities monitored Vito's reaction to the news. "Why do they go after an old man?" he asked family members in Italian during wiretapped telephone conversations. He had to vent, his voice filled with fury. There had always been much affection between Vito and his father. The transfer of power between them had been so seamless that it was impossible to say exactly when it happened. They had always presented themselves as a team, and now Vito was very much alone. For all his anger, Vito's reaction was different from when he'd learned of the murder of Nick Jr. He didn't seem to think anyone would ever do such a thing to his son. His father's death was painful too, but less of a surprise. For all of Vito's adult life, people had sought to murder his father. It was a tribute to the old man that he had lived as long as he did.

There had been eighteen gangland murders, sixty-seven arsons, eighteen attempted murders and two disappearances in Montreal since the start of 2007. Vito had predicted his removal from the country would mean increased chaos in the Montreal underworld. His words now bore a nasty ring of truth.

Four days after Zio Cola's murder, a Canadian Tire security camera in Montreal picked up a middle-aged blond man wearing a Rolex stuffing merchandise into his coat pockets. The store was about five kilometres from where Nicolò was slain. Among the filched items were a black balaclava, a handgun holster and a pouch for ammunition. When staff moved in to apprehend the thief, one was shoved and another was bitten in the hand. The employees eventually won the struggle, which caused the would-be shoplifter to drop a roll of more than three thousand dollars in hundred-dollar bills.

Once subdued, the man identified himself as Vincenzo Sestito, the name that appeared on his Italian passport, issued the previous July, as well as on his temporary Ontario driver's licence, current international driver's licence and debit card. The identification seemed genuine. When his fingerprints were run through a police database, however, the results showed he wasn't Vincenzo Sestito but rather forty-six-year-old Nicola Cortese of Halton Region outside Toronto, a cousin of Toronto-area Calabrian mob boss and convicted killer Vincenzo (Jimmy) De Maria. De Maria was on lifetime parole for second-degree murder after shooting a man to death in 1981 over a debt. De Maria's parole conditions forbade him from associating with Cortese.

A little more investigation showed that Cortese was wanted by Niagara Regional Police in Ontario for his role in a $15-million marijuana grow-op bust that included cultivating the drug in a former Ukrainian church in nearby Thorold. One of his co-accused in that case was James Tusek, an associate of hit man/restaurateur Salvatore (Sam) Calautti. Cortese was also sought by Halton Regional Police, west of Toronto, following his arrest and incarceration for a complicated multi-million-dollar mortgage fraud that involved inflated property values and falsified invoices and lease agreements. The Justice of the Peace at Cortese's bail hearing in the mortgage fraud case was told by a family member that Cortese was on his way to the courthouse when he fell and broke his ribs. Rather than return to court, Cortese assumed the identity of Vincenzo Sestito and vanished, until his ill-fated Canadian Tire shoplifting bust.

Cortese would later vaguely tell another parole board hearing that he bought the fake identification at a store in Italy, during his two years at large from Canada. He was a self-confessed former heavy drug user with fifty-three convictions, including fraud, breach of trust, assault, robbery, assault with intent to resist arrest and possessing weapons. He'd also had charges withdrawn for armed robbery, possessing unregistered/restricted weapons, sexual assault with a weapon, forcible confinement and assault with a weapon.

Police detectives tend to mistrust coincidences, so it was natural to wonder why Cortese was in Montreal so close to the time of Nicolò's killing. Was it also a coincidence that two of Paolo Violi's relatives had been seen in Montreal the week before the murder? Given all the 'Ndrangheta connections and activity around Montreal at the time, and the inside co-operation that seemed to have been part of the recent killings, it was easy to wonder if Vito had been sold out by Calabrian members of his own crime family.

Cortese lasted one night in Montreal's Bordeaux Prison, where prisoners had treated Nicolò with such respect just a short time before. Cortese then pleaded with corrections staff to be transferred. *Fast.* There were a number of Rizzuto men from the Colisée roundup on the same cellblock range and he wanted to be at a safe distance from them. He was quickly dispatched to safer quarters.

In the hours before Nicolò's funeral, someone left a black box with a white cross taped on it on the steps of Notre-Dame-de-la-Défense church. Fearing explosives or body parts from the missing *consigliere* Paolo Renda, police evacuated the area and summoned bomb disposal experts. Police were relieved to find only a note inside, a cryptic message written in Italian that seemed to allude to the funerals of the Violi brothers three decades earlier at the same holy spot in Little Italy, with words to the effect of: "Let's stop this church being the church of the Mafia and start it being the church of everyone." To someone with a Mafia frame of mind, it was easy to see the odd message as meaning: "You've suffered the way we suffered. Let's put an end to this sad story." Or maybe it was just a member of the public, tired of his place of worship becoming widely known as the church of the Mafia.

Inside, Nicolò's funeral was much like that of Nick Jr. less than a year before in the same church. Powerfully built men wearing earpieces and black leather gloves scanned the entrances to make sure no gawkers or enemies tried to enter. Four guards inside the church carefully eyed attendees. Not all of the eight hundred seats in the church were filled, and there were notably no representatives of the Bonanno crime family.

The ceremony was a simple one, in Italian, with no members of the Rizzuto family rising to say a word. There were no personal comments from anyone about the deceased, although the priest did thank those who sent their condolences but did not attend. White roses adorned the altar, with other white flowers on the golden casket. The only ostentation was in the form of some two hundred wreaths, arranged from floor to ceiling. A soaring rendition of "Ave Maria" filled the church. A choir sang hymns in Latin. A single trumpet sounded a tribute. Selections played on the organ, strings and brass ranged from melancholy to uplifting. Finally, the godfather was carried from the church under the eyes of mourners in sunglasses and dozens of police and media. His casket was escorted to St. Francis of Assisi cemetery by limousines carrying stacks of floral tributes, including at least one from a real estate developer.

Libertina looked stoic. Often, mobsters have lovers on the side to help them cope with the stress of their work and the constraints of arranged marriages, but that had not been the case with her devoted Nicolò. Libertina's composure was all the more remarkable in that she was grieving once again without Vito there to comfort her. She knew well how life so often ended in their world, which meant her only son could be next.

Nicolò abhorred sloppiness, and he would have been impressed by the undertaker's job, which had rendered even his wounded neck suitable for an open casket. He would also have appreciated how his family now guarded Mafia Row with private security firms, which used trained bodyguards and discreet auto patrols. Most of the people flooding to the cul-de-sac were gawkers, but the security men took down all their licence numbers anyway. It all seemed too little, too late, but it had to be done.

No one from Vito's group did a thing to avenge the latest bloodletting. His men were all either in prison or ineffectual or they had defected to the other side. Whatever their reasons, their inaction compounded the insult.

———

While the elder Rizzuto was meeting his fate, Antonio Coluccio quietly slipped back into North America from the United Kingdom with his bodyguard/driver. In November, he arrived in New York City, then travelled to Niagara Falls, NY. His visitors there included an Ontario man specializing in high-level money management who had been close to Vito.

Early in January 2011, vandals firebombed the Complexe Funéraire Loreto in Saint-Léonard. They did little actual damage, but attacking the Rizzuto-owned business was a powerful public statement nonetheless. It was open season on Vito's family.

Just a few months later, Big Joey Massino made history by becoming the highest-level rat in the history of La Cosa Nostra when he testified against his successor, Vincent (Vinny Gorgeous) Basciano. In the course of his testimony, Big Joey calmly explained how he hadn't really wanted to kill Vito's friend and associate George (George from Canada) Sciascia back in 1999, after the Montrealer broke mob protocol and criticized a Gambino family member. Big Joey made it sound as though he was just a worker doing his job. "As much as I didn't want to kill him, I had to kill him." News of this latest Bonanno defection brought a screaming headline in the New York Post: NOMERTA! MAFIA BOSS A SQUEALER. The April 13, 2011, story began: "There isn't a hunk of cheese big enough for this rat." If anything, it was confirmation that Vito—despite his family's desperate need for friends—had been right in his decision to pull away from the Bonannos.

On March 31, 2011, police found the body of Antonio Di Salvo in his home on Perras Boulevard in Rivière des Prairies. The forty-four-year-old had been a low-profile member in the Rizzuto group, with ties to Francesco Del Balso and Compare Frank Arcadi. The assassination occasioned no real surprise, despite Di Salvo's peripheral association. How could anyone be shocked by a murder after Nicolò was gunned down in his own house, at the feet of his wife and daughter no less? This was a fight to the death, but it was still impossible to identify all of Vito's enemies. The family's attackers remained in the shadows, and some still posed as friends.

CHAPTER 24

Tale of betrayal

ebruary 11, 2011, was shaping up to be a busy day. Toronto and York Regional police intelligence officers, part of the anti–organized crime Combined Forces Special Enforcement Unit, had plans to stake out the funeral visitation for Cosimo Stalteri, the grand old man of the Ontario 'Ndrangheta. He had just died in hospital at age eighty-six. An original member of the Toronto *camera di controllo*, Stalteri had recently been promoted from the rank of *santista*—the shadowy organization's equivalent of a senior lobbyist with senior mainstream people such as bankers and politicians—to *vangelista*—the 'Ndrangheta version of a respected senior statesman. It was a safe assumption that Stalteri was never in the pro-Vito camp, as he was Calabrian, from Toronto and on good terms with some of Vito's die-hard enemies. At the absolute minimum, Stalteri was a neutral in the hostilities that were surgically disassembling Vito's empire.

Also scheduled for that Friday was surveillance of the fiftieth wedding anniversary celebrations of Paolo Cuntrera at Hazelton Manor in Vaughan. On the surface, Cuntrera would appear to be on Vito's side in the current tensions, as he and his brothers Pasquale and Gaspare were cousins of Vito's recently murdered ally Agostino Cuntrera of Montreal. Paolo and his siblings had garnered considerable interest from Italian authorities for decades. Pasquale Cuntrera was considered a kingpin of a network that—the late Italian judge Giovanni Falcone estimated—had washed $77 billion in drug money in Canada, England and five other countries. The 1992 murder of Falcone, and that of his fellow judge Paolo Borsellino only months earlier, created pressure for Venezuelan authorities to finally extradite the three brothers (the fourth, Liborio, moved to England in 1975 and died there of natural causes in 1982).

Once back in Italy, Pasquale was convicted on charges of running a drug ring between Italy, Canada and Venezuela. In 1998, the sixty-three-year-old somehow managed to escape custody, even though he now appeared to be confined to a wheelchair. A week later, Pasquale was rearrested in Spain while strolling down a beach with his wife, the wheelchair nowhere in sight. As he went back to prison, his brothers Paolo and Gaspare settled in the Toronto area after their Italian legal difficulties had run their course. Both men were Canadian citizens and the move was entirely legal, although police maintained an interest in them.

Stalteri's funeral visitation came first on the agenda for the surveillance officers. They noted that attendance was solid, as might be expected for a man who was feared, respected and liked for decades. Back in his hometown of Siderno in the Italian province of Reggio Calabria, Stalteri had convictions for assault causing bodily harm, theft and carrying an unregistered revolver, but he received an amnesty from Italian authorities before he immigrated to Canada in 1952. He had no further criminal record in Canada, despite appearing in numerous police reports for his 'Ndrangheta associations.

In 1962, Stalteri was appointed to the *camera di controllo* in Toronto by Giacomo Luppino of Hamilton, Paolo Violi's father-in-law. Also in that governing body were Michele (Mike the Baker) Racco, Vincenzo (Jimmy) Deleo, Rocco Zito, Salvatore Triumbari and Filippo Vendemini. It was a tough group for a tough environment: Triumbari was murdered in 1967 and Vendemini slain in 1969, and neither murder was ever solved. They also didn't take opposition lightly. Zito was later convicted of beating a man to death with a liquor bottle during the Christmas season. Stalteri returned to Italy in 1973 for a visit and killed a street vendor in an argument over a toy. Italian authorities sought his extradition over the murder, then let the warrant expire when they falsely determined that he had died. He was also believed by police to be involved in alien smuggling and heroin trafficking in Toronto, although neither suspicion was ever proven.

What the surveillance officers saw immediately after the funeral visitation might have shocked even Vito. Stalteri's mourners climbed onto a chartered bus and rode off to the anniversary reception for the Cuntreras.

How could this be possible? Weren't they mortal, blood enemies?

And yet it *was* clearly happening. Members of both the Sicilian and Calabrian factions of Canadian organized crime, including representatives from Hamilton, York Region, Ottawa, Montreal and Sherbrooke, Quebec, were breaking bread together as if they were on some mob version of homecoming week.

Among the three hundred guests were several members of the Commisso crime family. It was no secret that they didn't mix well with Vito, but that wasn't the thing that would have shocked him most about the gathering. One of the welcomed guests at the Sicilian celebration was Salvatore (Sam) Calautti, the hard-core 'Ndrangheta hit man who was the suspected killer of Gaetano (Guy) Panepinto and a prime suspect in four other unsolved mob murders—one of which was the slaying of Vito's father.

The fact that the Sicilians could entertain a Calabrian hit man who was believed to have killed their most esteemed member was breathtaking. That they could sit down and socialize also with Calautti's bosses and confederates suggested a fundamental change in the underworld. Blood ties didn't seem to matter any longer.

It was unthinkable, but it was happening right in front of the intelligence officers. What police witnessed was bonding between the Ontario Sicilians and the 'Ndrangheta, less than seven months after the murders of Agostino Cuntrera and his bodyguard in Montreal, and two months after the murder of Nicolò. It had been widely assumed that the Sicilian and Calabrians mobsters were at war in Montreal, but that was clearly not the case in Toronto.

There had never been impenetrable divisions between the 'Ndrangheta and the Sicilian Mafia, nor its American cousin, La Cosa Nostra, especially when the Cuntrera–Caruana family was involved. The flow of money has a way of washing away even the most rigid barriers. Criminals who weren't touched personally by vendettas remained open for a deal. Business was business when blood didn't cry out for revenge.

If the men at the anniversary party could form a working relationship with the Desjardins–Mirarchi group, they would have a death grip on the Port of Montreal. In a new power alliance between them, the Coluccio–Aquino Calabrian 'Ndrangheta faction and the Caruana–Cuntrera Sicilian Mafia group, Vito would be the odd man out.

CHAPTER 25

Outlaw in-laws

J oe Di Maulo was an easy guy to like, which explained why he and
Vito had often golfed together and shared tables at downtown
nightclubs. Smiling Joe had a quick sense of humour, liked to
banter and carried himself with natural confidence. His roots ran
deep, to the old Cotroni crime family, who predated the Rizzuto group
in Montreal. When strangers approached—like the summer day in
1993 when a *Toronto Star* reporter arrived unannounced at his café—he
was apt to be more amused than perturbed. That day, at his business
in the Métropolitain Est–Viau Sud area of Saint-Léonard, kitty-corner
to his nightclub, he smiled broadly and kept his bodyguards at bay. Di
Maulo looked cool and casual in an understated silk Hawaiian shirt,
even as he checked the scribe's wallet for hidden recording devices. The
journalist began asking questions about the Mafia's interests in casino
gambling, which wasn't totally speculative since Di Maulo and his older
brother Vincenzo (Jimmy) both had extensive interests in the gambling
machine industry.

It was doubtful anyone knew more about what was going on in the
milieu than Smiling Joe, whose roots ran deep and also wide. The Di
Maulos and the Cotronis had been neighbours on downtown Saint-
Timothée Street long before gentrification (or lawns) arrived in the
neighbourhood. In a moderately upward move, the families departed

together for Rosemont. Joe Di Maulo rose high enough in the old Cotroni organization that he was chosen to travel with Paolo Violi in November 1973 to a New York City Bonanno family meeting for a leadership vote. That New York meeting came a year after Nicolò had fled to Venezuela, to escape Violi's gunmen.

Also in the early 1970s, Joe's older brother Vincenzo (Jimmy) began a life term for murder while Joe was acquitted of a triple murder in his Casa Loma nightclub on Sainte-Catherine Street downtown. Joe's conviction was overturned when a key witness dramatically changed her testimony in a related trial. Whatever the truth of the three killings, they certainly added to Joe Di Maulo's aura, although he remained an affable, chatty man, cultivating friendships with lawyers, politicians, businessmen, judges, artists—as well as Sicilian and Calabrian mobsters, the thugs of the Québécois Dubois family and assorted others in the underworld, including Lebanese drug smugglers. This combination of knowledge, contacts and charm put him in a prime position to mediate disputes as well as reap profits.

Sitting in his Montreal café, Di Maulo glibly announced to the visiting Toronto reporter that the best way to keep any new casinos clean was to let the Mafia run them. "That would be the best thing," Di Maulo said with a broad smile. A robust young man who looked like a slightly spruced-up biker, with a sweeping moustache, a black T-shirt and a pager, smiled too, as if on cue. "There would be no prostitutes, no pickpockets," Di Maulo continued, like a nightclub comedian. He laughed heartily at his own joke and the notion of being put in charge of keeping crime out of casinos. The husky young man in the black T-shirt laughed some more too.

A few minutes later, Di Maulo frowned deeply when reminded of recent clouds of controversy over the casino gambling industry in general and himself in particular. His sidekick picked up on the shift in mood and glowered. A month before, Richard McGinnis, head of the Montreal police organized crime squad, had warned the Quebec National Assembly about the dangers of mobsters in the video poker business and cautioned that casino gambling could only heighten the criminals' wealth. McGinnis claimed video poker machines were already the second-highest money-maker for the Montreal mob, behind only the drug trade.

Di Maulo barked out, "Bullshit!" to the reporter, dismissing reports he had approached the Quebec government about getting involved in incoming casinos. Despite the harsh language, he still appeared entertained as the line of questioning continued, as though he were untouchable. When he talked about negative reports linking his name to illicit gambling, he had the dismissive air of a much-maligned celebrity. In fact, he was proud of helping out some of the province's entertainers in the early stages of their careers, providing a nightclub stage on which they could cut their teeth. He was a patron of the arts, of sorts. He was also extremely proud of the fact that he had never been linked to drug trafficking. "It's strictly propaganda," Di Maulo said to the reporter. "They're using our name to get publicity." He declined to say who "they" were or why "they" wanted publicity. He smiled and added, presumably suggesting a law-enforcement tendency towards corruption, "Ninety percent of the machines are owned by police."

During the chat in his café, Di Maulo appeared to be the very essence of self-control and good spirits. Between conversations in French on his ever-present cellphone (one is even visible in his daughter Mylena's wedding pictures), he dismissed further questions about connections between organized crime and casino gambling. Then he muttered something about ten million dollars. Pressed to expand, he frowned and declined. As serious questions subsided, he ridiculed the idea that Ontario planned non-smoking casinos. "Why don't they turn the country into churches?" he laughed. The husky man in the black T-shirt chortled also.

There were few serious challengers to the Rizzutos as the crime family cruised through the early 1990s. It was easy for everyone to exude goodwill when they were all pulling in good money, so long as they could stay out of prison. His casual air at his café notwithstanding, Joe Di Maulo was an active man at the time. He was part of a Mafia group that tried in 1993 to get a $450-million commission to help liquidate three billion dollars' worth of gold stashed in banks in Hong Kong and Zurich that had been stolen by former Filipino dictator Ferdinand Marcos and his men.

Smiling Joe was charged in August 1995 with offering an RCMP officer $100,000 to destroy evidence against his older brother Vincenzo, after Vincenzo was charged in one of the largest money-laundering sting operations ever conducted in Canada. Also charged in that case was Vito's childhood friend from the old Villeray district, Valentino Morielli. The case against Joe Di Maulo was eventually dropped, although Morielli went to prison for a related drug charge and Vincenzo wouldn't see parole until the new century.

Smiling Joe Di Maulo was embedded in the underworld by marriage as well as his own criminal activity. His wife was Raynald Desjardins's sister and his daughter married Francesco Cotroni, the son of Frank (The Big Guy) Cotroni, not long after Francesco was released from prison after serving three years for his role in a contract killing. The Di Maulo–Cotroni nuptials were called "the marriage of the year in the Montreal *milieu*" by respected *Journal de Montréal* crime writer Michel Auger and further cemented Di Maulo's already formidable contacts.

Throughout the late 1980s and early 1990s, it seemed that Vito, Desjardins and Smiling Joe Di Maulo really were untouchable. Desjardins and Smiling Joe had risen so high by this time that it was easy to forget they had both once been waiters. Desjardins's name— and Vito's—kept coming up in massive drug investigations, but charges never stuck. Smiling Joe preferred to stay away from the drug trade, finding other areas in which to prosper. Then, in 1994, came Desjardins's arrest for cocaine smuggling. In that scheme he worked with the Hells Angels, and he oversaw at least eighteen other plots in an attempt to import seven hundred kilograms of cocaine. Vito's shadow hung over the whole effort, but he was not charged. Desjardins proved unmanageable when finally in custody. A parole report later noted: "While at Parthenais, you were found in possession of two blades and you also assaulted another inmate in the face and injured his eye." Worse yet, he tried to get two prisoners to murder another offender.

Desjardins could have done considerable damage to Di Maulo and Vito if he had been a weaker, chattier man. Even after he was sentenced to a fifteen-year term, Desjardins remained solid. Ratting out Vito or Joe Di Maulo would have bought him preferred treatment with prosecutors, but Desjardins didn't give up the names of his associates. Desjardins quickly established himself as a feared man inside Leclerc medium-security institution in Laval. Guards felt he was trying to run Range 4AB. Known by fellow inmates as "the Millionaire," he managed to get a jogging track repaired at his own expense and somehow secured a truck filled with three thousand dollars' worth of seafood. It was "a spectacular way to show your strength and power within the institution," the parole board said in a ruling, commenting on the exercise facility. He also managed to gain control of prison refrigerators and telephones and secure a computer for his cell. He and his cellblock cronies made daily calls to conduct business, even though that was obviously against prison policy.

By the end of 1995, Desjardins's conduct was deemed so bad that he was transferred to maximum-security Donnacona Institution, about forty kilometres west of Quebec City, because of concerns for the safety of staff and inmates. Generally, prisoners are transferred from medium- to less restrictive minimum-security facilities, but Desjardins proved to be a dangerous exception. The parole board later claimed the move was necessary because of his extremely aggressive behaviour, which included his role at the centre of a war between two prison clans.

"These concerns included information from reliable sources relating to your need to control and intimidate; your links to the Hell's [sic] Angels and involvement in the Italian Mafia; and the 'contracts' you put out on inmates and staff, including an alleged contract to murder inmate (name withheld) and one to poison inmate (name withheld). The Board of Investigation on the (name withheld) incident indicated that a 'war' existed between you and (name withheld) and that you put a 'murder contract' on him." Exactly why he acted so aggressively was anyone's guess, as he refused examination by psychologists or psychiatrists.

Faced with a criminal record that stretched back to 1971, authorities denied Desjardins day parole on October 31, 2000. "After reviewing all of the information, the members found that the attitudes and values that led you to this lifestyle in the first place had not changed," the parole board ruled. "They found no indication of real remorse." On

August 29, 2002, the parole board again turned him down for day parole, rejecting any likelihood that he would steer clear of the life he'd left behind. "In the years immediately before your arrest, you led a life full of advantages: a luxurious residence, pleasure boats, a fleet of luxury cars, vacations, evenings out," the board ruled. It concluded that he would likely resort to violence if he left prison.

Desjardins was finally freed on statutory release on June 2, 2004. By this time, he had drifted away from Vito. It also seemed doubtful that Desjardins would be hooking up publicly with his old chum and accomplice Vincenzo (Jimmy) Di Maulo, who was freed on day parole in 2004 after serving nearly a decade for his money-laundering conviction. Jimmy's parole conditions were tight, barring him from associating with people "related to the drug milieu and/or organized crime, including your brother Joe Di Maulo, who is known as an influential member of the Montreal Mafia."

Upon his release from prison, when Desjardins grandly announced that he was going to become a "construction entrepreneur," plenty of skeptics in Quebec didn't think a move into the construction industry was synonymous with going straight. If anything, it was a freeway into the province's heartland of corruption.

CHAPTER 26

Fault lines

L orenzo (Larry) Lo Presti grew up on Mafia Row, a few mansions down Antoine-Berthelet Avenue from Vito's home. His aunt was married to Vito's uncle, Domenico Manno, one of the tight circle of Rizzuto men involved in the Paolo Violi murder. Larry's high school was Father McDonald Comprehensive, which Vito's daughter, Bettina, also attended. There, Lorenzo talked like someone who wanted nothing other than to be a Mafioso, and he travelled with a muscular black youth who later became his bodyguard. In his high school yearbook, he declared "money is everything" as his motto and listed his ambition as "to be like my father."

For many high school boys, the ambition of carrying on the family business would have been seen as mundane or perhaps sweet. For Larry, carrying on the family tradition was more complicated and dangerous. His father, Giuseppe (Joe) Lo Presti, was a partner with Nicolò Rizzuto in D.M. Transport, which was registered in 1972. The senior Lo Presti was also a suspect in the Paolo Violi murder back in 1978, although nothing was ever proven. Joe Lo Presti certainly was considered a man of some influence in the *milieu*, even though he deliberately went out of his way to keep a low profile, with muted suits and a soft monotone in conversation. Living in such grand accommodations, he also clearly had a lot of money for someone who was not in town much to tend to his construction or trucking businesses. In reality, Joe Lo Presti was the Montreal mob's ambassador to the New York Bonanno family, and spent a good deal of his time south of the border brokering international drug deals.

After high school, Larry worked for a time running video poker machines with Nick Rizzuto Jr. Larry's perspective changed forever late on the night of Wednesday, April 29, 1992, after police found his father's body wrapped in plastic and dumped by the side of railway tracks in northeast Montreal. Joe Lo Presti's pager was ringing as police approached his corpse. When they contacted the caller, they found it was twenty-three-year-old Larry, who was summoned in to identify his father at the Parthenais Street morgue.

The working police theory was that the senior Lo Presti had trusted his killer up until the final instant of his life, when someone put a small-calibre bullet in his head. Whoever he met in a downtown restaurant that day had likely set him up for murder, and perhaps also drove him to his death, since Lo Presti's Porsche was found parked outside the restaurant. Perhaps that so-called friend even fired the fatal bullet. Did Lo Presti suspect anything was wrong as he left the restaurant? The killer left some four thousand dollars on the body, a sign of either arrogance or respect. The execution remained unsolved, but it was widely accepted by police that Vito's hand guided the crime.

One theory concerned five kilograms of heroin that had gone missing in France. That heroin had been Lo Presti's responsibility, and the gangsters who paid for shipment were in no mood for excuses. A second possibility was that New York mob boss John Gotti had ordered him killed for undisclosed reasons. With Gotti's mercurial temper, lives often ended quickly with little explanation. Although Joe Lo Presti was Vito's neighbour and close associate, if the second theory was true, Vito had apparently conceded to Gotti's demand to sate the American's anger.

Vito attended the funeral, and perhaps he felt true sadness, if not guilt, as the killing had been for business and not personal reasons. Not long after that, the Lo Presti family home on Mafia Row went up for sale and the family moved away. Any friendship Larry felt for Nick Jr. soon evaporated.

In the wake of his father's death, it wasn't surprising that Larry Lo Presti gravitated towards the American newcomer Montagna. Also leaning towards Montagna were Antonio (Waldo, W., Tony Suzuki) Pietrantonio and Domenico Arcuri Sr., who took it upon himself to introduce Montagna to others in the *milieu* who might become useful allies. One was Giuseppe (Closure) Colapelle, who was freed on parole back in June 2004, although he would prove more comfortable in the orbit of Raynald Desjardins.

As they jockeyed for new alliances, no one was about to publicly declare war on Vito's family or anyone else. No one even wanted to acknowledge that the *milieu* had split into opposing camps. Far better to feign friendship and strike unexpectedly. On the surface, Vito's former allies still got along and shared BlackBerry PINs. The smart phone's purportedly unbeatable encryption capability was sought out by businessmen and politicians, including American president Barack Obama and the US Defense Department. Not surprisingly, for the same reasons, it was also popular with criminals.

Perhaps there was no need for a war with the Rizzutos. Vito's family hadn't retaliated after the murder of Nick Jr. or the disappearance of *consigliere* Paolo Renda. No response followed the murders of long-time Rizzuto family loyalist Agostino Cuntrera and his bodyguard Liborio Sciascia. The family appeared passive after the slaying of Nicolò. So it was understandable that many of Vito's former associates found the prospect of aligning themselves with Salvatore Montagna or Raynald Desjardins to be a reasonable response to this new post-Rizzuto underworld order.

There were still a few glimmers of life on Vito's side, if one looked hard enough. Vito loyalist Rocco (Sauce) Sollecito was paroled in June 2011. Police had already warned the sixty-two-year-old behind bars that his life was in danger. "Your file contains extensive information in connection with your safety," a parole decision read. Sollecito replied to parole authorities that he planned to support himself through legal activities and his pension.

Calogero Renda's immigration papers. Renda accompanied Vito Rizzuto's namesake grandfather to the USA from the family's Sicilian home village of Cattolica Eraclea.

Vito Rizzuto Sr. landed in New Orleans in 1925. He would die in New York state in 1933, never again seeing his young son, Nicolò.

Thirty-year-old Nicolò Rizzuto arrived with his young family in Halifax in 1954, including eight-year-old Vito and his six-year-old sister, Maria.

In Montreal, the Rizzutos would clash with the more established Paolo Violi, seen here at his Reggio Bar.

Vito (in black) and other members of the hit team (Gerlando Sciascia, left; Joey Massino, right; other, unknown), the day after the 1981 Three Captains mob killings in Brooklyn. The murder cemented Vito's standing with the Bonanno Mafia family of New York, who considered Montreal their turf.

Nicolò and his wife, Libertina, herself the daughter of a powerful Mafia don in Sicily.

Nicolò, arrested and charged for cocaine trafficking in Venezuela in 1988. He returned to Montreal in 1993.

Like Vito, Smiling Joe Di Maulo was a mediator on the streets.

The Consenza Social Club in Saint-Léonard, chief meeting place and hangout for senior members of the Rizzuto crime family.

'Ndrangheta members Cosimo Stalteri and Michele Racco. By the 2000s, octogenarian Stalteri would be the most senior of the Ontario group's ruling *camera di controllo*.

Raynald Desjardins was Vito's right-hand man, until a major cocaine bust put the Quebecer behind bars for a decade. He returned an embittered rival and major threat to his former boss.

An invitation to golf with Vito was often tantamount to a performance review.

A high school dropout, Vito carried himself like a CEO, though his suits tended to be a little too flashy for the corporate world.

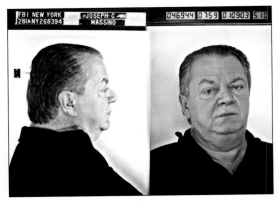

In 2004, Bonanno boss Big Joey Massino becomes the highest ranking member of La Cosa Nostra to cooperate with police, worsening the already fragile state of the Mafia family.

Salvatore Montagna hoped Vito's prison stay was the Bonanno family's chance to re-assert its claim on Montreal, a crucial entry point for smuggling drugs into North America.

Spaniard Juan (Joe Bravo) Ramon Paz Fernandez was briefly reliable muscle for Vito on the streets of Toronto. The bodybuilder pounces on an unlikely target for a photo.

Nicolò and his trusted inner circle in 1999: Paolo Renda (right), Rocco Sollecito and Francesco Arcadi.

Restaurateur/hitman Salvatore (Sam) Calautti was a never ending problem for the 'Ndrangheta.

Former pro football player Constantin (Big Gus) Alevizos was muscle for Panepinto's Toronto group.

Gaetano (Guy) Panepinto ran Vito's Toronto crew after Fernandez was imprisoned.

Nick Rizzuto Jr. tried to maintain his father's criminal empire after Vito went to prison. The effort cost him his life.

Hells Angels Montreal Nomad leader Maurice (Mom) Boucher, one more Vito ally lost to prison.

Salvatore Cazzetta (centre, seated), founder of the Rock Machine biker gang.

Ducarme Joseph was a Montreal street-gang leader Vito could rely on—for a time.

Vito's war continued with the daytime assassination of 'Ndrangheta drug smuggler and street boss Carmine (The Animal) Verduci.

Vittorio (Victor) Mirarchi was left by his late father to Desjardins' care and thrived under his mentor, just as Desjardins had once thrived under Vito.

'Ndrangheta killer Domenic Napoli had been part of a hit team in Siderno but ran afoul of Panepinto for encroaching on his video-gambling turf in York Region.

In Bagheria, Sicily, Fernandez tried to wait out Vito's war and maintain loyalty to both the godfather and his enemy Desjardins.

Portuguese national Fernando Pimentel brought Fernandez extra muscle in Bagheria.

Fernandez underestimating the extent of police surveillance in Italy.

Fernandez with Andrea Fortunato Carbone, Michele Modica's bodyguard who escaped the California Sandwiches shooting unscathed.

Fernandez with mobster Pietro Scaduto, also present at the North York shooting and deported.

Vito and Fernandez in happier days. In Vito's last war, no slight went unpunished.

———

By the middle of 2011, there had been so much change for everyone in the *milieu* to process. To help his boss, Desjardins, keep up with the times, Giuseppe (Closure) Colapelle assumed the role of a full-blown underworld spy, keeping tabs on the movements of Montagna and his camp. Colapelle feigned respect for the New Yorker while at the same time mocking him behind his back, often calling him Nancy—"NY" for New York, apparently, with the rest added to feminize it.

Colapelle reported that Montagna had moved out of his home in Saint-Hubert and was staying in a hotel. Did that have something to do with his girlfriend being in town? Or was he trying to hide out from Desjardins? Why hadn't he already moved to Woodbridge, Ontario, as planned?

Desjardins was on holiday in Europe with his wife in early August when Colapelle couldn't shake the feeling that something was about to explode. The Desjardins camp dripped with contempt for Montagna. When not calling him Nancy, they called him Mickey, short for Mickey Mouse. It was hard to take the newcomer from New York too seriously when he boasted that his guys would come by the dozens to support him. He sounded like a mouthy kid on the schoolyard, bragging about his tough big brother. Exactly where was his power base? What was left in New York? Was he talking about new contacts in Toronto, perhaps? Did the New Yorker really believe he could just show up in their city and take control?

As Desjardins chilled in Europe, black street gangs started venturing into cafés on Vito's old turf and requesting envelopes—protection money. They weren't collecting for themselves. If Montagna's loudmouth men hadn't already failed to impress Colapelle, here they were using black gang members as collectors, which he didn't particularly like; somehow, it seemed more respectable when extortion payments were demanded by Italian mobsters.

Meanwhile, Colapelle worried about the possibility of an informa-tion leak in the Desjardins group and called upon them to change their

BlackBerrys immediately. Whoever won the battle in cyberspace would likely win the war for the streets, and Closure didn't plan to make these hostilities easy for his enemies.

At 5:34 p.m. on August 15, 2011, Desjardins returned to Trudeau International Airport in Montreal on Flight TS711, after thirty days in Italy, Corsica and France. When police later checked his passport, they would find no trace of the extended trip. They did find other out-of-the-country jaunts, including a trip to Colombia from February 7 to 24, 2011, and another trip there a few months later, from April 11 to 21. His passport was stamped for a trip to the Bahamas in November 2009 and to the Dominican Republic on December 28, 2009. Interestingly, that was the day of Nick Jr.'s murder. The Quebec Hells Angels had set up a charter in the Caribbean island earlier that year, giving themselves and Desjardins a place to tan and talk, hopefully away from the eyes of Canadian police.

Colapelle had much to tell his boss. There was the trouble with the black gangs, but their new boss remained the priority. They needed to keep a constant eye on Montagna, who had recently changed his cars. They also needed guns.

By late August, Colapelle heard talk that some of Montagna's group would be playing golf in a tournament in a week's time. Perhaps Mickey would be on the links with them; despite the American's bluster, Colapelle had noticed that he actually kept a low profile. It would be a good chance to assess Mickey's Montreal power base. Perhaps the Arcuris would be there in their golf togs. Colapelle had no doubt that the family of Domenico Arcuri Sr. was now deeply entrenched in the Montagna camp. Domenico Sr. had once been considered a Rizzuto ally, but those days were long gone. The Arcuris had a history of backing winners, stretching back to the Rizzuto–Violi wars. Domenico Sr. was believed to have taken part in setting up Paolo Violi's 1978 execution, and it was Domenico Sr. who took over Violi's old ice cream business afterwards. Soon he became known by the happy title of "King of Ice Cream." Aside from making a tasty product, he also helped the company grow by bombing a competitor in 1983 who dared sell his wares at Italian banquet halls. If the

King of Ice Cream wanted to continue backing winners, he had no more need for the Rizzutos.

Desjardins agreed to buy four tickets for the golf event, just to keep up the appearance of getting along. If the Desjardins side met with the Montagna people at the golf tournament, they would likely break out smiles and not guns. Civility helped keep an enemy off guard. Meanwhile, the Desjardins side looked about for more "toys," a code word for guns. Pretence could keep the buildup of arms and resentments under wraps for only so long.

By mid-September 2011, there was talk among the Desjardins camp of another clumsy extortion attempt by the Montagna people. As the story went, some of Montagna's men went to a baker who had recently set up shop and told him he could no longer sell cold meat, just bread. The squeezing of the baker was typical of Montagna's aggressive, greedy push for *pizzo*, extortion money, which they preferred to think of as a tax.

Squeezing too hard on people outside the underworld—or "legits"— was a recipe for disaster. Squeeze legits too hard and they run to the police. Montagna didn't seem to understand or care.

CHAPTER 27

Time for Tims

The rifle shots made a harsh, metallic sound. Not the soft *pop-pop-pop* firecracker report of lower-powered automatic pistols, these sounded like iron hammers pounding on steel spikes. A little after 9:30 a.m. on September 16, 2011, two dozen shots were heard, rapid-fire, from Lévesque Boulevard near the Highway 25 toll bridge. They sounded close to Desjardins's luxury house on the Rivière des Prairies, in Laval's Saint-Vincent-de-Paul district. They were so loud they startled a lone passenger on a passing bus.

The gunfire originated near a clump of bushes on Desjardins's property, close to the river, where he often met with contacts. He was getting into his new black BMW X5 when the shooting began. Bodyguard Jonathan (Kid) Mignacca was sitting half in his Jeep. He fired twice at the black gunman, who was at a disadvantage as he was shooting uphill. Mignacca's show of force was enough to chase the assailant back to a waiting red Sea-Doo. Desjardins's BMW was pock-marked with bullets, but he didn't suffer a scrape. Mignacca received only minor wounds. The sole casualty that morning was the Sea-Doo, which was later discovered on the Montreal side of the river, torched.

Streets were closed off. Ford Fusions swarmed the area. Fusions were the cars of choice for undercover cops trying to look inconspicuous; several of them in one part of town was enough to make a pistol-packing gangster's heart race. Members of Desjardins's group let out a collective sigh of relief when they learned that their leader—known in the group as "Old" and "China"—was okay. He had spent only a little time in the back of a police cruiser for questioning. Mignacca was in hospital, but doing well. While police found no gun on him, there were gunpowder traces on his hands and he faced charges for discharging a weapon.

Desjardins was remarkably cool during the questioning by police. Someone with a machine gun had just tried to fill him in and he didn't look a bit rattled. He also showed absolutely no interest in giving police any clues. They seized his car and Mignacca's BlackBerrys, hoping analysis would reveal information the gangster wouldn't.

The Montagna side reached out to Desjardins. Within hours of the attempted murder, they asked Giovanni Bertolo's younger brother Giuseppe to set up a face-to-face talk between Montagna and the Bertolos' boss as soon as possible. Giuseppe wasn't sure it was a good idea. It sounded like another attempt to get at Desjardins.

A Sûreté du Québec surveillance team watched as a black BMW X5 pulled into the Tim Hortons at 10005 Louis-H. Lafontaine Boulevard in Montreal at 3:23 p.m. Not long after that, a black-and-grey Ford Flex also appeared at the doughnut shop. Domenico Arcuri Jr. got out of the Beemer and Montagna stepped from the Flex, and they headed inside. Bertolo texted Vittorio Mirarchi to say the face-to-face meeting with the Montagna group was about to begin—without Desjardins.

Police watched from a distance as Montagna led the discussion. Montagna stressed that it wasn't his group behind the Desjardins murder bid. The real would-be assassins, according to Montagna, were the "family." Montagna suggested that new Rizzuto leadership had now been established: Vito's mother, Zia Libertina. As he described it, all power flowed from the octogenarian. If Montagna was telling the truth, this was a development to be feared, not laughed off. Zia Libertina was a Mafia don's daughter, and she had recently lost both her husband and her eldest grandson to gunmen while her only son rotted in an American prison cell. It sounded absurd, that the acting boss of a New York Mafia family could be afraid of the wrath of a great-grandmother, but Mickey Mouse was clearly nervous.

Montagna described Desjardins as the only ally he could count on in Canada. Montagna's men would be happy to meet him anywhere. Montagna nervously tapped his hand as he made his pitch. Bertolo thought he could see tears in Arcuri's eyes.

Montagna pleaded in the doughnut shop for Arcuri to believe he had nothing to gain from Desjardins's death. As the American told things, now, more than ever, the Desjardins and Montagna sides needed to stick together. Clearly, the New Yorker was rattled. The fact that Desjardins chose not to meet with him spoke volumes: it was easy to conclude that the hunter and the hunted had shifted roles. Montagna seemed almost relieved by the heavy police surveillance.

The meeting over, Montagna climbed back into the Flex and retreated from sight. The attempt at détente with Desjardins hadn't been a success, but it could have been worse. At least he hadn't been shot.

Not long after that, the Desjardins side looked for help from a sixty-nine-year-old man nicknamed Toilet. Jack Simpson's nickname came from his plumbing business, but his long criminal record was what made him interesting. His life had been on a downward swirl since he was eleven and his father died. He did time in a delinquent boys' home, and then prison stretches after convictions for counterfeiting in 1962 and 1980. He had escaped prosecution while running a car dealership that served as a front for Rizzuto family car thefts, but was nabbed again for his role in an attempt to smuggle a planeload of three hundred kilograms of cocaine. That netted him a twenty-eight-year prison sentence in California, which was reduced to sixteen years in 2000 after he was transferred to Canada.

Simpson's wife and mother died while he was behind bars. Now out on full parole, he was living on Île Vaudry, a working-class/commuter neighbourhood on a small island about fifty kilometres north of Montreal. For all his efforts in crime, Simpson was close to broke. He had a job that paid him seven hundred dollars a week and massive debts that required him to file for bankruptcy and obtain a second mortgage on his home.

Desperate, criminally inclined and with no history of violence: Jack Simpson was just the sort of man who might have a chance of getting close to Mickey Mouse.

CHAPTER 28

The hunt for Mickey Mouse

No one answered on September 19, 2011, when Sûreté du Québec detective Simon Beauchemin and sergeant Benoit Dubé knocked at the door of Raynald Desjardins's unassuming yellow brick home overlooking the Rivière des Prairies in Laval. They left a business card in the mailbox and drove off to the nearby home of Joe Di Maulo, close to a private golf course where Vito had often played in happier times. No one answered there either.

Their next stop was Desjardins's workplace in an industrial park on the 10000 block of Secant Street in Anjou, Montreal. Desjardins was there when the officers arrived and listened politely as they tried to appeal to his sense of public safety. It was to no one's benefit to ignite a mob war. The pain caused by the biker war between the Hells Angels and the Rock Machine/Bandidos in the late 1990s and early 2000s was still fresh in everyone's mind. That conflict ended at least 160 lives, including that of an eleven-year-old boy, which made it easy for politicians to pass much tougher anti-gang legislation. There had been no winners in that war, only survivors.

Desjardins stuck to his line that he was now into construction, not destruction. "I'm a victim of this situation and I'm a peaceful person." The officers left him a business card before they drove off.

At 1:00 p.m., the officers were at a café in Saint-Léonard, looking for

Vittorio Mirarchi. He wasn't in and they left a business card with a manager.

Their next stop was an office on the 4000 block of Jarry East, Saint-Léonard, where they left a business card for Di Maulo. At 2:20 p.m., they followed a gravel road to Montagna's red brick home outside Saint-Hubert. Again, no one answered and they left a business card.

At 5:00 p.m., the detectives received a call from Di Maulo's lawyer, Pierre Morneau. They told him they wanted to speak with Di Maulo informally about the bungled attempt on his brother-in-law Desjardins's life. Five minutes later, Di Maulo called Detective Beauchemin, saying he and his lawyer would meet with them later in the day. The location of the meeting was undetermined.

At 5:10, the officers were back at Montagna's house in the country. A white Cadillac Escalade with New York plates was parked in front of the garage, but the woman who answered the door said he wasn't in. Detective Dubé left his card and a message that he urgently needed to speak with Montagna.

At 6:15 p.m., Morneau called the officers to say that he and his client could meet now at Pizzédélic on Labelle Boulevard in the off-island Montreal suburb of Rosemère. Fifteen minutes later, they arrived and joined Di Maulo and Morneau at a table. The officers pressed Di Maulo to use his influence to lower the tension and keep a war from exploding.

Smiling Joe did his best to shrug it off. "The media is making this story more than what it is," he told them.

Through all of the drama, Moreno Gallo laid low. The Montreal mob had split into distinct factions, but no one seemed to know where he stood. Perhaps he realized he held the balance of power. Perhaps he thought he could somehow stay neutral and ride out the chaos.

Gallo wasn't well known to the public, beyond those who bought pastries at his bakeshop, but the millionaire commanded a considerable reputation in the *milieu*. He was Calabrian, but had once been considered an ally of Vito. Maybe he maintained a low profile because of his own character, or perhaps it was a result of his lifetime parole conditions, after he was convicted of second-degree murder in the slaying of drug dealer Angelo Facchino in 1973.

Gallo was granted parole in 1983, fading into the background until he appeared on Project Colisée wiretaps in the mid-2000s. His voice was intercepted six dozen times in the backroom of the Consenza Social Club, as he mediated tensions between mobsters and between mobsters and the Hells Angels. Now, as tensions mounted, it was natural to wonder if Gallo might step up to provide badly needed support for Vito or join with Montagna or Desjardins and his rebels. Most likely he knew it was suicidal even to suggest mediation to Vito. For the time being, he chose to remain a wild card. If he was to make a move, there was no point in telegraphing his intentions.

By September 21, 2011, Desjardins's man Closure Colapelle had the uncomfortable feeling that he and his associates were being followed. They were right: the RCMP had set up surveillance on them. Police and Colapelle were both trying to locate Montagna. Since his failed attempt to meet Desjardins in the Tim Hortons, the New Yorker was reachable in cyberspace but a phantom on the streets.

Colapelle regularly texted Montagna and his crew, and Montagna still pressed him for a face-to-face with Desjardins. Through text messages, Montagna maintained the pretence that he and Desjardins were allies and that they must join forces against Vito's family. Did Montagna suspect yet that Colapelle was a spy? Were they smart enough to plant false intelligence with him? Perhaps Mickey's men had already planted a GPS on his vehicle.

Colapelle heard that Montagna and his group would be at a wedding in late September. The temptation was to attack quickly, while the enemy was liquored and relaxed. True to form, Desjardins played it cool when he heard the news and did nothing but joke with his men.

Police seemed everywhere on the streets now. There was a growing sense among the Desjardins camp that they would move in soon. That was logical. A bust would at least postpone gunfire. In the meantime, better to deter violence with a strong police presence.

Finally, Desjardins sent out word in a text that he would meet with Montagna. Before that meeting, however, Desjardins planned to attend to family matters. The wedding of his daughter Vanessa was scheduled for October 1, 2011, at the Le Mirage golf club in Terrebonne, owned by singing megastar Celine Dion and her manager/husband René Angélil. It would likely be monitored by the RCMP, so there was little chance the Montagna group would attack them there.

When the wedding day arrived, the Mounties made no effort to be discreet. They made notes on who was in attendance, capturing many on camera and video also, including Colapelle, Di Maulo, Jack Simpson, Felice Racaniello, Giuseppe Bertolo, Calogero Milioto, Tony Volpato, Desjardins's bodyguard Jonathan (Kid) Mignacca and Desjardins's nephew Hugo Desjardins. Colapelle gave a wedding envelope of $5,000, followed by Di Maulo at $2,000, Simpson $800 and Mignacca $500.

The Desjardins camp worried too that Montagna must be planning to do something about Colapelle. Montagna's group must suspect something by now. Colapelle refused to slow down. Retreating wasn't an option and it also wasn't his nature. His men began tailing Larry Lo Presti, hoping he would lead them to Montagna. Colapelle was hearing plenty, even if he hadn't yet located the Bonanno boss. By mid-October, Colapelle heard of a meeting involving an old Toronto Italian and the Montagna group. There were also more rumours of an imminent police operation. Who would be the target of the operation remained a mystery.

Rumblings from New York suggested more trouble for Montagna. The Gambinos had just suffered a big hit with early morning raids on a major sports betting ring, and the feeling was that the Bonannos were next on the police to-do list. In Montreal, there was also word that Montagna had pissed off a serious biker, although details on that were sketchy.

Colapelle could feel he was closing in on Montagna. He heard that the New Yorker was now living on the South Shore with his mistress, and frequented two restaurants in the area. Insiders in the Desjardins camp gave him yet another nickname: Lugie, as in phlegm. Colapelle still had people watching Larry Lo Presti. Sooner or later, he had to lead them to Montagna.

Lo Presti, who had dreamed of growing up to be like his father, got his wish on October 24, 2011. He was smoking a cigarette on a condominium balcony on De la Côte-Vertu Boulevard. in Montreal's Saint-Laurent borough, when someone pulled the trigger on him. At the time of his death, there was talk that Montagna had plans to "do" him, meaning to make him a full Bonanno family member.

Apparently, the junior Lo Presti wasn't killed by anyone in the Desjardins group, as they appeared clueless as to the cause of the murder. Word from them was that the Lo Presti job was the work of black street gang members. Whatever the case, his assassins remained unidentified, like those who had killed his father.

On October 25, Mirarchi was in downtown Toronto with another man, meeting in the upscale Yorkville area with a violent Albanian immigrant who was seen as an emerging crime boss, as well as a representative of the Commisso crime family and a couple of others. The next morning in Montreal, police visited Desjardins's office to talk about Lo Presti's murder, but he wasn't there. Police finally hooked up with him later in the day, when he was accompanied by his lawyer. Police again appealed to Desjardins to use his influence to avoid another all-out gang war.

Colapelle noted that Montagna didn't want any of his men to go to Lo Presti's funeral, as it was to be held out of the Rizzutos' Loreto funeral home. Anyone who showed up would be "dealt with." Colapelle was starting to think that Montagna was losing it. If any more proof was needed that he was nuts, this was it. Colapelle heard that the American had delusions of grandeur—ruling Montreal and then Toronto and then planting his flag on the tiny tropical island of St. Martin. It was his deportation fantasy, the way others might have retirement plans.

For their part, the Desjardins side sought out military-grade automatic weapons: AK-47s, .223s, AR-15s. An underworld gun supplier let it be known that they could get high-end Heckler & Koch, Walther, SIG Sauer and Beretta firearms bulk for $3,500 each.

And the hunt for Mickey Mouse continued.

CHAPTER 29

Mickey's bad day

I t was as if Montagna was getting crazier by the day. He seemed frantic as he tried to reassure his loose coalition that he wasn't behind the hit on Larry Lo Presti. How could anyone suspect such a thing? He had respected Larry's late father and would not touch his son. Also, Closure reported to Desjardins that Montagna was talking about a mysterious person lurking in Montreal called "36." Montagna was spreading word that "36" worked with the "family." Montagna was still pushing the idea hard that it was Vito's group—now along with "36"—who had tried to kill Desjardins.

While lots of noise was coming from the Montagna side in early November, it was still proving hard to divine exactly where the man himself was.

Desjardins didn't like going out at night now because he didn't carry weapons, which would be a breach of his parole conditions. If police caught him carrying a firearm, he would be back in prison to serve out the remaining five years of his drug-smuggling sentence.

The Québécois mobster heard a rumour that Moreno Gallo would have been very nervous to know was circulating. Word was that Gallo had given "files" to Montagna. If true, then Desjardins could be sure that Gallo was firmly in the American's camp. "Files" referred to the records kept by major organized crime sports books, and Gallo had run

Platinum for Vito. A gambler's "file" was made up of significant financial records, such as mortgages and banking information. It also included the names and addresses of a gambler's parents and other close relatives. This information would be carefully studied before the operators of a sports book determined how much, if any, credit he could be granted. The information also let the sports book operators know where to go calling if a gambler couldn't make good on debts. That degree of financial diligence could be overlooked if the prospective gambler was related to someone of interest, such as a professional athlete. In those cases, it was better for the gambler to run up a major debt, so that the book's operators could suggest to the athlete that all would be forgiven in exchange for the fixing of a game or the provision of inside information on a team. If Gallo had indeed turned over files to Montagna, then not only did Desjardins know what side the millionaire baker had taken, it also meant a major betrayal of Vito, punishable by death.

In the third week of November, Mickey Mouse finally resurfaced. He still wanted to meet with Desjardins, the man he had almost certainly tried to murder just two months earlier. Mickey's paranoia was feeding off itself and he talked again of bringing up guys from New York to bolster their ranks.

For his part, Desjardins continued his effort to make nice, as if he and Montagna were old friends bonded by common enemies. Desjardins warned him that he had just heard that Operation Whale would hit later that month. Perhaps they could meet to talk about it. There had been a leak about the list of names of targets in the raid. Leaks about upcoming police raids were commonplace when the targets were Hells Angels or the mob, with the result that the wanted men were often missing or had cleaned up their environs by the time police arrived. Oddly, Desjardins's reported list of warrants also contained the names of some honest people. He spoke with conviction as he called for a get-together and warned Montagna to be careful. Within a couple of days, Montagna seemed to believe the police operation was all about him.

The hunt for Mickey Mouse appeared to be almost over.

The wife of a Desjardins associate gave birth to a boy on the morning of November 24, 2011—American Thanksgiving Day. The baby came into the world around the time a video camera captured a white Ford F-150 pickup driven by Jack Simpson leaving Île Vaudry and heading north on Celine-Dion Boulevard. Around that same time, Sal Montagna seemed to be alone as his car entered the metro parking lot, his movements recorded by a security camera.

Moments later, Montagna walked into the lobby of the Hôtel Champlain and descended into the subway. It's unlikely he was afraid to meet up with seventy-one-year-old Simpson, who had no record of violence.

An hour later, a neighbour of Simpson's on Île Vaudry heard two shots in quick succession. Next came the sound of shattering glass. A stranger dashed down a slope, away from Simpson's house. The fleeing man slipped and disappeared from sight. Seconds later, he jumped back into view, frantically attempting to cross the narrow Assomption river. There was a splashing sound in the icy waters. Then nothing. Thirty or forty seconds later, another man, with glasses and backcombed salt-and-pepper hair, climbed into a white pickup truck. As a witness called 911, he saw the white four-door Ford F-150 pickup drive out of view on Celine-Dion Boulevard.

Neighbours ventured out to discover the soaked, bloodied body of a man lying face up in the snow on the riverbank. It looked like the same man who had leapt into the river minutes earlier. He had managed to cross the river, leaving blood in the snow on both banks.

At 10:10 a.m., police arrived to see the motionless body of Salvatore Montagna lying on the snowy shore. At 11:34, the acting boss of the Bonanno crime family was pronounced dead at Le Gardeur hospital.

As police analyzed the crime scene, a Montrealer flew to Toronto Island airport and went to a restaurant in Yorkville. There, he sat down with two members of the Commisso crime family. The lunch over, he returned to the airport and immediately flew home to Montreal.

Later that day, some of Desjardins's men finally had time to do something truly pleasant: visit the newborn baby in hospital.

One life had ended and another had just begun.

CHAPTER 30

Someone's watching

Raynald Desjardins couldn't shake the feeling that he was being watched. Again. Were those Italians that his wife saw in a navy blue Explorer near his home? What about that suspicious-looking man wearing a cap in a grey Mitsubishi? It was hard to sneak up on Desjardins at home, as the front of his house faced the river, with little room to park, and the back of his home was carved out of stone, with no yard. Still, the failed attack by the hit man on the Sea-Doo reminded the Montreal mobster that there was always room for improvement when it came to home security.

There was talk in Desjardins's circle about how Montagna had met with some relatives of Paolo Violi in Toronto along with "Turkey," the nickname for Moreno Gallo. They weren't worried about revenge for Montagna's murder, though. Neither the Violis nor Gallo were likely to care enough to avenge his death. Gallo likely had his own security concerns, as police notified him shortly after the murder that they thought his life was also in danger.

Meanwhile, Mirarchi stressed when he thought of the well-being of his son and daughter. If something happened to him, hopefully it wouldn't be at a time when his family was present. The rest he could take.

By midday November 26, 2011, RCMP officers were eyeballing a suburban townhome on Queensbury Drive on the outskirts of Ottawa, which served as Jack Simpson's hideout. Inside, grey-haired Simpson grew more restless by the hour. Just hanging out in Ottawa's colourless suburbs felt like a near-death experience. Perhaps he could rent a motel room with a weekly rate in Montreal. He could return by bus. Maybe they would give him a phone and another to his girlfriend so they could at least talk.

There had been a seventeen-piece brass band and twenty-three cars laden with flowers for the funeral of Vic (The Egg) Cotroni. At the funeral of the Egg's younger brother, Frank (The Big Guy) Cotroni, a white dove was released for each of the seventy years of his life. Matters of ceremony were far more restrained when it came time to put Salvatore Montagna into the cold ground of a country where he was born but never really accepted.

Just six dozen people showed up on November 27, 2011, for his funeral service at Notre Dame de Pompei church on Sauvé Street East, near Saint-Michel Boulevard. That paled against the hundreds of mourners at the recent funerals of Nicolò and Agostino Cuntrera. There were only female members of the Arcuri family paying their respects. Domenico Arcuri Sr. had introduced Montagna to members of the Montreal underworld, but now he was too fearful for his security to see him off. Just two limousines carried wreaths of flowers for the New Yorker. The most notable arrangement was from Montagna's daughters, which read: *we will never forget you.*

The day after Montagna's funeral, Jack Simpson still couldn't overcome his overpowering sense of restlessness in Ottawa. Crashing down from the adrenalin rush of Montreal's *milieu* to being housebound in the staid nation's capital in the dead of winter was a shock. His boredom ended that day when officers arrived at his door with a warrant for his arrest on parole violation, as he wasn't supposed to leave the province of Quebec without permission. His explanation that he was job hunting didn't impress anyone, and he was ordered to drop to the floor and was handcuffed. On a coffee table, in plain view, was his BlackBerry. There was a bundle of hundred-dollar bills in a bag on his bed, adding up to ten thousand dollars.

Fear seeped into the Desjardins group until it was all-consuming. Would police come calling for them next? Could there be a rat in their group? They heard on November 30, 2011, of the arrest of someone in their circle nicknamed "Moe." Moe was close to Simpson. Was there a connection between the two arrests? Next came word that someone had been shot, but the identity of the victim was unclear.

With the new boss of the Bonanno crime family lying dead in a cold Canadian grave, the silence from the organization's power base spoke volumes. Montagna had boasted of the dozens of New York mobsters who would rally to his side. Racked by informers and arrests, the once-proud Bonanno family was in no position to mete out vengeance or even to divine what had just happened north of the border.

Montagna's assassination left plenty of mobsters in Montreal nervously wondering: what happens to Montagna's allies now that he's dead? Antonio (Tony Suzuki) Pietrantonio got his answer when a gunman opened fire on him on December 13, 2011, outside a Jarry Street East grill, just south of the Métropolitain expressway. Pietrantonio survived, despite serious injuries. The would-be assassin's getaway car was found blocks away, near the corner of Jacques-Casault and Joseph-Quintal streets. As Tony Suzuki recovered, there would be plenty of time for his would-be killers to reload.

Within hours, Sergeant Benoit Dubé and Detective Sergeant Martin Robert of the Sûreté du Québec drove back to Desjardins's Laval home in an attempt to talk about the failed hit on Tony Suzuki. Police asked if he had received any threats and Desjardins replied that all was well and he didn't need a thing.

That afternoon, the detectives drove out to Tony Suzuki's home on pine-tree-lined Des Ancêtres Street in Sainte-Adèle, to discuss the attempt on his life. They didn't get closer to him than his outdoor intercom. They asked if he had received any threats. He replied that all was going well and he too didn't need a thing.

Jonathan Mignacca had been free on bail since November 16, 2011, but his conditions included one against him going into Laval, except for court appearances or to see his lawyer. He specifically was not allowed to associate with Raynald Desjardins. That wasn't much good if he was supposed to be the mobster's bodyguard. On December 28, 2011, an old blue four-door Volkswagen sat parked in front of Desjardins's Laval home. It might be nothing. In happy times, gangsters cruise the streets in Escalades and BMWs. When they're trying to sneak about, they turn to Fusions and Volkswagens.

Jack Simpson was already behind bars in Kingston Penitentiary on December 20, 2011, when he was charged with first-degree murder for the death of Salvatore Montagna. Also that day, the Sûreté du Québec arrested Vittorio Mirarchi and seized his BlackBerry. Calogero Milioto was also charged that day with the murder of Montagna and possession of firearms. His BlackBerry Curve was seized from a coat pocket.

The SQ executed a search warrant in the Anjou apartment of twenty-seven-year-old Felice (Pony) Racaniello, where they found the construction worker's chrome and black BlackBerry 9300 in a kitchen wine rack. A BlackBerry model 9800 was found in a pocket of Racaniello's coat and it was confiscated as well.

The SQ arrested and charged Desjardins without incident at his office at 10310 Secant Street, and seized a BlackBerry and an iPad. Mirarchi, who up to this point had enjoyed a low public profile and had no criminal record, was hit with the same first-degree-murder charge as his mentor. Forty-year-old Calogero Milioto and fifty-nine-year-old Pietro Magistrale were arrested on weapons charges as police unearthed a small arsenal of rifles and handguns.

In total, some two hundred officers from the SQ, the RCMP and the municipal forces of Montreal, Longueuil and Laval executed sixteen search warrants on December 20, scooping up pistols, bulletproof vests, large sums of money and several more BlackBerrys. The Desjardins crew could only hope their devices' message security was as good as the company's reputation.

Desjardins stopped and looked towards the waiting news cameras as he stepped out of the prisoners' van. Officers on the rooftop with military-level rifles scanned the assembled journalists as he waved to someone in the group. In some quarters, the native-born Quebecker was now considered to be Quebec's most important organized crime player, and he looked every inch the part. He appeared confident and solid, like someone who felt in control, even if he was getting out of a police van in shackles to face a murder beef. It was much like the V-for-victory pose Mom Boucher of the Hells Angels had struck for press cameras after he had been initially acquitted on two murder charges. If the media had to take their photos and video, Vito's former sidekick wasn't going to blink in front of the cameras.

CHAPTER 31

Homeward bound

M oreno Gallo liked to describe himself as a family man and a Little Italy baker who gave back to the community. That was accurate as far as it went, but hardly a complete description. The Canada Border Services Agency was less charitable, calling him someone with an "active implication in organized crime." Authorities also noted that he was vulnerable for deportation. Gallo had lived in Canada since 1954, when he arrived from Calabria at age nine to join his father. He had never bothered to take out citizenship, and that came back to bite him hard in the winter of 2012, when he was a sixty-six-year-old man.

For a time, the wealthy baker protested his innocence through lawyers and fought the deportation to Italy. "I was nine when I arrived in Canada," he told court through his lawyer. "I have no recollection of Italy." He suddenly reversed course in late January 2012, agreeing to leave of his own accord. He sold his $1.2-million home in Laval, on the shore of the Rivière des Prairies, apparently deciding that life outside Canada was preferable to a possible burial in Montreal. "He understood that if he had stayed here, he would have been vulnerable," his lawyer, Stephen Fineberg, told reporters. "He chose to live in total freedom overseas." Gallo might once have been considered a mediator in the underworld, but these were tough times for peacemakers. The underworld was split into Vito's friends and Vito's enemies, with no safe ground in between.

In March 2012, a *New York Post* story suggested Vito was slipping emotionally. The article quoted an unnamed source from the Florence, Colorado, prison as reporting that Vito said: "I do not just want to be the godfather of Canada. I want to be the godfather of the world." The report also quoted unnamed American police sources as saying they believed the hit on Sal Montagna was ordered by Vito. The first statement about Vito was questionable. The second one was clearly wrong, but the fact that it was believed was a tribute to Vito's former stature. It was also an accepted truth that Vito would have to return to Montreal once he was released in early October 2012. Vito was a proud man, and to avoid the city after the murders of his son and father would be a public admission of defeat.

Gallo's decision to flee Montreal seemed wise, as bodies kept falling in his old *milieu* and paranoia was the new norm. Closure Colapelle chose to stay. Around 6 p.m. on March 1, 2012, a bullet caught Desjardins's spy as he sat in his SUV outside a pub in a Saint-Léonard strip mall near the intersection of Langelier and Lavoisier boulevards. Closure had always felt that killers would come after him, if they couldn't get to Desjardins and Mirarchi. The dead spy had been right.

Giuseppe (Joe) Renda feared he was possibly next in line for a hit man's bullet. A decade ago, he had been one of Vito's point men in Ontario. Then it had seemed a safe bet to hitch his saddle to Montagna, but those days too were long gone, and now it was time to duck and look for cover. The murder of Larry Lo Presti had shaken him. Then there was the attempted murder of Tony Suzuki and a visit by police saying his life was in danger. Still, he had to make a living. He presented himself like a rich man but had a crushing mortgage on a luxurious stone home on De Maisonneuve Boulevard in Westmount and outstanding utility bills and taxes to the tune of almost $600,000.

On May 4, 2012, he reportedly had a business meeting with someone from the old Agostino Cuntrera camp. At ten-thirty that morning, he said goodbye to his wife Benedetta (Betty) and walked out the door. Betty notified police when he didn't return by suppertime. His car was later discovered on Saint-Urbain Street in Little Italy. Forensic testing yielded nothing. Six days after he went missing, police searched a building under renovation on Jeanne-Mance. Again they didn't find a thing. The fifty-three-year-old left no clues behind, just a massive debt. His home was sold for $1.15 million and his widow declared bankruptcy, sold her Mercedes and moved into a condo with relatives. Her husband had been known as a discreet man. Now she and police believed he was the victim of an equally discreet abductor.

The remains of Vito's side took a hit in July 2012 when Rocco (Sauce) Sollecito was arrested on a parole violation, after he was spotted in a Laval bar with men who had criminal records. He had been free for a year and was due for full, unconditional release in October, less than two weeks after Vito was due back in Canada on parole. By then he wouldn't have to report to parole officers at all, but now he'd spend the time until his statutory release back in prison.

Sollecito's rearrest came a week after his son Giuseppe (Joe) Sollecito was sentenced to six months in jail and fined $200,000 for keeping the Rizzuto family gambling house on Jean-Talon East, along with Nick Jr. Joe Sollecito also ran a thrift store and pizzeria in Florida. Nicola Di Marco had already been hit with a $50,000 fine and an eighteen-month jail term in the case. Another co-accused was Giuseppe (Closure) Colapelle, but he had met his fate before the case got to court.

There weren't huge headlines when, on Sunday, July 16, 2012, sixty-year-old Walter Ricardo Gutierrez was killed in a hail of gunshots while walking towards his west-end home. There were nods that Gutierrez had been involved in the mid-1990s with Vito's group in money laundering, along with lawyers Joseph Lagana, Richard Judd and Vincenzo Vecchio. Back then, Vito was always reported in the press as too elusive for police ever to capture. More recently, the Montreal *Gazette* had taken to referring to his family with the phrase "once-powerful."

Still, Vito's group seemed to have bite. His name was whispered after street gang leader Chénier Dupuy was shot dead that August as he sat in an SUV outside a restaurant. Hours later, assassins ended the life of Dupuy's friend Lamartine Sévère Paul outside his apartment building in Laval.

There was talk that Dupuy had recently attended a meeting of street gang leaders in Sainte-Adèle, where he refused to join a new street-gang alliance run by black biker Gregory Wooley, who was close to Vito. There also was talk that an intergenerational war was tearing apart the Reds street gang, also known as the Bo Gars (Cute Guys). While older members had an association with Vito, younger ones were hungry and frustrated at being left little more than crumbs.

The same week as the murders of Dupuy and Paul, Riccardo Ruffullo, a man with Mafia links, was slain in his Côte-des-Neiges penthouse condominium. Not surprisingly, the mood in the *milieu* was one of hyper-alertness and caution. Vito was coming home soon and people would be called to account for their actions, or lack of action, while he was gone. Maria Mourani, author of two books on street gangs and a Bloc Québécois member of Parliament, told the Montreal *Gazette* that others in the underworld were equally stressed: "One of my sources said there are people sleeping in hotel rooms under false names."

When it might be safe to return home was anyone's guess, but for those who'd laid claim to a piece of Rizzuto turf in Vito's absence, things were about to get a whole lot worse before they got better.

CHAPTER 32

Vito's return

There is a monument in a small square in Cattolica Eraclea to honour Giuseppe Spagnolo, the town's first democratically elected mayor. It reads simply, *Giuseppe Spagnolo, sindaco, leader politico, ucciso dalla mafia*, for the union leader and politician, assassinated by the Mafia in 1955. It was Spagnolo's son Liborio who would later recall Nicolò Rizzuto as a confident young *campiere*, charming and tough, preferring words to violence. One of Giuseppe Spagnolo's killers was hidden by a local priest before fleeing to York Region, and convicted *in absentia* of the murder after he was on Canadian soil. He was Leonardo Cammalleri, a member of the *cosca*, or crime group, of Mafia boss Antonino (Don Nino) Manno. The convicted killer Cammalleri was also the father-in-law of Nicolò Rizzuto 's son, Vito. In the Mafia, such stories wither and drop from view, but they seldom really end. They just wind into other narratives.

Italian authorities never pressed for Cammalleri's extradition and Canadian authorities showed no interest in pushing the case further, despite emotional entreaties from Spagnolo's daughter, who also settled in the Toronto area. On November 26, 1966, Cammalleri was concerned enough about the possibility of his arrest that he stayed outside a Toronto church in his car while Vito married his daughter

Giovanna. Among those who made the trip from Montreal for the wedding that day was rising mobster Paolo Violi.

Meanwhile, Rosario Gurreri, one of the witnesses who helped Sicilian police with their investigation, moved to Montreal, where he opened a small restaurant in the city's Plateau neighbourhood. That was where his body was found on March 5, 1972, hacked a dozen times with a hatchet. As a final insult, a knife was stuck deep in his heart. No one was ever arrested for that crime either.

Technically still wanted for the Giuseppe Spagnolo murder back in 1955, Leonardo Cammalleri drew his final breath in late September 2012 at age ninety-two in his north Montreal home. Vito was due to be released from prison on October 6, so it was only natural to wonder if he would attend his father-in-law's funeral. It was still up in the air whether Cammalleri would be buried in York Region, where he lived much of his life, or in Montreal, where he spent his final years. The website of Complexe Funéraire Loreto contained no announcement. Wherever the funeral was to be held, it seemed imperative that Vito serve notice that he was not afraid to appear in plain sight of his enemies. Attendance at the funeral and visitation would also give him a chance to see who had the nerve to support him publicly and who would reveal where they stood by their absence.

With only last-minute notice, Cammalleri's funeral rites were performed on the morning of Friday, October 5, at almost the same moment that the Colorado prison doors finally opened for Vito. His release date had been moved up a day, with no explanation. The timing of the funeral averted the media circus that would certainly have accompanied Vito's attendance. Leonardo Cammalleri had largely managed to avoid the media and police in life, and now he had done so in death.

Shortly before midnight, Vito Rizzuto stepped off a direct commercial flight to Toronto, amidst speculation that he planned to settle there. His five-bedroom home in the Ahuntsic–Cartierville region of Montreal was up for sale. It was certainly an appealing property. The stone-faced house had only one owner and the 1,300-square-metre lot backed onto green space, albeit the same wooded area that had provided cover for the sniper who killed Vito's father. Cabinets in the kitchen were mahogany, all of the bedrooms had bidet-equipped ensuites, and the granite and stairway in the front entranceway were worthy of a *Gone with the Wind* remake. Press accounts of the mob war certainly didn't help the real estate agent trying to move the mansion, nor did the media's affection for the nickname Mafia Row. The asking price had dropped from almost $2 million to $1.5 million, showing the seller was clearly motivated. It went without saying why Vito didn't want to resume his life there.

If Vito chose to move to the Toronto area, he would have to do so without the muscle of Juan Ramon Paz (Johnny Bravo) Fernandez. Vito's lieutenant had been deported to his native Spain for a third time months before, after being paroled for plotting the murder of former pro football player and Panepinto crew member Constantin (Big Gus) Alevizos, as well as conspiring to import a tonne of cocaine. Big Gus survived the initial murder attempt that put Fernandez in prison. He was finally slain in January 2008 while walking across the parking lot of a Brampton halfway house. His enemy Fernandez had a rock-solid alibi: he was in prison at the time.

No one doubted that Fernandez was capable of murder. A parole board panel wrote to him in May 2011: "Several correctional officers witnessed death threats you made to another guard who was attempting to search you. During this incident, you seemed to flaunt your well-established ties to traditional organized crime in an effort to further intimidate the guard; this implies you remain connected to the same criminal lifestyle that enabled your considerable drug dealing activities."

The letter also cast suspicion on his connection to a lawyer who routinely visited organized criminals like Fernandez in prison. "Your ongoing visits from a lawyer who has worked for persons identified as being part of organized crime further reinforces your continuing involvement with this criminal subculture," the letter states. The parole review board lamented his "considerable lack of progress" on rehabilitation while behind bars. "Your lack of treatment in this regard is especially relevant in the context of your involvement in an inherently violent drug subculture."

The letter added that Fernandez would be a better than average bet to reoffend quickly when finally released: "A statistical risk evaluation places you in a group of offenders where 60 per cent will commit an indictable offence within three years of release. This predictor is concerning in light of your significant criminal history, which includes a variety of serious drug offences and violent crimes."

Vito was himself now legally free to fly anywhere in the world without restrictions, save the USA, where he would be on probation for three years, and Italy, where he was facing massive money laundering charges. The latter were a nod to Vito's considerable reach. Italian authorities claimed that, while awaiting extradition in the regional prison reception centre in Sainte-Anne-des-Plaines, a forty-five-minute drive north of Montreal in an area replete with maple sugar shacks and petting zoos, Vito somehow helped direct a massive fraud that led to a series of arrests across Italy and France in 2007. Police moved against twenty-two companies and arrested nineteen people, while freezing nearly $700 million in assets. Part of the evidence was wiretap recordings of Vito talking to another suspect in Europe. How Vito managed that was hard to fathom, since it goes without saying that inmates aren't supposed to be placing overseas calls to plot crimes. The calls from custody notwithstanding, the fraud itself was a particularly audacious one: mobsters were trying to scam their way into a six-billion-dollar contract to build a bridge across the Strait of Messina between the Italian mainland and Sicily. The scheme represented what was possible when criminals worked together, as it involved both the Sicilian Mafia and the 'Ndrangheta on the southern mainland.

Italian investigators were determined that Vito Rizzuto was somehow the puppet master of the whole operation. "We believe that even from jail they are able to control the organization," Silvia Franzè, an investigator with the Direzione Investigativa Antimafia, told the press in Rome. For the Italian media, Vito Rizzuto gained a new title: "Godfather of the Bridge."

Vito certainly had the money to retire somewhere warm where he could indulge his passion for golf year-round. His enormous wealth and ability to speak four languages gave him plenty of options. He had always liked the Dominican Republic, and his friends in the Quebec Hells Angels had recently set up a charter there. Perhaps Vito would float between Montreal and York Region. Wherever he travelled, it would be with the realization that he would never again share a smile or a word with his father or his eldest son. No amount of money or wine or female companionship was going to change that. All he could hope for was the dull satisfaction of revenge. Perhaps that would also give his mother some cold comfort.

As Vito headed back to Canada, he appeared robust enough for the challenge. During his sentencing, he had made mention in court that he might have a spot on a lung, but apparently this fear had passed. His prison records contained no mention of cancer, although he remained a cigarette smoker, and Canada Border Security records make no note of serious health concerns. Indeed, he wouldn't even bother to reactivate his government-issued health card.

On his flight home, Vito got a taste of the attention that lay ahead. A Radio-Canada journalist at the back of the airplane began to pepper him with questions, as a camera zoomed in tight on his face. Vito was stuck in his seat and had nowhere to go, like a zoo animal in a cramped cage. People with cameras and microphones clearly weren't afraid of him now. What might he expect from people with pistols and rifles?

Once on the ground, it took less than an hour for Vito to shake the RCMP surveillance team and journalists following him. The reporters then filed news items that alternately portrayed him as the most powerful man in the Canadian underworld and as a dead man walking. Both theories could be supported, up to a point. Meanwhile, embarrassed police made hopeful plans to pick up his trail the next morning as Vito disappeared into the Toronto night.

CHAPTER 33

Old haunts

Vito's first days of freedom were spent with a small group of men whom he genuinely trusted. One of his valued York Region contacts lived in a mansion behind a walled compound in King City, with a fish-eye security lens on the front gate allowing a wide view of the street. Vito had been welcome there in the past and there was no indication that they had turned against him. He knew many mobsters, businessmen and politicians, but there was just a short list who had earned his absolute faith. Vito had remained solid in prison, and now he needed to be around equally solid men as he sorted through eight years of intelligence. Vito had well-placed sources within policing as well as on the streets, so there was plenty of information. There was also much to consider. Men who valued the motivations of business over those of blood would be quick to betray him, if they hadn't already.

Vito felt he could also still count on his father's old lieutenant, Rocco Sollecito, who was due to walk out of Leclerc Institution on October 16. In Vito's absence, Sollecito had been number four in the Rizzuto group, but the murders of Nicolò and Agostino Cuntrera and the kidnapping and disappearance of Paolo Renda pushed him up the ranks. Sollecito had been responsible for construction and bookmaking as well as managing the Consenza Social Club; Vito would need him to do even more now. He was a tough, experienced man who was good with numbers and had contacts on both sides of the Atlantic Ocean. He was finally getting freed on statutory release, meaning he wouldn't be subject to any parole conditions, which made him all the more useful to his boss.

As Vito settled into his new life, the general public was strangely engaged with his private war and personal odyssey. There was strong Internet debate about where he would live. One rumour had him setting up camp in a property north of Toronto believed to have once belonged to pop superstar Elton John. There was no substance to the speculation, but it filled the need for cyber-chatter, until the next gangland slaying.

While Vito had finally returned, the country he had returned to was irreparably changed. So was Vito. What man could be diplomatic after the murder of his father and son? There was also his mother to consider. What would please his mother most: revenge for fallen family members or a long, quiet life for her only son?

Some things remained clear. There was no possibility of any common ground with relatives of Paolo Violi. Vito had never really liked members of the Commisso–'Ndrangheta family. How things stood with Carmelo Bruzzese wasn't so clear. They had once been friendly, but Bruzzese's son-in-law was Antonio Coluccio, and the Coluccios seemed central to the 'Ndrangheta's attempt to push into Montreal. Bruzzese had problems of his own, as the federal government was pushing to deport him to Italy.

Another important man in the shadows was Peter Scarcella, once considered a Vito ally. Scarcella was free on statutory release after his nine-year sentence for conspiracy to commit murder, conspiracy to commit aggravated assault and possession of a prohibited weapon. That prison time stemmed from his contribution to the failed group effort to have Modica murdered, which resulted in the crippling of innocent mother Louise Russo. Like Vito, Scarcella was now a marked man in some quarters. Scarcella's parole release form warned that he shouldn't get too comfortable: "On April 5, 2012, based on new information indicating a threat to your life, the Board altered an existing condition and imposed additional conditions including a condition that you reside at a Community Correctional Centre, or Community Residential Facility (such as Private Home Placement) approved by the Correctional Service of Canada, until the warrant expiry date."

There was nothing novel about criminals concluding it was a good idea to murder Scarcella. Back in the early 1980s, he was a target of the Commisso crime family. In 2007, while in custody, Scarcella was stabbed by another inmate. That year, he began psychological testing and violence prevention counselling. His parole file concluded that "you do not meet the criteria for the designation of psychopathy," but also added, "clinical impressions suggest that you represent a higher likelihood for indirect involvement in criminal activity for which you would not be prone to detection or apprehension. Clinical impressions also suggest a higher likelihood of involvement in indirect, instrumental violence should you feel the need for it."

In short, blue-eyed Peter was a mobster but not a lunatic. The report continued: "Indications are that you have held entrenched criminal values, and professionals assessing you believe there is a significant likelihood of you returning to your criminal lifestyle." Scarcella's parole conditions included the usual prohibition against associating with criminals. So while Scarcella was free, he was also a carefully watched man, both by the parole board and by underworld enemies. Meeting with him would be difficult and dangerous.

Some of the other men Vito had trusted also weren't much good to him now, even if they had remained loyal. *Compare* Frank Arcadi was serving a fifteen-year sentence as a result of the Colisée crackdown. Even with Canada's often-generous parole system, Arcadi was out of the *milieu* for the foreseeable future, and Vito needed help *now*. Francesco Del Balso and Skunk Giordano were both key lieutenants for Arcadi and their loyalty wasn't in question. However, they were both also in custody because of Colisée.

Vito's old biker contacts in the Quebec Hells Angels were mostly in prison. Mom Boucher would likely be a very old man before he was free again, after his first-degree murder convictions for ordering hits on two jail guards. Some of the London, Ontario, Hells Angels were working now with the York Region 'Ndrangheta, but they might still be useful. Also, there was Gregory Wooley. He had run the now-defunct Rockers, a Quebec Hells Angels support club, and was considered the originator of the Syndicate, a teetering alliance of Red and Blue street gangs with clout in Montreal's downtown.

Obviously, Vito could no longer call upon Raynald Desjardins. Quite the opposite. If the rift had begun when Desjardins got fifteen years for a drug scheme while Vito walked free, that rift became a chasm after Vito's men murdered Desjardins's friend Giovanni (Johnny) Bertolo. Another name now embedded in the enemy camp was that of Domenico Arcuri Sr. He had helped the Rizzutos take out the Violis thirty years before, but after making introductions for Salvatore Montagna when the New Yorker first arrived in Montreal in 2009, he had opened the floodgates for the man who had turned Vito's life into hell.

Giuseppe (Ponytail) De Vito was never a true insider in Vito's group; he'd pulled away after the murder of his boss and friend Paolo Gervasi. Ponytail had dangerous friends, but after four years on the run he was a convict now, starting a fifteen-year sentence for narcotics conspiracy. Ponytail was in isolation in Donnacona, but protesting that he wanted to be returned to the general population. Since the deaths of his daughters, he was apparently a man without fear and perhaps also without the will to live. According to a prison report explaining the isolation, De Vito was now a threat to the safety of the Rizzuto clan, even behind bars.

Joe Di Maulo had backed his brother-in-law Desjardins in early stages of the attempt at a consortium with Montagna, Mirarchi and Arcuri, and his loyalty to Desjardins was unquestioned. Still, Smiling Joe was something of a man of peace in the *milieu*, his three old murder charges notwithstanding.

Vito would also have to get used to new cityscapes in Montreal and Toronto. The old hangout of the Consenza Social Club was now just a memory, converted into a clothing store. Also gone was the Laennec coffee bar in Laval, where the second tier of the crime family once held court. Laval was now home to more than three dozen significant players in Vito's world, as the core of power shifted from Mafia Row to luxury Laval neighbourhoods such as Val des Brises and Sainte-Dorothée. The homes on Antoine-Berthelet had once been a statement of wealth and separation from the cramped houses of downtown Little Italy; now Vito couldn't rid himself of his old home and its memories of defeat and death.

For the time being, Vito had left the safe confines of the walled compound in King City and was holed up in a downtown Montreal *pied-à-terre* condominium with Giovanna. When he stepped out, it was into a $100,000 armour-plated car he had special ordered from the States. Only his tiny inner circle knew his address.

Clearly, there were informers in Vito's midst. Someone in his world had betrayed Agostino Cuntrera and Paolo Renda, and maybe also Nick Jr. Perhaps the traitors even smiled at them just before sending them to their graves. A few words in a quick text or phone call and there might be a funeral for Vito too. As he regrouped in his new apartment, there was no way to judge if Vito felt afraid, or if he was so prepared for imminent death that he had already gone cold inside.

CHAPTER 34

The other mediator

In many ways, Smiling Joe Di Maulo was like Vito: likeable, tough, confident, smart and capable of getting along with a variety of people. The fact that they were in different camps now called to mind the old Woody Allen joke: "Why are we fighting? We both want the same thing."

There had never been a time in the *milieu* when clear, sharp, trusted thinkers were in more demand. If a third of the underworld was on Vito's side, another third yearned to see him dead. The remaining third would enthusiastically support whoever emerged as the last man standing. Smiling Joe knew as well as anyone who was in what camp.

For all the current turmoil, there was no record of Vito and Di Maulo ever fighting. Di Maulo had been the first to rise to power, alongside Paolo Violi and Moreno Gallo. While Vito ultimately surpassed Di Maulo in power, Smiling Joe always enjoyed a certain elite status. On the surface, Vito and Di Maulo were long-time golf buddies, with Vito playing in Di Maulo's hospital fundraisers. These were classically Montreal events, with well-dressed criminals wrapping themselves around a good cause to cleanse their image and public institutions making deals with the devil to gain funding. The golf fundraisers also drew at least one city councillor and strip club owner Paolo Gervasi, in 1992, 1993 and 1994, before Vito had Gervasi killed. Joe's older brother

Jimmy had also been in the trusted circle of Vito's golf buddies. Vito and Joe Di Maulo travelled together to Casa de Campo in the Dominican Republic with three others in 2003. Even after Vito's arrest, Di Maulo had attended the 2005 wedding of Frank Arcadi's daughter, suggesting at least some level of solidarity with the old Rizzuto group.

Maybe Di Maulo sensed something bad was about to happen when, back in December 2011, he agreed to meet with *La Presse* reporter Daniel Renaud in the third-floor office of his loans business on Jarry Street, at Viau. Di Maulo had been upset by a story the veteran journalist had written that linked him to a drug trafficker—Di Maulo had no record for drug trafficking—and left a message on Renaud's voice mail saying as much. The two met behind two locked doors, in a room with no decorations or bodyguards. Di Maulo was calm and friendly as he insisted he never had anything to do with selling drugs. Sounding like a man trying to cleanse his image for posterity, he told the respected journalist: "I have grandchildren, and I do not want them to have this image of me."

The talk took place a few days after Desjardins was arrested for murdering Salvatore Montagna, so naturally the topic of his brother-in-law was inescapable. Di Maulo wasn't about to step away from Desjardins, even though he would be one of the men in Vito's sights now. "Raynald Desjardins, he is my family and I cannot deny him," Di Maulo told Renaud. "He is still my brother." Di Maulo then continued, in French, to talk about how he felt about his own security. Di Maulo was thinking of his place in underworld history as he continued: "I'm seventy years old, and there are people who are seventy-five years old and should be afraid for their lives, crossing the street. They could get hit by a bus and die. I do not have bodyguards and I do not look behind me when I walk in the street. I walk with my conscience, and my conscience is clean."

There was talk in the *milieu* about Di Maulo receiving several visits in 2010 from a Hamilton Mafia family that hated the Rizzutos. Vito most likely was angered when he heard of this. Around the time Vito stepped back into Canada, police warned Di Maulo that his life was in danger, much as Paolo Violi had been warned before his murder a generation earlier. Di Maulo apparently responded just like Violi, with a shrug.

When was a man in his *milieu* not in some danger? It was like asking when a fish was not wet. He wasn't about to run from his luxury home in suburban Blainville, just a chip shot from a well-manicured, tranquil golf course. Di Maulo wasn't a nervous man like Agostino Cuntrera, and eschewed armour-plated cars, bodyguards, bulletproof vests and thoughts of suicide, although he did refresh his weapons collection with what his brother-in-law liked to call a small "toy." Di Maulo realized that if his enemies really wanted to kill him, they would do so. All he or the police could hope to do was postpone it. Death was inevitable, but death with dignity was still an option.

On November 4, 2012, no one reported hearing any gunshots outside the home of Joe Di Maulo as his body collapsed onto the driveway. Perhaps the gunman used a silencer, as Di Maulo was shot at least twice in the head. His wife, Huguette Desjardins, discovered her bleeding husband lying near his Cadillac Escalade. A neighbour said the first sound he heard from Di Maulo's home that night was the widow's screams, leading him at first to wonder if it was a heart attack. After Nicolò Rizzuto 's murder at home, the businesslike conduct normally expected in mob slayings was clearly being set aside in favour of an intensely personal approach.

Smiling Joe's murder incited comment from as high up the political ladder as Quebec's public security minister, Stéphane Bergeron. He said police had been placed on high alert, as he didn't want to see a repeat of the 1990s biker war. "We certainly want to avoid vigilante justice in the streets," Bergeron told reporters. "When scores are settled, there's a real danger of collateral victims."

It wasn't that long ago that Vito had been the one who would settle disputes to preserve the common interests of criminal enterprise and keep police at bay. It was Vito who urged Mom Boucher of the Hells Angels to talk with the Rock Machine in September 2000. That push came when Vito heard that tough anti-gang legislation was in the works, after the near-fatal shooting of reporter Michel Auger. Boucher met with leaders of the Rock Machine on neutral ground in a conference room at the Palais de Justice. Then they made their truce public by breaking bread in a crowded and trendy Crescent Street restaurant in the city's downtown on October 8, 2000. The move was designed to quell public fears about organized criminals. Veteran crime reporter Claude Poirier and a photographer from the Quebec tabloid *Allô Police* were summoned to record the Thanksgiving feast that included Boucher and Rock Machine leader Frédéric Faucher, and about twenty of their lieutenants. Vito was the unseen hand behind the public relations move—but that was several lifetimes ago, and his place in the Montreal underworld had radically changed.

Smiling Joe Di Maulo had many friends, contacts and relatives, but the turnout for his funeral was poor. He would have understood their reluctance to step forward publicly. In uncertain times, funerals after mob hits are seldom well attended. Among those notably absent from Di Maulo's funeral was Vito. More telling yet, Di Maulo's visitation was not held at the Rizzutos' upscale Complexe Funéraire Loreto in Saint-Léonard. Vito's family didn't attend or send a wreath as a sign of respect. Flowery best wishes appeared in the form of a white wreath from Raynald Desjardins, who was in the Rivière des Prairies penitentiary. The Cotroni family sent flowers, as might be expected from in-laws. Di Maulo's casket was open, so that mourners could see the rosary in his hands, and there were no signs of violence on the body. The undertaker had done his job as well as the hit man.

Mourners heard Di Maulo described as "a man of honour, a man of courage." With no explicit mention of his role in the underworld, he was remembered as a lover of golf, wine and the music of Frank Sinatra. Others paid tribute to a man who gained respect "in the world of business, arts and politics." Although Di Maulo had ties to the GTA, there were no out-of-province licence plates outside. When the service was almost over, Di Maulo's widow, Huguette, and other close family members released white doves into the sky.

The *Journal de Montréal* reported talk that Di Maulo had been summoned to a meeting with Vito shortly before his death. Had this been Smiling Joe's day of reckoning? Raynald Desjardins reportedly went into segregation in jail after his brother-in-law Di Maulo's murder, but he was up to date on the news and clearly annoyed when some stories claimed that the Complexe Funéraire Loreto had flatly refused to deal with the Di Maulo family. That kind of speculation about tensions between Vito and Desjardins's camp might excite fellow inmates and further endanger his life. After a request from Desjardins, a Loreto official sent out a public letter to say that Di Maulo's family hadn't asked to hold Di Maulo's service at their establishment. There had been no snub from the funeral home. That still didn't explain why no member of the Rizzuto camp—including Vito—attended the funeral. No explanation was needed, really, for those who understood Vito's rage.

In fact, it was becoming impossible not to read dark motives into what otherwise might be considered accidents or coincidences. On October 8, 2012, seventy-nine year-old Domenico Arcuri Sr. dropped by to see how things were going at a Pompano Beach, Florida, construction site where his son, Domenico Jr., had been working as a subcontractor on a one-storey industrial garage for more than a week. Father and son lived in the same condominium development on the 4000 block of Galt Ocean Drive, Fort Lauderdale, as did a dozen Montreal-area construction and real estate business owners and their families.

As Domenico Jr. later told police, it was late in the morning and he went to retrieve something from his car. Before he reached the vehicle, he heard a crashing sound, turned and saw his father lying under the garage's collapsed roof. After getting up, Domenico Sr. seemed his gamely self, even though he was seventy-nine, and claimed to have hurt only his shoulder. Domenico Jr. said that he decided to take his father to the hospital after he saw him turning pale and blood coming from the back of his neck. When an officer went to see him at North Broward Hospital, he was told to wait because the senior needed a CAT scan. Before the day was over, Domenico Sr. surprised hospital authorities by passing away.

It might have been considered a sad if somewhat commonplace death if not for Arcuri's long-time criminal associations. Since August 17, three Montreal construction companies and an Italian ice cream company connected to the Arcuri family had been hit by arsonists. Domenico Arcuri Sr. had assumed control of the Ital Gelati ice cream firm after Paolo Violi's murder in 1978. He had connections to both the Violi and Rizzuto sides in the murderous feud, and at one time was considered a potential peacemaker. For this, the Violi side ultimately considered him a traitor, as did Vito's men.

Enterprising Montreal *Gazette* reporter Paul Cherry dug up the coroner's report into Arcuri's death, and it outlined reservations about whether or not the death was accidental. Rebecca MacDougall, associate medical examiner for Broward County, wrote in her report on the death that it was an accident, but "the context is worrisome." MacDougall continued: "By report, the decedent was under a roof when the roof collapsed. Although the context of the death is worrisome, the manner of death, at this time, is best classified as accident. Should any probative information pertaining to this case become available, such information may be used to amend this report at that time." The report didn't elaborate on the context of the death. However, Domenico Jr. had been threatened in the month before the collapse.

Was it a coincidence that the dead man was the one who introduced Montagna to others in the *milieu*, setting in motion the decimation of Vito's group while he was in prison? Was it also coincidental that, a generation earlier, he had helped lure Paolo Violi to the card game where he had been murdered? Or was it revenge, served stone cold?

CHAPTER 35

Friends in high places

Montreal has a long history of spirited efforts to shine light on its underworld. In 1909, a Royal Commission into municipal wrongdoing heard the head of the Light, Heat and Power Company testify that an alderman had leaned on him for ten thousand dollars in campaign contributions. Less than two decades later, Supreme Court of Canada justice Louis Codèrre conducted a probe of the city's police force and found it sorely lacking. "Vice has spread itself across the city with an ugliness that seemed assured of impunity," the justice concluded. The failed experiment with Prohibition only made things worse, enriching the underworld and semi-legitimizing it in the eyes of the public. During Prohibition days, the Montreal Customs House was used as a criminal terminal of sorts, where smugglers unloaded American tobacco, silks and narcotics to the point that a Crown attorney called it "one of the greatest clearing houses for stolen goods in Canada." In the 1930s, French police ranked Montreal as the world's third "most depraved" city, behind Port Said and Marseilles. Vic (The Egg) Cotroni was at the time a part-time professional wrestler who worked on "baseball bat elections," mustering voters to support whatever candidates paid him.

Vito's family hadn't yet landed in Canada when crime-fighting prosecutor Pacifique (Pax) Plante probed corruption in Montreal's municipal politics and police force with a Dick Tracy–like zeal during the late 1940s and early 1950s. In a series of articles written for *Le Devoir* with journalist Gérard Filion, Plante catalogued how police "protection" buttressed certain figures in the underworld. Future Montreal mayor Jean Drapeau was a junior member of Plante's camp, as Plante's crime-busting appealed to both the younger man's puritanical streak and his political ambitions. Together, they gathered information that led to the arrests of several police officers.

Try as they might, their fevered efforts weren't nearly enough to stem the river of sleaze. Martin Brett wrote in his potboiler novel *Hot Freeze* in 1954 about the enduring reach of the city's organized crime establishment: "The Syndicate was probably the most subtle organization of its type in North America, tentacles reaching anywhere and everywhere, with pressure all the way." Brett, the *nom de plume* of CBC Radio announcer (Ronald) Douglas Sanderson, described Montreal through the eyes of his protagonist, private detective Michel Garfin:

> "It makes me puke," I said savagely. "Look at it. An illuminated cross stuck up on the mountain, street after street full of the reverend clergy, a self-congratulatory city council, pious editorials in all the newspapers, and as much vice and aberration and corruption as any city this side of Port Said. One level stinking and the other level smirking, and in between a layer of supposed public servants trying to stuff their greasy pockets with graft. Oh sure, we have a vice probe every decade or so. It goes on and on, year after year, and then finally it peters out under the sheer dead weight of its own evasive evidence. A few honest officials are disgraced, a few more get eased gently out of their jobs, a couple of writs for slander are issued and settled out of court, and everyone sighs with relief and goes right back to smirking abnormal."

That pretty much captured the tenor of things in the generations between the days of Pax Plante and Vito's time. More huffing and puffing about cleaning up Canada's underworld was heard in the mid-1960s, when the stench of corruption again became too rank. Some of this came from embarrassing revelations about the actions of long-time Montreal mobster Lucien (Moose) Rivard. His underworld contacts ran to Vic (The Egg) Cotroni's younger brother Giuseppe (Pep) Cotroni and a network of Corsican heroin smugglers who later became known as the French Connection. Rivard also had strong Cuban criminal connections. In 1956, Rivard moved for a time to the island, working both the Communist and capitalist sides of the political spectrum as he supplied guns for Castro's revolutionaries while also running a nightclub.

By March 1965, Rivard was in Montreal's Bordeaux Prison on fresh narcotics charges. He somehow managed to escape, after someone on staff let him outside onto the facility's grounds and provided him with a garden hose to flood the skating rink. Suspicions naturally arose, as his ice-making duties took place on a warm spring day and the hose he was issued was strong enough to allow him to scale a jail wall. A jail employee told the *Toronto Star* that this could only be done with inside help, and that the going rate for such assistance was ten thousand dollars.

The press jumped on the story, dubbing Rivard the "Gallic Pimpernel." Rivard basked in the attention, writing Prime Minister Lester Pearson from wherever he was hiding: "Life is short, you know. I don't intend to be in jail for the rest of my life." The full story was never disclosed, but a 1965 inquiry surprised no one when it concluded the justice department should have investigated reports that he tried to corrupt several key members of the Liberal Party.

Corruption remained a constant, and former Liberal cabinet minister Pierre Laporte was notorious for his relations with mobster Francesco D'Asti until Laporte was murdered by FLQ terrorists in 1970. In October 1974, Paolo Violi "invited" a political candidate to his ice cream shop, where he was successfully convinced that it would be best for all concerned if he abandoned his campaign to become mayor of Saint-Léonard.

Brett's mid-century observations about the stinking, smirking nature of vice in Montreal, and its reliance on "a layer of supposed public servants trying to stuff their greasy pockets with graft," rang true through the 1970s, when then Quebec premier Robert Bourassa called upon Robert Cliche to head up a public inquiry into construction violence. Cliche was assisted by thirty-six-year-old lawyer Brian Mulroney, a future prime minister of Canada. Cliche's report, released in May 1975, spoke of "an organized system of corruption without parallel in North America," with tales of ex-con union organizers who taught underlings how to break legs and goons willing to strangle the pets of people who stood in their way. Union leaders and cabinet ministers were discredited, as Cliche concluded that construction union corruption would not be so rife without active government support. Cliche's final report contained a paragraph that was eerily reminiscent of *Hot Freeze*: "The work that this commission has done will matter little, even if the undesirables are purged from the positions they hold, even if the laws governing the construction sector are improved, if those who make the laws do not have the will to apply them and see that they are respected."

Vito's public profile was still low in the 1970s, when a parade of Montreal underworld figures was called to appear at another series of crime commission hearings. When Paolo Violi refused to testify, he was sentenced to a year in jail for contempt. Violi's status was undermined by revelations that he had lowered his guard and inadvertently allowed undercover police officer Robert Menard to live above his ice cream parlour for years, secretly recording conversations of the mobsters downstairs. That created the opening Nicolò Rizzuto needed to move against him. The world of vice described so well by Brett survived the inquiry, but it did spell the beginning of the end for the Violi brothers. Small wonder that Nicolò had chosen the seventies to take his family to Venezuela, where he was close to his cocaine contacts in the Cuntrera family and far from the guns of his rival Violi and the spotlight of the public inquiry.

Now, as Vito settled back into life in Canada in the fall of 2012, Quebec was awash in fresh stories of corruption. The revelations of a former Montreal chief of police and a series of investigative stories from Radio-Canada's award-winning *Enquête* program set the stage for the public hand-wringing of yet another commission. The City of Montreal was awarding some $1.4 billion in contracts annually, providing plenty of opportunities for graft. Public confidence in the system was at a nadir. A Montreal *Gazette* reader wrote, with more than a little sarcasm, that perhaps Vito should run for mayor now that he was back in town:

Think of just some of the benefits:

No need for city councillors and the like; he has his own organization.

He has extensive experience with high finance.

He's very familiar with Montreal's infrastructure and construction needs.

There would no longer be a need for bribes, payoffs and the like; middlemen would be eliminated.

He might even give the blue collars' union an offer they couldn't refuse.

Essentially, I think Vito Rizzuto would run a much more efficient operation at city hall and probably save the taxpayers a pile of money in the process. What have we got to lose?

CHAPTER 36

Greasy pockets

Former Montreal police chief Jacques Duchesneau leaked a secret 2008 transport ministry report to the media, knowing it would change his life forever. The head of a government anti-collusion unit feared authorities wouldn't act on it otherwise. The leaked Transport Canada study concluded this graft was costing taxpayers heavily. The bid rigging and protection money meant that it cost 37 percent more to build a kilometre of road in Quebec as compared with Ontario. The move cost Duchesneau his job but did attract attention. The province was also embarrassed when RCMP sergeant Lorie McDougall testified at a Mafia trial in Italy in 2010 and spoke of payments to the Mafia in the Quebec construction industry. He described how several firms in Quebec paid out a tithe of 5 percent of their contracts to the Mafia, as though it were another layer of government.

When the din of stories on corruption became too loud to ignore, an inquiry was called to expose connections between the mob, politics and business. Appointed to the helm of this latest tour of underworld sludge was Quebec Superior Court justice France Charbonneau, a hard-working, highly competent legal bulldog best known as the Crown prosecutor who put Hells Angels leader Maurice (Mom) Boucher behind bars for murder. His was one of some eighty murder cases she had prosecuted, with sometimes ferocious zeal. She was also durable. During the eighteen-month Boucher trial, she took only five days off. This time she was given a two-year mandate to expose corruption that had taken generations to put in place.

One might have expected the RCMP to welcome such an inquiry, especially considering the relatively limp results of its multi-million-dollar, four-year Colisée operation against Vito's family. However, when Charbonneau's staff requested voluminous tapes from the RCMP, they were met with a tough, taxpayer-funded fight. Among its many lines of legal reasoning, the RCMP argued that it had gathered some 1.5 million wiretap intercepts and 35,000 hours of video and prepared numerous reports as a *federal* agency, and shouldn't therefore be obliged to comply with a *provincial* inquiry. The commission ultimately won the right to play the intercepts, but only after subpoenaing the police documents and using more taxpayers' money to fight for them in court. Criminals clearly weren't the only ones prone to infighting at the public's expense.

Generations of mobsters had survived similar inquiries, but Vito recognized the danger he faced. The crime commission of the 1970s had helped set the stage for his father's usurping of Violi's place at the top of Montreal's underworld. Now, the public was about to hear and see secret recordings from the old ground zero of Vito's family, the Consenza Social Club. Vito might even be called to testify.

There were limits to the inquiry's scope. It couldn't deal with federal matters and it only reached back fifteen years, meaning it wouldn't look into the Rizzuto family's activities in the 1950s and 1960s. Nicolò had listed his occupation in 1956 as "cement contractor" when buying his fourplex on De Lorimier Avenue. The apparent success of his Grand Royal Asphalt Paving seemed at odds with the much smaller number of government contracts for things like sidewalk and sewer repairs in those years.

Linda Gyulai of the Montreal *Gazette* dug up records that showed Nicolò managed to set up five construction-related companies between 1962 and 1972, often with underworld associates and relatives. In September 1966, Nicolò and his half-brother Liborio Milioto were officials with Franco Electric Inc., even though they had no background whatsoever in electrics. By 1972, Nicolò was an official with D.M. Transport with his uncle Domenico Manno and Joseph Lo Presti. Manno was also an officer in four of Nicolò's other construction companies. Nicolò's construction activities slowed down but didn't cease in 1972, when he relocated in Venezuela.

With its limits in time and scope, the enormously ambitious Charbonneau Commission wasted no time in getting to the point. Hearings opened with Duchesneau saying as a witness what many suspected: Quebec politics are financed by criminal proceeds. "Dirty money finances elections," Duchesneau told Charbonneau. "This clandestine empire I'm talking about comprises links between the construction world and the illegal financing of political parties," he continued. "According to the testimony [we gathered], we have before us a widespread and brazen culture of kickbacks."

The former police chief described a corrupt system in which political organizers solicited money from engineering firms, who in turn pumped up their invoices and passed the added costs on to the public. As Duscheneau described the scheme, the mob was a silent partner, demanding *pizzo*, or protection money, from a select circle of just over a dozen construction firms.

Among the inquiry's early witnesses was Detective Constable Mike Amato of York Regional Police, whose jurisdiction included Woodbridge, Ontario. In carefully measured comments, the veteran officer told the inquiry that 'Ndrangheta crime families originating in Italy's Calabrian region dominate the Ontario mob landscape, while Quebec has been largely under Sicilian families. He added that, in the Toronto area, the 'Ndrangheta and Sicilian groups seem to coexist more easily, sometimes even helping each other. "Obviously, at times there's conflicts," Amato said. "There's murder. There's violence. There's bombings." For the most part, however, Ontario preferred to keep its corruption buttoned down and behind closed doors.

Still, the province had secrets that would have no doubt elicited colourful disgust from the late novelist Martin Brett. In the late 1970s, county court judge Harry Waisberg wrote a Royal Commission report on violence in the province's construction industry. It described the strafing of a North York construction company office with a machine gun, arson and plenty of bribery. The report also spoke of a meeting between industry executives, some with strong political connections, and an "array of sinister characters," including Toronto mobster Paul Volpe, who was later murdered and dumped in the trunk of his wife's leased BMW at Toronto International Airport. Waisberg's report inspired a brief flurry of headlines and then it was back to business as usual.

At the Charbonneau inquiry, Amato's comments buttressed those of Italian scholar Valentina Tenti, who earlier told the commission that Mafia organizations around the world have infiltrated legitimate business. The commission heard that Ontario mobsters work as restaurateurs, trucking company executives, construction entrepreneurs, lawyers and accountants, and run banquet halls, nightclubs and garden centres, among other things. "They don't want us to know about their legitimate businesses; they don't want us to know about their wealth; they don't want us to know about interaction in public life," Amato said. ". . . There are persons who are criminals, who are suspects in murders. . . . They're integrated into the community and most people don't even know who they are."

They also donate to charity, raise money for political parties and take part in community services. "It legitimizes your own persona," Amato said. "It legitimizes your criminal past. It's almost like absolving your sins." Amato balked when asked about Ontario Mafia groups winning government contracts. "That question there is too close to something that we are working on right now," Amato said. He certainly didn't dismiss the question. It was a well-accepted truism that Mafia figures are only as powerful as their links to so-called respectable society. "If you accept that [the Mafia] exists, you have to accept that public corruption exists," Amato said.

The commission heard that mobsters had been able to fly under the radar in Ontario because violence is kept to a minimum. "If there is numerous murders, if there's a lot of violence, if there is a lot of bombings, it attracts attention. It attracts attention from politicians, it attracts attention from the community, it attracts attention from the police,"

Amato said. "You cannot build a successful criminal enterprise if you are continually being investigated and monitored by the police. If you stay under the radar, you are going to expand."

While the Charbonneau Commission was generating daily headlines about corruption, Montreal police quietly moved to stem Vito's influence within their own ranks. In November 2012, just a month after Vito's return, at least two Montreal officers were fired for leaking sensitive information to the Mafia. In the months that followed, leaks of information to Vito's group continued, as there were clearly many moles inside the police force.

Towards the end of 2012, the public learned that the excitement from the witness stand had only just begun. Raynald Desjardins would be compelled to testify at the inquiry, despite his pending murder charges for the Montagna killing. And in a move that promised both headlines and security nightmares, Vito had been subpoenaed to testify. Unless something drastic happened, Vito was going to move from well below radar to the full glare of a public spotlight.

Inquiry lawyers would want to probe him on his deep and central role in construction corruption. It was a complex and deeply entrenched system, which predated Vito, though he protected and refined it. If he took the stand, he would certainly face questions about how he seemed to control family interests, even while in custody. Lawyers would like to know how firm his grip was on a $10-billion union investment fund, but their questions would probe far beyond unions, through bureaucrats to politicians. Vito's hands were everywhere on the wheels of corruption, and all of this would be up for discussion if he took the stand.

Vito himself had other things on his mind—namely revenge—but he could not take the subpoena lightly if he hoped to avoid returning to jail. Paolo Violi's refusal to testify in the 1970s hearings had meant prison, and Vito had already been away from his empire for too long. He would have to say enough to satisfy the bulldog Charbonneau but not so much that his world was overturned. Even for a man with Vito's finesse, it would require the performance of a lifetime. If anyone was nervous about what Vito might say, this was the time to silence him forever.

CHAPTER 37

Trusted few

At seventy-nine years of age, Domenico Manno was a well-seasoned Mafia artifact, with a massive skull, the body of a fridge and the pained expression of a constipated elderly bull. Wrinkled and creaking as he was, he was still the younger brother of Zia Libertina and beneath her in the family pecking order. Their Mafioso father, Antonino (Don Nino) Manno, had been trying to immigrate to Canada for a decade before he finally arrived on September 11, 1964. Don Nino lived in Montreal until his death by natural causes on October 1, 1980, at the age of seventy-six. He was entombed in a mausoleum alongside his wife, Giuseppa Cammalleri Manno, and their daughter Giuseppina Manno, younger sister of Libertina and Domenico Manno.

In the minds of many involved in law enforcement and law-breaking, Domenico Manno would always be connected to the hit that changed the Montreal underworld forever. Manno was present when a call was placed to his brother-in-law Nicolò Rizzuto from Montreal hours before Paolo Violi was killed in a card game in his old ice cream shop. In the telephone message, Nicolò was told, "The hunting has begun." Hours later, just after Violi's death, Manno was also present in the ice cream shop when another call south was made, saying, "The pig is dead."

For his role in the Paolo Violi murder, Domenico Manno eventually pleaded guilty to conspiracy to commit murder, along with Agostino Cuntrera and Giovanni Di Mora. The identity of the man who pulled the trigger of the *lupara* was never disclosed, and no one publicly dragged the names of Nicolò or Vito into the proceedings. On the stand, Manno was the very personification of *omertà*. When a prosecutor pressed him about the murder, he replied: "I don't remember." Pushed further, he said, "I don't remember, I don't remember," just in case the first lie wasn't enough. All he could remember, he said, was having a cup of coffee and buying cigarettes in the café where Violi was slain, hours before the murder.

Manno's wife was the sister of Joe Lo Presti's wife, making him the uncle of the recently murdered Larry Lo Presti. If Manno held a grudge against Vito for his presumed role in that murder, it didn't show. These uncomfortable things occasionally happened in this life they led. Like the senior Lo Presti, Manno was also heavily involved in the drug trade. He pleaded guilty in Florida in 1998 to plots to traffic heroin, cocaine and counterfeit money, which included an effort to smuggle twenty kilos of cocaine into Florida in a suitcase on a commercial flight. For this, he was sentenced to twenty years in prison.

As he prepared to leave Fort Dix prison in New Jersey for Montreal in December 2012, Manno must have contemplated the fates of the cadre of killers behind the murders of the Violi brothers. It seemed that a time of reckoning had fallen upon them. Agostino Cuntrera, Paolo Renda and Domenico Arcuri Sr. had each played a role in Violi's murder, and now they were each murdered or abducted or dead under odd circumstances. And of course Nicolò Rizzuto, long understood to be the invisible hand guiding the Violi execution, was murdered most infamously of all.

Manno looked hulking and threatening back at the time of the Paolo Violi murder, with sweeping sideburns and long black trench coat to give him the full disco-era hit man look. He returned to Montreal a lumbering old man, but age wasn't much of a concern in the mob.

In late December 2012, word came that another senior citizen might join Vito's ranks. Seventy-five-year-old Pierino Divito was also expected to return from an American prison. Divito had been arrested in 1994 in

Nova Scotia for drug smuggling and later extradited to a Texas prison. Times were tense and Vito could sorely use all the men he could trust, even if they were a tad long in the tooth.

Meanwhile, in the courts, the foundation of the prosecution's case against Raynald Desjardins, Vittorio (Victor) Mirarchi and others charged for the murder of Bonanno crime boss Salvatore Montagna was something entirely unprecedented: encrypted BlackBerry messages.

One of the first clues that the case was travelling through uncharted territory came when Quebec Court judge Maurice Parent made the unprecedented decision to deny Desjardins access to some of the evidence against him in the Montagna murder case. Sealed documents in the Joliette courthouse included an affidavit and wiretap warrants used to intercept communications between the suspects. Federal prosecutor Yvan Poulin cryptically said it was in the public interest to keep the documents about the intercepted messages totally secret. "Read the authorization [for the warrants] in your office," Poulin told the judge. "It speaks for itself. . . . I can't say anything more about it. . . . This is an exceptional case."

A publication ban blocked the media from reporting the contents of intercepted BlackBerry messages. It was thought that the messages in question were sent by plotters before, during and after Montagna's murder in November 2011 on Île Vaudry. In short, the prosecution was building its case in large part on the surveillance of Montagna conducted by a murdered underworld spy: Giuseppe (Closure) Colapelle.

It wasn't totally unprecedented for BlackBerry manufacturer Research In Motion to comply with search warrants. After a case in Pakistan, RIM issued a statement saying: "Like others in our industry, from time to time, we may receive requests from legal authorities for lawful access assistance." The statement added: "We are guided by appropriate legal processes and publicly disclosed lawful access principles in this regard, as we balance any such requests against our priority of maintaining the privacy rights of our users." By the time of the news release, some criminals had already moved on to messaging systems such as WhatsApp and Viber, the latter trading on ultrasecurity and boasting on its website that "Not even the staff at Viber have access to your data with UltraSafe enabled." There was also the Dark Web, or the Deep Web, which allowed communicators to burrow deep between the layers of the conventional Net, paying their way into exclusive, uncharted cyber tunnels.

It was looking as if Desjardins's trial for the Montagna murder would take place in the spring of 2013. No one expected public outrage if he managed to plea bargain. There had been minimal public response to Vito's relatively light sentence for his role in three gangland assassinations. The victim in the case was a major organized crime figure and a prime suspect in the failed hit on the accused. Who besides Montagna's wife, three daughters and mistress really mourned his death? Even the Bonanno family showed no sign that it was upset over the assassination of its leader.

It's a time-honoured tactic for mobsters like Desjardins to argue self-defence after killing another criminal. Desjardins could make this argument quite strongly after the failed attempt on his life. And if Desjardins played along and cut a deal of his own, the public also wouldn't hear embarrassing disclosure about the underworld's relations with the politically connected business people whom Montagna had tried to squeeze a little too hard. He had made plenty of money extorting businesses in New York, but he wasn't in tune with the climate of Montreal's *milieu*. Montagna hadn't just broken the law; he had upset the finely tuned balance between mobsters, politicians and business. There had been many reasons to kill him.

CHAPTER 38

BFF

Bodies had kept falling that autumn, like leaves from the trees. On November 15, 2012, Montrealer Tony Gensale was shot dead leaving a martial arts class in what might have been a case of mistaken identity. He bore a dangerous physical resemblance to tough guy Giuseppe Fetta from the Arcadi faction of Vito's family. Not just targeted mobsters were in danger now, but their look-alikes too.

Fetta was just the kind of soldier Vito needed. At thirty-three, he was a battle-tested fitness and firearms enthusiast. He weathered an attack in an east Montreal jail while awaiting Project Colisée charges. In that confrontation, he was stabbed with box cutters and plastic knives and still managed to break a leg of one of his attackers.

On November 17, a gunman opened fire on Mohammed Awada in front of his north Montreal house. With that, another tough guy was suddenly gone from Vito's ranks, although there was a good chance that Awada's slaying wasn't directly linked to Vito's war. More likely, his death was a settling of old scores. That sort of thing happens often during an underworld war, as it's easier to hide murders with personal motives when everyone is focused on the bigger picture. There was also no one like Joe Di Maulo, Moreno Gallo or Vito on the streets now to peacefully mediate mid-level disputes.

Whoever ended the life of restaurant owner Emilio Cordileone on

December 8 clearly wanted to make a statement. His bullet-riddled body was transported to his street in Ahuntsic and left there inside his white Range Rover. He had once been close to Vito, but he was even closer to Joe Di Maulo. If he was killed by Vito's men for his association with Di Maulo, he received a token of forgiveness, as he was buried out of Complexe Funéraire Loreto.

On Friday, December 14, a masked gunman burst into the Café Domenica-In next to the Métropolitain highway at mid-afternoon. When he left, thirty-seven-year-old Domenic Facchini lay dead from a gunshot to his head. Another man fled to the nearby Montreal Choppers motorcycle store, bleeding from a non-fatal shot to his neck. Montreal Choppers was the old business of the aggrieved former Rizzuto soldier Ponytail De Vito, who was now in prison for cocaine smuggling.

At 10 a.m. on Monday, December 17, gunmen arrived for the real Giuseppe Fetta. This time there was no mistake. He was dropped by shots to the legs and throat as he stepped out of his car on Saint-Laurent Boulevard, and died close to where his look-alike Gensale had been cut down.

Police responded to the wave of violence with a handful of arrests and a whole lot of theories. Among them, authorities speculated that 'Ndrangheta members from Toronto and Violi's hometown of Hamilton were involved in some of the trigger pulling. There was so much to ponder: Was New York still interested in tightening its ties to Montreal? The Bonanno family still had a pulse, albeit a weak one. Was the murder of Agostino Cuntrera the death knell of the old Sicilian-born, Rizzuto–Caruana–Cuntrera alliance that had fended off the Bonannos in the past?

As the body count grew, Vito's war became something of a public spectator sport, but it was hard for anyone but an insider to keep score. Twenty Montreal mobsters had been shot dead over the past thirteen months and there was no sign of a slowdown. If the war spread to Ontario, police and other observers could finger at least a dozen more prime candidates for assassination. For those in the know, Vito was ahead in the body count, but not by much. And still, no one had reported seeing the godfather himself since he'd shaken police and journalists the night of his arrival in Toronto.

Throughout the year before Vito's return, as gangsters were killing and getting killed, Montreal police had the unsettling feeling that someone from their own ranks was trying to profit from the bloodshed. Word sifted out that a list of two thousand confidential informants was being shopped around the underworld for one million dollars. Considering the damage that list could do, the asking price was a bargain.

Retired Detective Sergeant Ian Davidson heard that the mole's name would be made public in the press on January 18, 2012. Davidson, a twice-divorced former criminal intelligence specialist, had recently left the force after thirty-three years' service with an unblemished record. Upon hearing the news, he left his home in Laval's quiet Sainte-Rose district and took a hotel room. He then texted his wife, "This is the end." Next, he swallowed the antidepressant trazodone as well as lorazepam, which treats anxiety and insomnia, and climbed into a warm bath. There he opened a vein and added his name to the list of victims in the underworld carnage.

Four months later, major crimes investigator Mario Lambert was found guilty of committing fraud by accessing a police database and funnelling information to mobsters. The veteran officer was caught in an elaborate sting, which included planting fake licence plate numbers into the system. For this, Lambert received three months' house arrest and a year's probation.

The first verified public sighting of Vito came in January 2013, more than three months after his return to Canada. It was as though he wanted to be seen as he strode through Dorval airport in Montreal, heading for a vacation in the sun. Pumped up and fit, Vito looked like a man who could handle a fight as well as a challenging round of golf. He often smoked, but there was no cigarette in his hands that day. Plainclothes police officers watched from a distance as he walked to the gate for a 5:30 a.m. flight to Punta Cana in the Dominican Republic. In an apparent show of nonchalance, the *sportif* mobster had no bodyguards in sight.

The Dominican had long been a comfortable spot for Vito, even before Quebec Hells Angels set up a charter there. On January 3, 2003, he had flown to the island nation for a fairway vacation at Casa de Campo seaside resort that included *Compare* Frank Arcadi, Paolo Renda and Joe Di Maulo. The resort had three golf courses, the best of which was the world-class Diente de Perro, "Teeth of the Dog." It was at that resort where Vito told Arcadi why he was avoiding setting foot in the United States, alluding to the Three Captains Murders. His description of the slaughter was a detailed one, mostly in an Italian dialect, with a few words of English. Vito described blood splashed all over the Brooklyn social club as Alphonse (Sonny Red) Indelicato, Philip (Philly Lucky) Giaccone and Dominick (Big Trin) Trinchera fell dead. Vito and Arcadi had no clue that the room in which they spoke had been bugged by Dominican police, at the request of the RCMP. Vito's January 2013 visit was also to Casa de Campo, suggesting he either didn't know he had earlier been recorded there or had sorted out the security problem.

While Vito was sunning himself, at least some Montreal assassins stayed home and worked through the cold spell. At suppertime on Tuesday, January 22, on the coldest night of the year, a video camera outside the Jean-Tavernier Street home of sixty-nine-year-old Gaétan Gosselin in the Mercier district captured his image as he stepped from his car. The high-resolution camera then picked up two men opening fire upon him before he reached the door of his home. Were the killers too stupid to know they were being filmed? Or were they so brazen about their craft that they didn't care?

Vito resurfaced in Montreal ten days after his departure, looking sporty and buff in jeans, a T-shirt and a baseball cap. Again there were no bodyguards in sight and again he looked as relaxed as anyone in the centre of a mob war could possibly be. He dragged his own suitcase while Giovanna shot an exasperated look at a team of *La Presse* journalists.

As Vito stepped back into the chill of Montreal, mourners paid their condolences to Gosselin's family. While he had no criminal record, there was no doubt where he had stood in the city's underworld: deep inside the camp of Raynald Desjardins. The murdered man had once been related to Desjardins through marriage and lived in a building owned by a Desjardins relative. He had been considered Desjardins's representative at the Blue Bonnets Raceway. Most interestingly, the Montreal *Gazette* revealed that after his release from prison in 2004, Desjardins ran a construction company, the majority shareholder of which was a numbered company. The president of that numbered company? Gosselin.

The murder came just months after the slaying of Joe Di Maulo, another Desjardins relative. Gosselin's obituary noted that he was survived by family and friends "but especially his best friend forever, Raynald Desjardins." The optics of taking down a man who declared Desjardins his BFF couldn't have been more poignant. For someone who had been written off as a dead man walking, Vito now looked surprisingly alive and dangerous.

In their search for Gosselin's hit men, police investigators soon zeroed in on the Reds street gang. The Reds were believed to operate under the umbrella of the Syndicate, especially since the murders of leader Chénier (Big) Dupuy and his lieutenant, Lamartine Sévère Paul, on August 11, 2012. The widely accepted explanation for their murders was that they had refused to be part of the Syndicate, with its Hells Angels and mob ties and control of the city centre. Such a move towards consolidation would help pave the way for Vito's resumption of control on the streets.

The investigation pointed to a thirty-three-year-old known on the streets alternately as Dirty Harry and Harry Up. His real name was Harry Mytil. His criminal history included a three-year prison sentence for his role in a 2003 home invasion in the Vieux-Longueuil condo of a defence lawyer. He had also been convicted for the gunpoint robbery of a drug dealer, with charges pending for reckless driving and failing to stop at the scene of an accident. He appeared to have acted as a talent scout in the Gosselin murder, picking the hit men and paying them.

Before police could move on Harry and his associates, they were called to his Laval home on April 16, where they found his body sprawled in his garage, pockmarked by several bullet holes. The door of the garage was still open. If there were links between Harry and Vito, they were suddenly as cold as the night Gosselin was murdered.

CHAPTER 39

Public spotlight

The Charbonneau Commission soldiered on, reputations and occasionally people falling dead along the way. Few people in the general public knew of Robert Rousseau, head of the Côte-des-Neiges–Notre-Dame-de-Grâce borough department of permits and inspections, until he sat under the bright lights of the inquiry. He was interrogated for hours in March 2013 by Quebec's anti-corruption unit about the construction of condos on Wilson Avenue by Tony Magi and Nick Rizzuto Jr., near the spot where Nick Jr. was murdered. He faced pointed questions about zoning changes, and also about a demolition permit approved by Rousseau for the site. Hours after the probing ended, the father of two children killed himself in his Châteauguay home.

That March, the city was faced with a difficult decision. After the snow and ice of a Montreal winter, plenty of potholes needed repair, but there were few companies with clean reputations to fill them. Mayor Michael Applebaum announced that the city had qualms about granting $5.2 million in road repair contracts to seven companies when at least three of them were accused of corruption at the Charbonneau Commission.

Giuseppe Borsellino knew plenty about how business got done in the world of Quebec construction. As president of Garnier

Construction, his company had won millions of dollars in public infrastructure contracts. As he told the Charbonneau Commission, city works engineer Gilles Surprenant was the prime mover in the wave of slime that coated the industry. Borsellino argued that the contractors were the victims and not the villains in the drama. The commission heard that Borsellino and two other major construction bosses paid the city thousands of dollars in cash from the 1990s on for what Borsellino called "tips."

"What I didn't like is the power that those people [at the city] had acquired," Borsellino said. "It became apparent that [the contractors] were in a system we couldn't get out of."

Justice Charbonneau wasn't impressed, saying "there are limits" to her credulity. "So you're telling me the great mastermind of all of this was Gilles Surprenant, when he was thirty years old?" Charbonneau asked.

"Yes," Borsellino replied.

Asked to comment on why he attended a Rizzuto family wedding, Borsellino told the commission that his parents were from Cattolica Eraclea, the same village as the Rizzutos. He explained that he didn't go to Rizzuto family events as a general practice. If he did attend the wedding of one of Vito's sons, it was probably after he was invited by the bride's family. Who could be sure of such things? "I think I was invited to one of the weddings," he said. "But I'm still not sure. And I knew it coming here, that maybe if we get to that, I wouldn't be able to confirm. But probably was invited to one wedding. And it's probably because the bride, I knew the parents of the bride. But I'm still not sure. And I'm not sure if I went."

Borsellino found conviction when speaking in more general terms about the mob, testifying that he had never had any business dealings with anyone associated with organized crime. "I'd rather hand over the keys to my business" than pay the Mafia, he said. "My parents came from Sicily," Borsellino continued. "[The Mafia is] something you hear about, you feel . . . it's never clear."

Perhaps the most interesting part of his testimony concerned a 2009 beating from three men that forced him to undergo seven hours of facial reconstruction surgery. Borsellino said he wasn't sure about the motive behind the attack, although it might have been for a construction project or unpaid debts. He admitted he did not report the assault to police.

Prosecutor Simon Tremblay offered two theories of his own to explain the pummelling. One was that Borsellino's actions might have forced a top official in the city's public works department to resign, when it was learned that Borsellino had paid the official's way to Italy. The second hypothesis was that Borsellino didn't pick Raynald Desjardins's firm, Énergie Carboneutre, for decontamination work at one of his construction sites. Domenico Arcuri Jr. also had an ownership share in the company.

For his part, Borsellino wasn't able to clarify anything further about the beating. He did say he had once been a political contributor, but halted his donations in the late 2000s.

"It was not ethical," he explained.

Accountant Frank Zampino spent twenty-two years in municipal politics, rising to become executive committee chairman under ex–Montreal mayor Gérald Tremblay. That made him the second most powerful official in Montreal's civic government. Before this, he had been mayor of Saint-Léonard. In the course of his mayoral functions, he was invited to some fifty weddings a year and attended many of them, including the July 6, 1991, union of the son of Frank Cotroni to the daughter of Joe Di Maulo. "It wasn't the most brilliant decision of the century to go to the marriage," he testified. "Perceptions are worth more than facts in politics." Commission prosecutor Sonia LeBel asked if he could recall a photo being taken of himself with Vito Rizzuto. Zampino replied that he did not know.

The commission's mandate didn't include a foray into federal corruption. National NDP leader Tom Mulcair told reporters of a conversation with police back in 1994 after someone tried to slip him a suspicious-looking envelope following a meeting between himself and Gilles Vaillancourt. At the time, Mulcair was a rookie provincial politician and Vaillancourt was five years into his six-term career as mayor of Laval, the municipality across the Rivière des Prairies from Montreal.

By the time Mulcair went public about the incident, in 2013, Vaillancourt was facing a dozen criminal charges, including influence peddling, breach of trust and gangsterism for directing a criminal organization. He had resigned after twenty-three years as mayor of Laval, pledging to devote his energies to proving his innocence. By May 2013, the City of Laval was placed under a trusteeship in hopes it would help contain the political mess.

Shocking as all this was, none of these public grillings and confessions felt like the inquiry's main event. Desjardins and Vito were still expected to take the witness stand. The inquisition was far from over.

CHAPTER 40

Non-stop hits

oing home for supper was now a life-threatening activity in the *milieu*. Everyone seemed a little quicker to settle things with a gun. Saint-Léonard neighbours of Vincenzo (Vincent) Scuderi called 911 at 6:10 p.m. on January 31, 2013, after hearing a volley of shots outside his home on Robert Boulevard. Police arrived to find a handgun beside the forty-nine-year-old's lifeless body on the sidewalk. He had ties to Ponytail De Vito, Raynald Desjardins and Giuseppe (Closure) Colapelle, suggesting his killer might be from Vito's camp.

Scuderi's old associates needed less than a day to respond. At 10:10 a.m. on February 1, fifty-one-year-old residential building contractor Tonino (Tony) Callocchia was felled by gunshots in a parking lot between two restaurants on Saint-Martin Boulevard West in Laval. Callocchia's history with Vito's group ran deep. He was busted in massive cocaine-smuggling and money-laundering cases in the 1990s by the RCMP. "You have . . . been identified on several occasions as an active member of the Italian Mafia," his parole hearing panel wrote him in 2001. "The offences you have . . . committed are large-scale and they required organization and planning at a level that only a highly organized group can hope to execute."

Good luck spared Callocchia's life that day in the parking lot. Bleeding heavily from several bullets to the torso, Callocchia managed to stagger into a restaurant. The gunman chose to drive away rather than venture inside and finish the job. There would be plenty more chances.

As the bodies continued to drop, Vito seemed to be pulling ahead in the undeclared Mafia war. Secretly bunkered still in his downtown Montreal condominium, he ventured out only in the company of guards and rode in his armoured car, nothing like the lithe and open Ferrari he sometimes drove in the salad days of the early 1990s. As a possible omen of good fortune, someone finally made an offer to purchase Vito's Mafia Row mansion in March 2013, almost two years after it went on the market. The offer was for $1.275 million, and it sold for almost three-quarters of a million under the original price. The new buyer would be a pioneer of sorts for Mafia Row, as listing broker Leon Derestepanian noted to the press that they were from a large family without organized crime connections. The Montreal *Gazette* had fun with the story, headlining it, THE OFFER VITO RIZZUTO COULDN'T REFUSE. Reporter Allison Lampert's account began, "Vito Rizzuto's former home in Ahuntsic has finally sold, but it appears the reputed Montreal crime boss has taken a hit."

Some members of the 'Ndrangheta in Ontario now quietly pined for the big money they used to make while working with Vito in the 1990s and early 2000s. So much blood had been spilled; whatever opportunity had once tempted them was now long gone, replaced by loss and confusion. Baker Moreno Gallo was an exile of sorts in Acapulco, where a friend owned a hotel, and where he was close to other significant Calabrians in the underworld. His wife and sons had never left Montreal, even though he had sold his $1.2-million home, and he retained construction interests in the city. While Acapulco was warm and exciting, Gallo remained a Montrealer at heart, and a homesick one at that.

He filed papers in May 2013 with the Canadian immigration board, arguing he had a right to be in the country even if he wasn't a citizen. He still had resident status, and he argued that this meant authorities didn't have the right to push for his expulsion. He further argued that it wasn't fair for him to be deported for serious criminality, since the murder for which he was convicted was committed before the Immigration Act was revised in 1978. His application included a letter of support from the Mammola Recreation Association, a six-hundred-member group of Montrealers of Calabrian background. Included in his appeal package was an affidavit from the association's president, Francesco Ierfino, praising the frequency and generosity of his charitable donations. Like Vito and Di Maulo, Gallo had a civic-minded side and his largesse included financial support for the Montreal Children's Foundation, the Breast Cancer Foundation of Maisonneuve, the Rosemont hospital and the Canadian Multiple Sclerosis Association.

Before any sort of meeting was scheduled with immigration author-ities, Gallo had a hearing before Vito Rizzuto. He was summoned to meet Vito on vacation in the Dominican Republic, along with a group of other Canadians. Gallo knew that his next round of golf with Vito could be a life-altering or life-ending event. For those in the *milieu*, a round on the links served as a performance review, and men like Gallo knew there wasn't much point trying to hide from Vito's invita-tions, as his reach was long.

Gallo didn't seem nervous about trying to come back to Montreal. Did he think Vito hadn't detected the depth of his betrayal? He was too smart and experienced a man to truly believe that. Did he feel he might somehow be forgiven for transferring Vito's sports book in the Toronto area to the Calabrians during his absence? Other sports book operations had been turned over to Montagna. In Vito's world, betrayed accounts were closed with bullets. Gallo knew all of this, and yet he agreed to the meeting in the Dominican.

As Quebec's criminal body count rose, so too did the political body count. At dawn on June 17, 2013, Montreal mayor Michael Applebaum's day began with an event that wasn't written into his itinerary: he was arrested at his home on fourteen corruption-related charges, including fraud, breach of trust and conspiracy. Pundits recalled how Applebaum had presented himself as a cleansing force for the scandal-plagued city when he replaced former Montreal mayor Gérald Tremblay the previ-ous fall, after Tremblay had resigned amidst construction bid–rigging allegations. "I solemnly vow that I will erase this stain on our city," Applebaum had promised, eight months before he was taken into custody.

His arrest was news around the world, coming at the same time accusations first surfaced that Toronto mayor Rob Ford was videotaped smoking crack cocaine with street-gang members. Suddenly, the mayors of Canada's two largest cities had become punchlines. The *Atlantic* magazine headlined its report "What the Heck Is the Matter with the Mayors of Canada?" and opened it with the line: "So a Canadian mayor was arrested Monday and, no, it was not the one you expect."

Just a few months earlier, Applebaum was the man who was expected to deal with the city's potholes. Now he was facing criminal charges and the axle-bending potholes had got worse. The seriousness of the city's deterioration was driven home on August 5, 2013, when a backhoe collapsed into a sinkhole in the downtown intersection of Sainte-Catherine West and Guy. The symbolism of Montreal's decay was impossible to ignore.

Other troubling symbolism came when the Charbonneau inquiry was shown a photo of high-ranking Fédération des travailleurs et travailleuses du Québec union boss Jean Lavallée and construction magnate Tony Accurso together on a vacation trip to the Virgin Islands in 2005. Lavallée, who ran the FTQ's construction wing, testified that he and Accurso had been friends for three decades. The vacation photo showed the union boss literally getting his back scrubbed by Accurso, as Lavallée stood waist-deep in the water, puffing a cigar. At the time the photo was taken, Lavallée was a board member of the federation's billion-dollar investment fund, which helped finance several Accurso-led projects. At the time the photo was shown, Accurso was facing charges for fraud and influence peddling.

Lavallée testified that he saw nothing wrong with taking about a half-dozen week-long trips as a guest aboard Accurso's luxury yacht, *Touch*. He balked at the suggestion that the trips swayed him to grant contracts to his friend.

"I didn't think it was a sin to go on a friend's boat," Lavallée said.

Martin Brett's writing from the 1950s seemed to echo through the halls of the inquiry, especially his description of the "smirking abnormal" balance between the city's respectable veneer and its underworld, "probably the most subtle organization of its type in North America, tentacles reaching anywhere and everywhere, with pressure all the way."

It should surprise no one when a yappy cocaine aficionado utters some shocking words at a party. But one day in January 2013, in a high-end Vaughan restaurant, this particular man's voice was perhaps the only strong pro-Vito one in a sea of supporters of Platinum Sports Book, and he didn't even look nervous. Platinum had, of course, once been Vito's fiefdom, before Moreno Gallo ceded control of it to his fellow Calabrians. Now, Vito's man was acting like someone with an unusual level of comfort and confidence, even for a man whose nostrils had been liberally dusted with white powder.

He had said something breathtaking in its simplicity and strength. They were words that affirmed Vito's genius for consensus building, even in these most difficult of times. The man said that Vito wasn't looking for money from them, related to Platinum. They could keep whatever they had made. That was a triviality. And Vito certainly didn't need their love. But Vito did need something from them, and it wasn't negotiable. Vito demanded their loyalty and a clear path to seek justice. For Vito now, revenge and justice were fused into one thing, and nothing short of his own death would stop him from achieving it.

With those magic words, Platinum SB quietly passed back from Calabrian into Sicilian control. It was an easy decision to make. The sports book operators had grown weary of the penny-pinching ways of the Calabrian 'Ndrangheta members, and the murders of Smiling Joe Di Maulo et al. showed that Vito's wrong side wasn't such a safe place to be.

"Whoever wants to switch to us, they don't have to pay money," was the emissary's message. "They don't have to share."

Those words had more power than bullets. With their utterance, Vito became once again the most powerful person in Canada's underworld.

His message, and the locale where he chose to have it spoken, was a direct affront to the 'Ndrangheta, who had played a guiding role in the attacks on his family. By the time Vito's man sauntered out of the restaurant, some of the York Region 'Ndrangheta were targets themselves, surrounded by people whose loyalty had just been purchased back by Vito—for free.

The words also signalled that something had changed profoundly about Vito. Before the murders of his father and eldest son, Vito was a man who always put business first. He was the man who created money-making opportunities out of chaos and blood. Now, Vito had all the money he would ever need. But without his eldest son to pass his businesses on to, and without his father to impress, his fortune had an empty feel to it. What could he offer his widowed mother that would make her remaining days less painful? All Vito had left was life in the present, and he didn't want to share a second of that time with his enemies, unless that second was spent killing them.

At the time of the Platinum SB party, the Bonanno family's credibility hung at a historic low, never having recovered from the defection of its former boss Joe Massino. The family's failure to avenge the murder of Salvatore Montagna had called particular attention to their weakness. In Ontario, the New York City crime families with the most influence now were the Luccheses and Gambinos, and to a lesser extent the Genoveses. The old Magaddino family of Buffalo was attempting a revival through loansharking at Casino Niagara on the American border. This revived La Cosa Nostra was more loosely structured now, and more of a network than a tight organization. Contacts, expertise and experience were shared across organizational lines, for mutual benefit. These weren't particularly friendly waters for Vito, but he had navigated far worse.

CHAPTER 41

Triangle of death

The surveillance team of *carabinieri* caught sight of its target at 9:25 a.m. on Friday, September 14, 2012. They were stepping off the direct flight from Madrid to Palermo's Aeroporto Falcone e Borsellino, named after martyred judges Giovanni Falcone and Paolo Borsellino, childhood friends who were murdered in 1992 by the island's Mafia.

The police target that day was former Toronto and Montreal resident Juan Ramon Paz Fernandez, a.k.a. Johnny Bravo, Joey Bravo and James Shaddock. The night before his arrival in Sicily, he called his local contact Pietro Sorci, asking him to show up at the airport to give him a ride. Fernandez wanted Sorci to arrive alone. Clearly, there were things he wanted to discuss in confidence.

Fernandez was moving fast and travelling light since his release from prison the previous April, after serving a ten-year term for an assortment of underworld offences around Toronto, including murder conspiracy and drug trafficking. After being deported to Spain, he quickly embarked on a trip to South and Central America, where he had tried to secure cocaine deals with associates of Vito's family. Now, as he landed on the island of Vito's birth, it was easy to think that Vito—a month before his release from Colorado, at this point—had devised an exit plan for him that would allow Fernandez to keep making money for the family.

The *carabinieri* had been tipped off by the RCMP about Fernandez's imminent arrival. The surveillance team followed Sorci's Hyundai Veloster along the only highway from the airport to Palermo. It was the same route that Falcone had travelled two decades earlier, until his armour-plated Fiat Croma reached a spot where the Mafia had hidden thirteen metal drums containing 350 kilograms of explosives in a drain-pipe. From a vantage point high on the white sandhills overlooking the highway, amidst the prickly pear and olive trees and cane thickets, a Mafioso pressed a detonator. With that small movement, he made instant martyrs—*cadaveri eccellenti*, illustrious corpses—of Falcone, his wife and three bodyguards.

There had been a time when the arrival of a Spaniard in Sicily brought terror. The Spanish Inquisition raged for almost two centuries there, beginning in 1592 with Tomás de Torquemada, the First Grand Inquisitor of Spain. So great was the terror that *mi spagnu*—*spagnu* referring to Spain—means "I have a fear" in the local dialect.

The *carabinieri* weren't fearful of this Spaniard, but they were wary. They kept pace as Sorci turned the Hyundai along Via Tornatore towards Bagheria, a Mafia-ridden town in Palermo province. They lost sight of the car for a brief time and then caught sight of it again, shortly before 10:40 a.m., when Fernandez was dropped off at his apartment at 18 Via Tornatore. At 4:30 p.m., the Hyundai pulled up outside a fruit and vegetable shop on Via Nino Bixio. The shop was run by forty-nine-year-old Sergio Rosario Flamia, who was considered by police to be the treasurer of the Mafia family of Giacinto (Gino) Di Salvo, top Mafia boss in the *mandamento*, or district, of Bagheria, which also included the towns of Altavilla Milicia, Casteldaccia, Villabate and Ficarazzi. Di Salvo's group ran a network of extortion and narcotics. Sorci got out of the car and went inside to talk with Flamia.

The next day, September 14, police overheard Sorci via wiretap in conversation with Carmela Starita, a woman living in Perugia whose husband, Luigi Scuotto, was in prison north of Naples for drug traffick-ing and possession. Sorci reached her at an unlisted number registered to a Senegalese drug trafficker living in Naples. Sorci talked about "it" and said "it" would arrive in twenty to twenty-five days. In case there was any doubt about what "it" was, Sorci asked the woman about the market price of *fumo*—slang for marijuana—in Perugia, a city known for rich international students at the University of Foreigners and the most enthusiastic per capita illegal drug consumption in Italy. Starita said she'd ask someone the next day about the going rate for *fumo*.

That evening at 10:33, Sorci and Starita were on the phone again talking about the fierce Spaniard who had just arrived in their midst.

"He is fifty-eight years old," Sorci said, overestimating Fernandez's age by two years, then added that Fernandez looked much younger.

Indeed, Fernandez appeared a decade younger than his real age, although he was a bit thicker around the waist than during his heyday. His arms were also a little thinner than when he had posed for that photo with Hulk Hogan back in the 1990s. Still, Fernandez remained a fit man and a black belt in karate—not someone you'd want angry at you in an alley.

"Yes, yes," Carmela said. "He looks more like a forty-year-old."

As Carmela laughed, Sorci said Fernandez hadn't slept in two days. "He kept me half an hour to talk, then you know what he says?" Before Carmela could answer, Sorci answered his own question: "'Now I'll go to the gym!'" Sorci expressed his amazement at the Spaniard's energy, using an impossible-to-translate local phrase—*buttana di tua sorella*—meaning roughly "whore your sister," then explained, "Fuck went to the gym for two hours."

Fernandez planned to settle down in a region whose name carried connotations of Mafia as strong in pop culture as in reality. Bagheria featured prominently in the *Godfather* movie trilogy, as Al Pacino's Michael Corleone character hid out there under the wing of a politically connected Mafia leader for two years after he killed a corrupt New York cop.

Not surprisingly, Bagheria was also a real-life stronghold of the remains of the Mafia-friendly Christian Democrat Party, which had run Italy for four decades. It sat in the centre of what locals called "the Triangle of Death," between the mountains and the Tyrrhenian coast. Once a country playground for Palermo's princes, it was a place of fantastical stories of abuses of power, the oddest of which were often true.

One of the city's prime tourist attractions was the baroque Villa of Monsters, built in 1715 for the Prince of Palagonia. It was decorated with hundreds of stone statues resembling handbags, dragons, griffins, hunchbacks, soldiers and centaurs, as well as a particularly hideous one that was said to be a caricature of his promiscuous wife. Chair pillows inside had been spiked with thorns, for the prince's amusement when guests were seated.

Bagheria was also home to Sicily's first "illustrious corpse," Marchese Emanuele Notarbartolo, an incorruptible director of the Bank of Sicily. On February 1, 1893, two well-dressed assassins stabbed him to death on the train to Palermo. The man behind the slaying was Raffaele Palizzolo, a former Palermo city councillor and a Member of Parliament. Bagheria also had the dubious distinction of being the only town in Italy to name a square after a suspected Mafioso, Pasquale Alfano. Following a public outcry, the square was renamed in 1993 for *cadavere eccellente* Beppe Montana, a police commissioner who was assassinated by the Mafia.

In the first decade of the twenty-first century, left-leaning youth began plastering the town with Wanted posters for seventy-three-year-old Mafia leader Bernardo (by then known as The Ghost) Provenzano, who had lived underground there for more than four decades. Police relied upon descriptions from informers and a police Identikit to create a portrait of a thin, grim man with a scar on his neck, who looked like a menacing farmer. Under the sketch the posters read, "Don't Be Afraid, Turn In the Mafia."

Anti-Mafia prosecutor Pier Luigi Vigna appeared on national television to call Provenzano "the invisible man" and read one of the notes written by the boss to guide his men. In the missive, the invisible man referred to an old nail factory in Bagheria that had once been a heroin production facility for Leonardo Greco, a former local Mafia boss. At the time of the letter's writing, the factory served as Provenzano's execution chamber. Provenzano wrote on the paper: "If you can, see if they've managed to put any cameras at the bottom end of the factory, close in or far off. Tell everyone not to talk inside the place or close to the machines. Even at home, they mustn't talk loudly."

Much of the slaughter in the old nail factory took place in the 1980s, after Provenzano graduated from being a senior member of the Corleone family to interim *capo di tutti capi*, or overall boss of the Mafia in Sicily. In one court case, former loyalist and one-time school-teacher Antonino Giuffrè called it a "factory of death" and continued: "Horrible things happened there. . . . Many people went there never to return home again." Giuffrè described how victims were strangled and tossed into drums of acid, then buried in nearby fields. He wasn't able to forget "the nauseous stench of bodies dissolved in acid." He told authorities that the Mafia thrived because of corruption, in a description that would have had resonance in Montreal: "It's very simple," Giuffrè said. "We are the fish and politics is the water."

By the time of Fernandez's arrival, the old nail factory had been seized by local authorities and transformed into a youth recreation centre for theatrical and musical events. Fernandez's old Toronto associates Michele (Mike, The American) Modica and Andrea Fortunato Carbone had resettled in Bagheria after the California Sandwiches shooting in Toronto. It hadn't taken long for Modica and Carbone to get back into trouble. They were now in jail for Mafia association, after Sicilian police heard they were plotting to murder Pietro Lo Iacono, acting boss of a Bagheria Mafia family. Modica and Carbone were due to be released from prison in April 2014.

On the streets, Fernandez had links with Carbone's brother Giuseppe—known on the streets as Salvatore—as well as Pietro Sorci and Sergio Flamia. His other contacts in Bagheria included former GTA residents Pietro and Salvatore Scaduto, brothers who had worked in Canada for Vito's family. The Scaduto brothers had lived in Canada for a quarter century, moving shortly after Pietro escaped a murder bid in Bagheria in 1990. Their father, Bartolomeo, had been slain in under-world feuding the previous year, and it seemed like a smart time to explore the possibilities of life abroad.

Now, the family ran an excavation business and L'Ultima Fermata ("The Last Stop") pizzeria at the corner of Via Togliatti and Via Papa Giovanni XXIII. Like Fernandez, they kept in frequent phone contact with a Montreal lawyer connected to Vito. Back in Sicily, they chafed at even the thought of Modica. Shortly after the California Sandwiches debacle, the Scaduto brothers had been arrested with a large stockpile of weapons. Faced with the prospect of a deportation hearing, they voluntarily left Canada. If not for Modica's arrogance and stupidity, they might all still be in Canada. They had made it to the promised land of nice cars and good money and Modica had got them expelled.

Fernandez sported a sparkling gold Rolex believed to have been given to him by Vito, back when he was known on the streets of Toronto as Johnny Bravo and his benefactor Vito valued business over revenge. The Spaniard opened up a karate dojo that doubled as a dance studio in his new town, but it would soon become clear that his passion remained crime.

CHAPTER 42

Man in the middle

lmost immediately after his arrival in Sicily, police overheard Fernandez talking about transactions involving "vitamins," "loaves of bread," "grandmothers," "girls," "illegal immigrants," "snapshots," "photos," "kimonos" and "things." All the references really meant OxyContin, or oxycodone, known on the streets as OC, Oxy and hillbilly heroin. Addicts crush it into a powder, then inject or snort it for a morphine-like buzz. In an effort to curb its sale on the black market, it was banned for sale in Canada in early 2012, but that only drove up the price of tablets to one hundred dollars on the streets. For drug traffickers with connections to unwitting or unscrupulous doctors, the ban was a godsend.

Police wiretaps recorded Fernandez talking to a Toronto man named Danny, who remained a close associate. Danny was someone you might want beside you in a dark alley, but you would never invite him to sit at the big table. He was the sort of cement head who would be sent into a business and wouldn't bother to cover his face when punching out the owner. He was capable of home invasions, extortion and even murder, and if he was nabbed, he would keep his mouth shut and do his prison time like an old-school criminal. Once, he enlisted a guard to help out with his drug ring when he was serving time. He was just Fernandez's type of guy.

In the fictional *Godfather*, the Bagheria mob boss owns local politicians. The reality wasn't any prettier. Police listening in to the mobsters' phones also heard how a regional mayor asked the Mafia for fifty votes. On October 17, 2012, they heard another politician paying three thousand euros to buy a package of votes in Bagheria, much like one might buy a herd of sheep.

Tapes also recorded talk of how Fernandez met with a Hamilton, Ontario, friend after the latter arrived in Sicily on October 27, 2012. He brought money with him for Fernandez, who had been buying bars and pizzerias around Bagheria. Each transfer from Canada totalled €999 to avoid anti–money laundering controls.

On October 31, at 8:36 a.m., Fernandez talked with his friend about contacting a doctor who could supply the pills. They also wanted the doctor to help them find an elderly patient to move the drugs to Canada. "Most older people, people over sixty years or so, no one looks at them," the friend explained.

A bug in Fernandez's BMW X5 SUV caught them on November 29 talking about Lorenzo Carbone going to Toronto for a week. Fernandez wanted to know if there had been checks at the Toronto airport about "things" on his possession. Carbone replied that it had been very superficial, with most of the questioning about whether he was transporting Parmesan cheese.

Fernandez considered sending the next shipment of oxycodone to Canada through the mail. "I do not see why not . . . because the vitamins, do not smell or anything like that."

On December 5, the second shipment of oxycodone from Italy to Canada was sent by courier post to Hamilton Mountain. The plan was simple and successful. On December 7, his friend Carbone bubbled over with the thought of getting fabulously rich. "I have always money, money is always."

Fernandez preached caution, warning his associates to be careful of walking under video cameras. In Palermo and Bagheria, sometimes the walls literally have electronic eyes and ears. Despite his words of caution, Fernandez was feeling positive. A Sicilian contact told him he could get him a batch of oxycodone within two weeks, using his medical contacts. When Fernandez said he had a problem getting money from Canada, the contact suggested he pay him with narcotics.

Then the contact bragged that he had a godson in common with fugitive Trapani province boss Matteo (Diabolik) Messina Denaro of the Corleone Mafia. Messina Denaro was considered a new Cosa Nostra leader after Provenzano's arrest on April 11, 2006, and *L'Espresso* magazine featured him on the cover with the headline HERE IS THE NEW BOSS OF THE MAFIA.

"Thirty-five years in hiding here in Sicily," the contact said of Denaro, with a touch of awe.

Fernandez was intrigued by talk that Messina Denaro was considered more powerful than even Salvatore (Totò, The Beast) Riina, Sicily's top Mafia boss in the 1980s.

"Say if it's true or not. Is he bigger than Riina?" Fernandez asked. "Bigger than him?"

"Yes."

"Fuck!"

Between January 10 and January 19, 2013, Fernandez talked many times by phone with two Toronto-area men. One of them owned the King City compound where Vito often stayed when he was in the GTA. They were both harsh critics of how Fernandez's man in Toronto, Danny, was acting, showing a disregard for the "old guard" of the Rizzuto organization there.

On March 25, a Canadian associate named David had arrived in Sicily, and he and Fernandez were almost immediately talking about smuggling weapons into Canada. That day, the conversation shifted to what would happen if anyone took action against Danny. "I will return there in a second if something happens to Danny," said Fernandez. "They all will be killed in the same day."

On March 26, Fernandez's voice was recorded talking with David. He said he was keeping an equal distance from both sides in the ongoing Canadian Mafia war. "I am good friends with Vito but also good friends with Raynald Desjardins," he said. Then he added that he was made a member of the Mafia with Desjardins during a ceremony presided over by Vito Rizzuto. Fernandez's tone was clearly aggressive. He demanded in English that his associate know that he wasn't a second-class mobster, just because he was a Spaniard who had lived in Canada.

He made his comments on a winding street, forgetting his own caution about the dangers of omnipresent police cameras and bugs as he announced that Vito Rizzuto "makes the fucking rules." He proudly announced that this meant he and Desjardins had been promoted to a status where they could sit as equals with fellow "men of honour."

"Vito 'made' me and my *compare*, Raynald," Fernandez said.

It was a breathtaking statement. The Spaniard's respect for Vito was obvious, but he had just said something that could cost him his life, should word ever get back to Vito. He had called Desjardins *compare*, a term far closer than "friend" in local parlance. He had also unknowingly said it on a police surveillance camera, in the midst of a war between Rizzuto and Desjardins.

His boast stunned his companion, who replied, "You're not Italian."

"No, no. Me and my *compare*." Then Fernandez restated that he and Desjardins were "made" men. Then he said the word again.

Did he not think that such words travelled?

For all his brashness with underlings and people on his level, Fernandez remained a suck-up when it came to bosses. When first trying to work into the *milieu*, he had courted the goodwill of Raynald Desjardins. When Desjardins brought him into Vito's elevated circle, Fernandez sucked up to him with equal enthusiasm. Now that Desjardins and Vito were deadly enemies, it was tough to see exactly which side Fernandez supported, since he appeared to have ties to them both. Fernandez did stay in touch regularly by phone with the Rizzutos' Montreal lawyer, who was also speaking with the Scadutos. It was as if Fernandez somehow refused to recognize the intensity of emotions involved in the war under way in Canada, as he traded on the names of both Desjardins and Vito.

As he and David wound down the ancient street, Fernandez also seemed to be disclosing family secrets. To be officially inducted into the Mafia, there is a ceremony, called *pungiutu*, which translates to "pinch and make blood," performed by a boss. It involves burning the photo of a saint while pricking then squeezing the inductee's trigger finger. He (all members are male) is then required to say, "I will burn in hell if I betray the organization."

It was possible Fernandez was telling the truth, and that Vito's Canadian organization was unique in inducting non-Italian members. That would be a first, but Vito was capable of breaking ground and certainly didn't lack for confidence. If so, it said a lot about life in the *milieu* that the first non-Italian inducted into the Mafia was now Vito's mortal enemy. It was also highly possible that Fernandez was lying. He was boasting to someone who was not a Mafioso. There are few real rules in the Mafia, but those that do exist tend to be hard and fast. Among the most strictly enforced of them is that you can lie to anyone but another member, and David wasn't a member.

Fernandez stressed again that he was attempting to remain neutral in the midst of the Canadian hostilities. "There is a small war over there and I am stuck in the middle between those people. . . . It's a war between two of my best friends, my *compare* Raynald and my other friend Vito." If Fernandez believed the hostilities were a spat that would pass in time, he couldn't have made a worse misjudgment of Vito's fury.

Then Fernandez told his guest that he wanted his Toronto friend Danny inducted into the Mafia too. There was a casualness to the comment, as if it was nothing more than joining a gym. "I want to make Danny a made man and I know that I can do it with some boss over there. We need a boss to do that. . . . If Danny would have come here, I could have asked Sergio [Flamia] to make him a made man right away."

That same day, the bug in Fernandez's car picked up the two men talking about moving guns between Italy and Canada. The conversation shifted to how a silencer for one of their guns had somehow been lost. Fernandez was upset because it was a quality item.

"These are fucking deadly, do not feel a dick," he said, simulating the soft sound of two shots fired with the muffler.

Then Fernandez described the pains he took when sending such items to Canada.

"It is difficult to send to you; you can also send in a package. . . . In a bundle, you put it in a bottle of shampoo, a big bottle with carbon paper, they cannot see through it."

On March 28, Fernandez's strength in Bagheria was boosted further with the arrival of his long-time associate, a Portuguese national named Fernando Pimentel. The thirty-five-year-old was Modica's and Fernandez's type: someone not afraid to do a home invasion and crush a face. He had a UFC look to him, with short hair, big buff muscles, a tattoo the length of his right forearm and a watch the size of Fernandez's Rolex. It was an international tough guy look that played just as well on patios in Mississauga or Madrid.

Pimentel had committed many crimes in Canada before he was deported for drug trafficking. From Portugal, he moved to Bagheria and lived there between 2006 and mid-2008 as a guest of sorts of Michele Modica. He had been arrested in the Azores for robbery and kidnapping in August 2009, and served three years in Portuguese prisons. He didn't plan to stay in Sicily too long this visit, as he had a return ticket to Portugal for April 18.

His time behind bars apparently hadn't made Pimentel any milder. He immediately jumped into a conversation with Fernandez on March 28 about beating up people in Sicily for associates.

"Brother, I had to beat people to make money!" he announced.

"This is a shit," Fernandez said.

The Canadians were showing up at a time when the old underworld of Bagheria was in a dangerous state of flux. A police wiretap at the time picked up Flamia talking to a friend named Enzo of how he was tired of the current state of affairs and needed change. "I'm tired, Enzo, to see these twisted things."

Enzo appeared to be pushing Flamia to distance himself more from the current leadership as he said: "I think you were wrong to sit down again at the table."

On March 29, Fernandez and Pimentel were cutting through Bagheria's traffic in Fernandez's BMW when a familiar location brought back memories.

"This is where I fucking killed that person," Pimentel said, out of the blue.

"Huh?" Fernandez replied.

"This is where I killed him, killed . . . I have beaten, I ripped the ear . . ."

They also talked in the car of the tragedy at California Sandwiches. Pimentel found humour in the bloodshed as he talked about Andrea Carbone, who was supposed to be a bodyguard for Modica that day. "He was shaking in his boots when those guys went at him . . . down there [at] California Sandwiches," Pimentel said. ". . . He had the thing [pistol], and don't even shoot back."

"I know, bro," Fernandez replied.

"So, *pfff*," Pimentel continued, mimicking a spitting noise. "Buddy M. [Michele Modica] had to fucking grab the thing and, you know . . ."

"Yeah," Fernandez said.

"Come on," Pimentel continued. "You have a thing and you are fucking scared to use it? Stay home next time! Don't come down like you are a hero. . . . Rather carry your water gun."

Pimentel had been close to Modica back then, and Italian authorities suspected he had been part of the unresolved hit on Peter Lo Jacono, the important man of honour whom Modica had plotted to kill back in 2008 in Sicily. Few things make mobsters more edgy than an unresolved murder. On March 31, the police bug in Fernandez's BMW picked up a cryptic conversation about what sounded suspiciously like another murder plot.

"So, what you do not understand . . . he told me that he had . . . said to M&M [Michele Modica] to do the . . ." At that point, Pimentel dropped his voice so that it was unintelligible.

Pimentel noted that they had spoken with the other man behind the plot recently.

"Yeah, what we met the other day," Pimentel said.

"Who?" replied Fernandez. "Not with me, as I know, he was the one that [inaudible] this is what . . . and was the other man in jail."

Bagheria was now flush with former Canadian residents. The Scaduto brothers had been back in Sicily since 2004, and where they stood in the current tensions wasn't clear. Since returning to Sicily, the Scaduto brothers had pushed to reassert their family's power, while staying in touch with Vito's lawyer. The brothers' ambitions also butted up against those of Fernandez's new associate, Sergio Flamia. The Canadians had the always tense city feeling ready to explode. The *carabinieri* pondered moving in and making arrests early on the drug charges. Otherwise, they could be sure they'd soon be investigating yet another murder.

CHAPTER 43

Several churches

Vito's long-time associate Pietro Scaduto had an appointment to meet with Fernandez and Pimentel on April 9, 2013, at the Bar Diva outside Palermo. It was a busy, modern stop just off the highway, where they shouldn't stand out on a Saturday evening. They weren't going to be there long anyway. The topic was to be marijuana seeds and cultivation, and it wasn't hard to get Fernandez to the table. "If there was money to be made, Ramon was the right person to deal with," Carbone recalled later. "He liked money."

Ever since he had inquired about the price of *fumo* in the university town of Perugia, Fernandez had sniffed an opportunity in local marijuana cultivation. He first needed a secure location for production and some seeds, and Scaduto had said he could help. As Fernandez prepared for the meeting, he went to great pains to be discreet. He drove a rented compact Renault Clio hatchback rather than his more eye-catching SUV.

Moments after they met in the Bar Diva at 7:15 p.m., Fernandez, Pimentel and Pietro Scaduto were together in the little Clio, heading for a house under construction in Contrada Incorvino in a rural area of Bagheria. It belonged to Giuseppe Carbone, and Giuseppe had stolen a key. It wasn't occupied yet and was surrounded by a fence, so they would have security and privacy. They passed through the gate of the house at 7:30 p.m.

Giuseppe (Salvatore) Carbone was waiting in the house with a loaded .765 pistol. Hiding in a large doghouse inside the grounds was Pietro Scaduto's brother Salvatore. His gun that evening was a dependable .38 revolver.

None of the men in the Clio carried weapons. Salvatore Scaduto had stashed a Spanish nine-millimetre pistol by a pillar on the gate. The plan was for Pietro Scaduto to exit the car to close the gate behind them, and for him to pick up the gun and start shooting. That was the cue for the others to come out firing.

The two targets didn't notice as Pietro Scaduto picked up the hidden gun and approached the car. Pimentel, oblivious to the danger, swung the Clio around so that he could make an easy exit after the meeting. "Ramon realized what was happening and he exited from the car and ran to open the gate," Carbone later said.

Pimentel realized he had seconds to act or his life would be over. He tried to accelerate towards the gate and accidentally hit Fernandez and then caught Pietro Scaduto, knocking him to the ground and injuring his shoulder.

Pietro Scaduto came up firing. "At that moment, Pietro and I, we started shooting," Giuseppe Carbone later said. "One shot after another. We shot at least thirty times." They fired so many times that Carbone had to reload his pistol, and then they fired some more on the unarmed men.

Pimentel was half in and half out of the Clio when the shooting finally stopped. Fernandez lay on the ground inside the compound. During a lull in the shooting, he had enough breath left to ask his killers a question.

"He looked at Pietro and asked, 'P., why?'" Carbone recalled. "And then he turned his face at me and said, 'Why, Sal?'" There wasn't much point explaining to Fernandez that there was no room for neutrals in Vito's war and no place to hide. "At that point, Pietro took my gun and shot him in the head. But Ramon was still alive. We just carried him in the trunk of the car and we gave him another shot in the head."

It was dark as Carbone drove the Clio, with the bodies crammed inside, to an old illegal dump in Contrada Fiorilli, a rural area between

Altavilla Milicia and Casteldaccia, overgrown with chest-high weeds and grass. Pietro followed on Carbone's Vespa scooter while Salvatore returned home in his Fiat Panda. The Panda had been a modest-enough vehicle when it was new, and that was more than a decade ago. Killers for the Sicilian mob often earned less than plumbers, and their scruffy vehicles reflected this.

Carbone heard a cellphone going off in the back of the Clio, where the bodies lay. He heard the sound at 8:46 p.m. and again at 9:44 p.m. and yet again after he pulled to a halt, and Pietro Scaduto arrived on the Vespa. The caller was Fernandez's girlfriend, Giovanna Landolsi, but none of the killers knew that at the time. Her calls went unanswered.

Pietro Scaduto's arm was hurting and his patience was gone. He smashed the phone and the buzzing finally stopped.

On April 19, Giuseppe (Salvatore) Carbone discussed selling Fernandez's Rolex with a jeweller on Via Paolo Emiliani Giudici in Palermo.

"I found a buyer for €3,500," the jeweller said.

"Ask if he can give 4,000," Carbone replied.

Later that day, Pietro Scaduto advised him against the sale: "Don't do anything. I have a potential buyer who can give us more money."

The next day, Carbone returned to the jeweller and retrieved the timepiece. After leaving the shop, he was stopped by the *carabinieri* in a routine check. When Carbone was unable to satisfactorily explain how he came into possession of the watch, a police officer seized it, but Carbone wasn't arrested.

Later that day, Carbone went back to the jeweller and told of his encounter with the *carabinieri*.

"Don't worry, I will say . . . if they ask me, that you asked me only to clean the Rolex, not to sell it."

Italian authorities decided it was time to move in. Charges were drafted against Fernandez for transporting oxycodone from Italy to Canada from August 2012 to the present. Other charges were drawn up for smuggling a kilo of heroin into Perugia and for illegally possessing a gun and two silencers.

There was a blitz of twenty-one arrests, but when *carabinieri* moved to serve the warrants on Fernandez and Pimentel, the former Toronto-area residents could not be found. The last record of a signal from Fernandez's BlackBerry was on the night of April 9, near the home of Carbone's cousin. "The current unavailability could be a result of a hasty escape," an Italian police document concluded. "We cannot exclude, however, that he may have been the victim of a double murder."

By the time of his latest arrest, Giuseppe Carbone was forty-three years old and had been in and out of prison since he was nineteen. He had grown weary of the grubby reality of Mafia life, in which he was on call 24/7 to murder associates without question. Maybe he found something particularly soul-destroying about peddling the Rolex he'd stripped from the wrist of a dead man who had once trusted him. Perhaps he also realized that someday he could become a target himself.

Whatever the reason, almost immediately after he was taken into custody, Carbone told authorities he wanted to talk. There were no tears on May 8 when he sat down to give a statement to two magistrates and four *carabinieri*. "For so many years I was a fugitive in America and I don't have any intention to hide anymore or to pay for things I haven't committed," Carbone told them. "I knew the risk was as soon as I leave jail I would be killed, so I want to collaborate."

Exactly why Fernandez and Pimentel were targeted for murder wasn't totally clear to him, and it wasn't his business to ask. That didn't stop him from wondering: "Most likely it was because Fernandez took the side of a Rizzuto enemy, a former right-hand man."

Fernandez knew much about Vito, but failed to appreciate the recent and fundamental change in him. Vito's priority now was revenge, and only revenge. There was no Plan B. Business just didn't matter. Fernandez's view of the world was the polar opposite: business was everything. "Ramon was one where, when he saw money, he really jumped on," Carbone said. "He didn't care about this Mafia or that Mafia. He knocked on all doors. He tried to be friendly with anyone. He didn't understand our mentality here. . . . [You] cannot be friendly with everyone."

Carbone said that Pietro Scaduto had made a similar comment after speaking with the Canadian lawyer who was in frequent contact with Scaduto and Fernandez. The lawyer had been sending money to Fernandez on a regular basis and Carbone noted that the investments directed by the Canadian lawyer were bound to change the balance of Mafia power in Bagheria. "Pietro Scaduto told me, 'I called there and this guy told me what to do.' He always told me that Ramon 'attended too many churches.'"

For all his brashness, Fernandez didn't realize that in Sicily a few genuine friends counted for more than several loose associates. He also didn't comprehend how there are times when blood takes absolute precedence over business. "He did not have his own church. Instead, he was like a priest that entered all churches. . . . I know that in Canada now there is a war. A Mafia war. Vito Rizzuto is involved on one side. On the other side, there is a *compare* of Ramon. . . . Ramon was saying he was friendly with both of them. So he was trying to keep his foot in two shoes [*tenere il piede in due scarpe*]."

Carbone spoke from the vantage point of a weary mob journeyman who had always just done his job. There would be no extra pay for taking part in the murders, and no promotion within the group was offered or expected. It was simply an unpleasant part of his duties, like how a farmhand knows he is supposed to muck out a stable or slaughter a chicken or a hog. "I had a good relationship with Fernandez."

Carbone had spent his entire adult life in the Mafia, although he had never been formally inducted. Old ceremonies and mystique didn't seem to matter much in Carbone's world. "No, no, we don't use those things anymore," Carbone said. "I've never been *pungiutu*. I never had a ceremony with anyone. We made all kinds of feasts where we had to eat with each other. But not *pungiutu*. Not those type of things."

Carbone said that, at first, the Scaduto brothers were guarded in what they said to him about Fernandez. "They were not telling me things because they were afraid I would tell things to Fernandez." Finally, they asked him, "You are with him or with us?"

"I'm not with anyone," Carbone replied. "What do we have to do?"

Carbone said that Pietro Scaduto then replied: "You have to arrange a place and we will tell you what to do after."

Carbone settled on his cousin's property. Since it was under construction, no one would be there at night. His cousin wasn't part of the plot: "He doesn't know anything because I stole the key."

Fernandez had earlier confided to Carbone that there had been tensions between himself and Pietro Scaduto when they travelled the previous year in Panama, Ecuador and Peru. Fernandez was a vain man and he cringed at the thought of being seen in public with Scaduto, although he didn't expand on why his companion embarrassed him so. "Ramon liked to talk. [He said,] 'I took a piece of shit there with me and he . . . embarrassed me.'"

That trip was a bust, and not just for the lingering ill feelings it created between Fernandez and Pietro Scaduto. The narcotics they sought were already sold by the time they arrived. Fernandez had hoped to get the cocaine into Palermo, where prices were premium, but now he had no product to sell.

Carbone heard from Scaduto that he was concerned the Spaniard Fernandez and the group collecting around him were growing in power. "The Scadutos were a little bit concerned that they were becoming stronger as a group and they could pull together against them."

The orders to kill Fernandez and Pimentel came from Canada in late March, Carbone said. "We planned to kill them ten days earlier," but Fernandez was constantly calling and texting Pietro Scaduto on his BlackBerry. Scaduto worried that it would be a red flag for investigators when they checked through Fernandez's cell records and saw that they had so recently been in such constant contact. Better to let the calls cool down a little before they made their move.

Fernandez had a pass code on his smart phone, which he frequently changed. But for all Fernandez's underworld experience, there remained a naïveté about him. During his frequent meetings with the Scaduto brothers, he appeared to have no clue that he and his group members were targeted for death. Carbone explained that the Scaduto brothers also intended to kill Sergio Flamia, and after that to eliminate Modica when he was released from prison in April 2014. Flamia was expected to be an easy target. He recalled Pietro Scaduto saying words to the effect of: "We can kill him [Flamia] in the middle of the street."

Modica was a particularly dangerous target: "If Pietro Scaduto didn't kill Modica, it was because of my brother. He always said, 'No, Michele Modica always was sleeping with a gun under his pillow.' Scaduto was a bit scared. [He said,] 'Let's kill him, because this guy will eventually kill us.'"

Carbone told the magistrates and the *carabinieri* that his memories of the Fernandez and Pimentel murders and the subsequent cleanup were vivid. It was so easy to do and yet so haunting. "They did not have weapons. Not at home nor when we killed them. Otherwise they would have killed us. Shot back. But they didn't suspect anything.

"It was dark," Carbone continued. "We arrived at the dump and we burned the bodies with naphtha along with some tires." The plan was to make them victims of *lupara bianca*, bodies that were never found. "The day after, we returned with Salvatore [Scaduto] and we covered the bodies with Eternit [a fibre cement]. The car of Fernandez and Pimentel, we left at the Bolonegnetta dump close to a river, where we put it on fire." Carbone wore coveralls for the grim work. When it was completed, they were splattered in blood.

He also went through Fernandez's home to remove any trace of their relationship. He scooped up photos of the killers with Fernandez in Peru with Vito Rizzuto's drug contacts. Aside from the pictures, there was little worth taking. "No money, no guns, no passports. I didn't find any of those things."

Carbone knew the victims were not innocents, but he still couldn't shake his memory of Fernandez's face as he uttered his final words. "'Why? Why?' I can't forget those words. They're still in my head. *Mamma mia*, I can't forget those words."

At the end of his ninety-three-minute statement, Carbone directed paramilitary officers through the tall weeds of the dump. There they found the charred bodies of Fernandez and Pimentel, riddled with some thirty bullets, just as Carbone had said.

When authorities told Pietro Scaduto of Carbone's confession, he dismissed it as the lies of a bitter man. He said that their relationship had become unpleasant when they were involved in cattle breeding together. "There were always fights for financial reasons related to our breeding business."

Scaduto also dismissed the idea that Fernandez was anything but a friend. "When I was in jail in Canada, he helped me a lot and I did the same for him when he moved to Sicily. Only for friendship. Nothing else."

Perhaps Carbone had grown weary of mob life because he could never really tell his friends from his enemies. Certainly, Scaduto's words called to mind an old underworld saying: *You never worry about your enemies. It's your friends that bury you.*

CHAPTER 44

Hit man gets hit

In May 2013, Vito's former soldier Giuseppe (Ponytail) De Vito was in the early days of an eleven-year, seven-month sentence for conspiracy to import drugs and gangsterism when he testified at the trial of his wife, Adèle Sorella. She had been charged with the murders of their daughters, Sabrina and Amanda. There the gangster spoke of guilt and loss.

"I blame myself, I guess—yes," Ponytail testified. "Maybe I could have been there. I could have done something, like a father should."

He knew that Adèle was distraught over his lengthy absence while he was on the run from police. He had left the girls at home in her care. He had done the only thing that seemed to make sense, and still his world had exploded.

"How did you learn about the deaths of your daughters?" a prosecutor asked.

"Like everyone else, through the news," De Vito said.

"Did you attend the funeral?"

"No. I was on the run."

A pathologist told court the sisters may have been killed "gradually, slowly, gently" in the airtight hyperbaric chamber Ponytail had purchased to treat Sabrina's juvenile arthritis. In the end, his wife was convicted, and Ponytail's entire family was either dead or behind bars.

At the time of his testimony, Ponytail had been trying to get transferred from a protective unit to the general population at Donnacona, despite word that there was a contract out on his life. He was finally granted his request after calling upon his lawyer. A month after Adèle was found guilty, early in the morning of Sunday, July 7, guards were unable to revive De Vito when they found him unconscious in his cell. There was nothing around his neck and no marks on his body. He had been in good shape, as one might expect of someone who had burned off stress in a gym. Prison staff would have to wait for an autopsy to know what had happened.

Joseph (Big Joey) Massino appeared before U.S. district court judge Nicholas Garaufis in Brooklyn on Wednesday, July 8, 2013, to say that he was sorry. That was the same judge who had sentenced Vito to his time in the Florence prison and the same judge who had once been the target of a Bonanno family murder plot.

"Every night I pray for forgiveness for all the people I hurt, especially the victims' families," Big Joey said.

That would take considerable praying, since Big Joey was serving two life sentences for seven murder convictions and was also facing an outstanding murder charge, which took place after the federal death penalty had been reinstated. Perhaps Big Joey was particularly sorry now that a trip to death row was a possibility. Whatever the case, as he stood before the judge in his two-toned sweatsuit, the highest-ranking rat in the history of the North American underworld apologized.

The judge said he had no illusions about Massino's reasons for co-operating. That said, there was no questioning the results. "Quite simply, Mr. Massino may be the most important co-operator in the modern history of law enforcement efforts to prosecute the American Mafia," the judge stated. "He has provided information about the highest levels of the Mafia, including testifying in open court, assisting dozens of investigations and helping lead to numerous additional arrests and convictions." Then the judge commuted his two life sentences to time served and allowed the man who ratted on Vito to disappear deep into a witness protection program, under a new name. The only proviso was that Big Joey was obliged to help prosecutors if they needed him in future cases. Vito already faced parole conditions should he return to the United States. Big Joey's ongoing relationship with American authorities was one more reason for Vito to stay out of the country.

With renewed confidence, Vito appeared in Saint-Léonard that summer, shaking the hands of old acquaintances and friends. There was a report of him dining in a downtown restaurant, and he was also seen teeing up on Montreal-area fairways. It was just eight months since he arrived back in Canada, after eight years in custody. The war for Montreal appeared to be almost won, just in time for golf season.

La Presse reported that there was some understandable unease at his old Blainvillier Golf Club, which billed itself as "a place of peace and tranquility." Vito still had a membership, a carry-over from when he played there in the 1990s. Since his return, he had played at least four times, including once in a foursome with Stefano Sollecito, son of lieutenant Rocco Sollecito. Vito had the reputation of being a good golf companion, and sometimes even a humorous one and a gentleman. Still, it was hard not to think of Smiling Joe Di Maulo. He had been a member there too and lived beside the course, until he was shot dead on his driveway.

As Vito took some time to savour his victories on the fairways, he knew he couldn't afford to get sloppy. He likely knew also that Salvatore (Sam) Calautti was one of five hundred guests attending a stag for a bookie at the Terrace Banquet Centre in Vaughan, Ontario, on the night of July 11. Stags are a chance for mobsters and folks from regular society, sometimes including politicians, to bump up against each other, double kiss each other on the cheek, and eat and drink. They're an opportunity to renew things with old friends and acquaintances, sometimes to betray them with false smiles and complimentary drinks. It was at such a function that Fernandez had posed triumphantly for photos with Vito, in happier times, before Vito turned assassins on him.

As usual, Calautti didn't travel alone when he went to the bookie's stag. He rode in his black BMW X6 with his long-time associate, James Tusek. At the age of thirty-five, Tusek had a violent reputation that included turning a baseball bat on one unfortunate soul. He had also been acquitted in the same marijuana grow-op as Calautti's friend Nick Cortese.

By the night of the stag, Calautti remained a suspect in five unsolved murders, including that of Nicolò Rizzuto. He must have trusted whoever walked up to him in the parking lot, within eyesight of the York Regional Police 4 District Headquarters, as the party wound down around one in the morning. The killer got up close before the gun came out and he opened fire, killing both men. "It's hard to think someone snuck up on him," a police officer familiar with Calautti said. "Sam was the type of guy who always carried a gun." Although there were still a hundred men at the stag, it took them some fifteen minutes to call 911, and by then the killer or killers were long gone. It was the mob's version of a public execution in the town square: a blunt assertion of its version of state power.

There was a time when GTA mob send-offs were impossible to miss, but on the morning of July 17 it would have been easy to drive past St. Margaret Mary Church on Islington Avenue and not take a second glance at the funeral of Salvatore Calautti. The modest turnout of 150 mourners certainly didn't compare to the January 1980 funeral of Michele (Mike) Racco, which snarled traffic along Toronto's St. Clair Avenue West for three kilometres after the elderly Mafioso died of cancer. Of course, Racco was a boss. Calautti was a murdered soldier whose killers were probably fixing on their next target.

Coincidentally, one of the grandest GTA underworld funerals in recent years was for a man that Calautti had killed: Gaetano (Guy) Panepinto. His mourners were defiant and appeared ready for a fight, if they could figure out whom to fight. The Discount Casket Guy was escorted to his final resting place by an estimated four dozen bikers on Harleys from the Para-Dice Riders, Vagabonds and Last Chance motorcycle clubs. There were no outlaw bikers in club colours at Calautti's low-key funeral, just a few scruffy men with tattoos. Only one truck was needed to take his wreaths away, and it wasn't totally full.

"They all stayed away because they don't want to be associated with him," said the police officer who knew Calautti. The funeral did draw waiters and banquet hall owners, which made sense, as Calautti ran an Italian restaurant. They got to hear that he wasn't all bad. Who is? His daughters got a chance to tell the assembled that he loved them and they loved him. Others privately said he was a stand-up guy, who once served jail time for a non-fatal shooting committed by a member of his crew. There was also talk that Calautti bragged about taking part in the Nicolò murder. Indiscreet bragging about Vito's family had cost Fernandez his life. As the mob hit man he was, Calautti ought to have known better.

Calautti's mourners included a GTA man who ran baccarat games for a local leader of the 'Ndrangheta. Almost all of Calautti's mourners were of Calabrian descent, and several were from the Niagara Region. That made sense too, since Calautti was a frequent patron of Casino Niagara. Pallbearers included long-time friend Kristopher Della-Pia, who appeared far less bulked up than back in 2001, when he pleaded guilty to conspiracy to traffic a controlled substance. That was when he was part of a gang that included former Toronto police detective constable Darin Cooper, who used his official police badge, revolver and body armour to rip off drug dealers. When the gang was busted, Cooper, a former steroid addict, was sentenced in 2001 to nine and a half years in prison, while Della-Pia received a four-year term.

Although Calautti worked for three of the GTA's seven 'Ndrangheta families, none of the heads of those families attended his funeral. One was on lifetime parole for murder, with parole conditions that barred him from associating with criminals. Another was an Italian-born man suspected in the murders of two of his brothers-in-law in Italy. One theory held that Calautti was set up for murder by local 'Ndrangheta members as a peace offering to Vito. Alternatively, it was a blunt message to whoever dispatched him to kill Vito's father.

It was easy to think that the next person murdered in the Toronto underworld would be well known. A week after Calautti's murder, there were likely plenty of sweaty palms at a stag in the GTA for a Rizzuto in-law. As on Calautti's fateful night, there were Calabrian and Sicilian underworld guests. If Vito's enemies were plotting revenge, the stag would be a good time to strike. The evening passed peacefully, however. One of Vito's money managers and a senior member of the Commisso crime family had chosen not to attend. The money man had crossed over to the 'Ndrangheta side when Vito was in prison, while the senior Commisso was friendly with the Desjardins faction in Montreal. Not long ago, abandoning Vito seemed like a prudent choice for men focused on money and power. Now, it was a good way to get killed.

CHAPTER 45

Unholy trinity

O n July 1, 2013, Vito Rizzuto took possession of a home in the upscale Sainte-Dorothée district of western Laval, across the Rivière des Prairies from Montreal and, not surprisingly, close to a number of golf clubs. The cut-stone, executive-style residence wasn't really a step up from the old one on Antoine-Berthelet, but it was a move away from the street with so many sad memories and the unfortunate nick-name Mafia Row.

Vito's new home was originally listed at $1,295,000, but he got it for $874,000. It was registered in his wife, Giovanna's, name and rumour was he paid in cash. Like the old home, there was no fence around it, so the bold could just walk up to the front door, unlike the bunker-like condos of his rivals by the Rivière des Prairies or the walled compound in King City. His new neighbours anonymously grumbled to the press that they worried their families might be caught in the line of fire if assassins came looking for Vito. Who didn't recall how Nicolò was shot dead in his own kitchen by a sniper? Vito's new house didn't look that much different from others in the neighbourhood. What if the killers showed up at the wrong house and opened fire? Anyone reading the papers knew it was too early to pronounce the Mafia war over.

That said, the move into the new home was a pronouncement of victory. No longer was Vito hidden in a downtown condo, whose address was jealously guarded. Between his release from prison and the time he turned the key to the mansion in Laval, at least five well-placed Desjardins associates had been murdered with surgical precision.

As Vito settled in, however, there were reports that some of his Ontario enemies in the 'Ndrangheta had driven to Hamilton to huddle with Vito's enemies there. Long-time organized crime reporter Claude Poirier reported that Vito went to a Laval golf club five times a week that July, meeting in a cottage with a small group of trusted associates. Before the month was over, there were reports of an arson at the cottage, and questions about whether Vito had got too comfortable, too soon.

Behind the bars of Bordeaux Prison, Raynald Desjardins was settling into new accommodations of his own, preparing himself for what threatened to be a long legal battle. He had some 3.4 million documents to sift through to plan his defence. For this, he was granted permission to have a laptop computer in his cell. Desjardins did have to pay for the computer and also the costs of disabling it from Internet connectivity, which was pocket change for the millionaire; the public was left with the expense of random checks of the computer. Desjardins's seventy-one-year-old co-accused, Jack Arthur Simpson, was also adapting to a new home that July. He had been held in isolation as he awaited his eventual trial for first-degree murder. Unlike Desjardins, he wasn't boning up on court documents to better argue his case. He was just trying to stay alive.

As court proceedings crawled along, intriguing questions emerged about whether the RCMP had managed to infiltrate top levels of the Mafia. If so, were police now taking extreme measures to protect their source? There were even whispers about whether it was being treated as a matter of national security.

Certainly, something felt odd about the pending court case. Court of Quebec judge Maurice Parent gave no explanation for why he limited access to disclosure information for defendants, access that is considered a given right in most trials. Clearly, e-mails and texts from the accused killers and their associates were at the heart of the prosecution's case. It was understandable if Desjardins, Simpson and the other accused were struggling now to recall exactly what they said in those interminable strings of texts, when they thought they were operating under the cloak of RIM's vaunted privacy system and when they changed their cellphones fourteen times in one calendar year. Was there a traitor in that lengthy message string?

CHAPTER 46

Circle of corruption

> . . . fraud, because of man peculiar evil,
> To God is more displeasing
>
> *The Divine Comedy, Inferno,* **Canto IV**
> DANTE ALIGHIERI

Sixty-four-year-old construction executive Nicolò Milioto was already known by a nickname at the Charbonneau Commission before he took the witness stand. He was Mr. Sidewalk. His testimony followed that of Martin Dumont, a former Union Montréal party worker, who testified that he had once badly mispronounced Milioto's name and was told, "You can call me Mr. Sidewalk." Dumont told the commission that Milioto had an equally memorable response when questioned about why his cost estimate for a sidewalk project was $100,000 more than a competitor's estimate. "You know, Martin, my sidewalk foundations are thick and deep," Dumont recalled Milioto telling him. "You don't want to end up in my sidewalk foundations."

When it was Milioto's turn to testify, it was natural to ask why his construction firm always seemed to land contracts for sidewalk work. Milioto protested his innocence: "If people told you that it was rigged, I'm telling you it wasn't. . . . I never rigged a contract."

He met very often with people under suspicion for doing exactly that. Milioto was picked up by RCMP cameras visiting the Consenza Social Club 236 times in two years. He wasn't alone in doing so, as vehicles of some seventy-four companies involved in the construction trades, from electrical to landscaping to air conditioning to asphalt, were also seen in the "Coz" parking lot. Milioto provided precious little help in explaining what was happening in the grey RCMP videos, other than the elder Rizzuto stuffing wads of money into his socks. Milioto cast this in an innocent, even folksy light. "It was so the money would not be stolen, or fall out," Milioto offered. Milioto told the inquiry that he was in the dark about anyone in Canada paying protection money, or *pizzo*. "I come from Italy, madame, I know what a *pizzo* is." But in Canada? In Montreal's construction industry? "I'm not a member of organized crime," Milioto continued. "I was the owner of a construction company."

The very mention of Dumont's testimony incensed the retired construction boss. "I never told him my name is Mr. Sidewalk. And my name, 'Milioto,' is not complicated [to pronounce], even in French. . . . I swear to you, before God, that I don't know him. He's either mixing me up with someone else or he's a professional liar and more."

He did admit to having known Nicolò Rizzuto since his boyhood days in Cattolica Eraclea. In Canada, he knew Nicolò as a respectable man and a frequent card player, not a Mafia don. "For me, he was a family father. He was a good person," Milioto said. The Mafia stuff came from the media and was not something he'd experienced personally. "I knew what the newspapers said. That didn't affect me. . . . For me, he was a good person." He offered an innocent explanation for why he was often seen playing cards with Nicolò: his butcher shop was in the same plaza as the Café Consenza and he often wandered in for a hand or two of cards. What did they talk about during those frequent games? "We talked about cards."

In one of the videos shown to the commission, Milioto puts money in his socks and walks out of the room. He returns with Rocco Sollecito. Asked about the scene, Milioto said: "I see Sollecito. I call and ask him to return the money to Rizzuto, and my job was finished." He made it clear it wasn't his job to ask questions. He was also videotaped taking a wad of money himself, but said it was possible he was just going to buy Nicolò meat, bread and bottled water. "He was eighty years old and I had a lot of respect for him and I could have made him such services." Pressed further, he said it might also have been a loan of $20,000 to $25,000 for debts or for his house or for the wedding of one of his daughters. Who could remember such details?

Sonia LeBel, the chief prosecutor for the commission, pressed him about Sollecito. "How can you trust Mr. Sollecito to give money to Mr. Rizzuto?" LeBel asked.

"Between Italians, we trust," Milioto replied.

As for Vito, Milioto professed to be clueless about why he was in an American prison at the time the videos were shot. It wasn't his concern. What did concern him was respect. "You respect me, I respect you. You abuse me, I can abuse you." Pressed further, he appeared baffled by talk that the Mafia even existed. "I don't know, madam. What is the Mafia? People who shoot people? People who sell drugs?"

In his week on the witness stand, Milioto told the commission "I don't know" more than two hundred times. He still made a contribution to the pursuit of truth, in his estimation. "Me, I'm giving you my truth, my version of the truth," he said.

If Nicolò Milioto was Mr. Sidewalk, then municipal fundraiser Bernard Trépanier was Mr. Three Percent. A bagman for Montreal mayor Gérald Tremblay's Union Montréal party, Trépanier's nickname came from the amount he allegedly skimmed from municipal contracts in kickbacks for his party. His own role wasn't a clearly defined one, but he certainly wielded power. "I was a guy who opened doors," Trépanier testified. "I helped people get from point A to point B with my contacts." A self-confessed drinking problem and some memory challenges apparently made it difficult for him to explain as much as he might like. And there were indeed intriguing incidents for him to explain. Alexandra Pion, who had worked for Union Montréal as a receptionist, told the commission how she was asked—and refused—to help Trépanier tally up how much cash was in a full suitcase. Former party staff worker Martin Dumont testified about a time at a fundraiser when

Trépanier's coat was so stuffed with money that he couldn't button it up. Dumont also recalled the party's safe being so rammed full of cash that it couldn't be closed.

Six weeks before his turn on the witness stand, retired Montreal city engineer Gilles Surprenant filled a leather briefcase with $122,800 in kickback money and dropped it off with police. "I didn't want it anymore," he explained to the commission. "I wanted to get rid of the money because, as I said, I was always uneasy with the money. It was filled with bad memories."

While Trépanier was Mr. Three Percent in the city's corruption pecking order, Surprenant was Mr. One Percent, if you accepted the testimony of former construction boss Lino Zambito. In his testimony, Zambito said that Surprenant demanded a cut of 1 percent of the value of a contract for his bid-rigging services. Then another 2½ percent went to the Mafia and 3 percent to the Union Montréal party. Such were the unofficial taxes of working in Montreal, and these fees, high as they were, could be recouped by hiking up the cost of city contracts.

Surprenant told the commission of an odd personal problem. He had far more money than could be explained by his annual salary of $80,000 for his position as a city engineer in charge of planning and budgeting for public works. There were expensive leisure activities that didn't jive with his earnings, like $12,000 season tickets for the Montreal Canadiens and exotic southern golfing vacations. Aside for the money and gifts, he also had to deal with a guilty conscience, as he told things. He said he coped with his guilt by gambling heavily at the Montreal Casino. Losing some $300,000 there was apparently his way of pumping money back into the public purse.

Surprenant testified that he spoke openly about corruption to his superiors at work but didn't take any further action. He might be guilty of a lot of things, but insubordination was not one of them. "I didn't think it was my role, as a simple bureaucrat, to call the police."

This was a common refrain throughout the hearings: something was clearly wrong but somehow it wasn't really the fault of any one person. Certainly no one blamed it all on Vito or the late Nicolò. For his part, Surprenant pointed an accusing finger at Montreal's construction entrepreneurs for colluding to rig tenders on public ser-vice projects such as those to repair dozens of sewers and aqueducts. Yes, he did co-operate, and yes, he did pocket hundreds of thousands of dollars, but in the end, should he really be blamed? "I am not a vil-lain. I am a bureaucrat who was corrupted," Surprenant testified. "No one at the City of Montreal wanted a system like this."

In words that Martin Brett could have written for him, Surprenant added: "There was an established system and I was caught up in it." Corruption was "an open secret" at work, and one that no one seemed eager to stop. "There was no initiative from our superiors to correct the situation . . . and no initiative on the part of [Montreal's] executive com-mittee," Surprenant told the commission.

If Surprenant was indeed a victim, as he suggested, at least he was a well-compensated one. The commission heard that Surprenant pock-eted about $706,000 in kickbacks between 2000 and 2008, plus another $25,000 under the table between 1995 and 2000 in the form of golf vaca-tions, dinners, bottles of wine and other handouts from entrepreneurs.

In the end, Surprenant said he would never forgive himself for his role in the city's corruption. "I bitterly regret everything that happened," he told the commission. "I must say, for me, the past ten years at the City of Montreal have been catastrophic. It should have never existed. I should have never accepted those sums. I should have never done that."

Ken Pereira could have been forgiven if, for a time, he thought his boss was Jocelyn Dupuis, director-general of FTQ-Construction. With six hundred thousand members and billions of dollars' worth of invest-ments in its Solidarity Fund, the FTQ was Quebec's largest labour federation and a major player in the province's construction world. At the time of the inquiry, Quebec had a unionization rate of 39.9 percent, compared with 31.5 for Canada as a whole. The rate was 27 percent in Britain and 12 percent in the USA. That meant plenty of dues to collect and invest in Quebec.

The Charbonneau Commission heard of the aforementioned social links between Antonio Accurso, a former construction mogul facing tax evasion and corruption charges, and top FTQ officials such as Jean Lavalée, but also of links between Accurso and Vito Rizzuto. Accurso entertained union chums on his yacht and in private dining rooms of his restaurant, L'Onyx. L'Onyx even hosted FTQ-Construction's annual Christmas party.

The commission heard that Raynald Desjardins and the Hells Angels had clout in the FTQ between 2005 and 2008, when Vito was behind bars and Desjardins was back on the streets after his prison stretch. When a Chambly strip club owned by a Hells Angels associate burned down, it was rebuilt at no charge by FTQ-Construction. Jocelyn Dupuis, director-general of FTQ-Construction, ran up expenses that included $2,000 for meals in Las Vegas, a $300 breakfast and $30,000 for meals at one restaurant in a single month, Pereira told the commission. He had his suspicions that many expense receipts were fake. In his testimony before the Charbonneau Commission, Pereira said that Dupuis attended Hells Angels' wet T-shirt parties and socialized with Normand (Casper) Ouimet of the Hells Angels' Trois-Rivières chapter, before Ouimet was hit with twenty-two murder and money-laundering charges. Pereira also considered the 2008 elections for FTQ-Construction's executive to be rigged in favour of a Dupuis-backed candidate, and that a rival candidate quit the race after a show of force by the Hells Angels.

Pereira told the Charbonneau Commission that Dupuis wasn't shy about his rough connections. On Dupuis's wall was a photo of union organizer Giovanni Bertolo, the former drug trafficker for Vito's group and the victim of a gangland murder. "He [Dupuis] made it known that the FTQ was his family, but that he had another . . . the Hells or the Mafia," Pereira testified.

When Pereira became disenchanted with what he was seeing, he broke into an FTQ accountant's office and scooped up six months' worth of expenses filed by Dupuis. He said he was offered a Mercedes for his silence, but declined.

While Vito was in prison, Desjardins seemed to think he was the boss of FTQ-Construction. Perhaps this is what Desjardins meant when, upon his release from prison, he spoke of becoming a construction entrepreneur. Pereira spoke of meeting Desjardins at a brunch, with ten goons standing guard at the door. As he recalled before the commission, Desjardins told him: "Listen, Ken, I don't know if you know me, but I did eleven years in jail. I kept my mouth shut, I did my time and that's the way it should be."

Next, Pereira said, Desjardins addressed the obvious tensions between Pereira and Dupuis, saying that he could get Dupuis removed from his job. Desjardins was intent on ending the union infighting as "we've got more important business to do."

It was then, Pereira testified, that he felt a jolt of fear and clarity: "At that moment, I discovered that Jocelyn Dupuis, who I thought was the boss, wasn't the boss. Raynald Desjardins was the boss."

As the Charbonneau testimony ground on, Montreal imposed new ethics codes for city employees. The price of public contracts dipped and new players finally won bids for city work. Still, the construction world hardly seemed a safe place for innocents, and there was talk of intimidation taking the place of bribery.

Certainly, police and government couldn't be trusted to make things right. Confidence in policing dipped on October 5, 2013, with the arrest of Benoit Roberge, a retired Sûreté du Québec biker expert, after investigators learned he was selling highly confidential intelligence to bikers. Roberge wasn't just someone who had handled sensitive witness protection files. He was also married to a top organized crime prosecutor and went to work for Revenu Québec in March 2013. Police offices were scanned for hidden microphones. Computer databases and reports were studied to see who had been reading them. A senior SQ officer even voluntarily took a polygraph test to show that he wasn't an underworld mole.

Good cops fell under suspicion while bad cops remained in the shadows. A veteran Montreal police investigator who specialized in organized crime and who had cultivated a string of informants was quietly transferred away from his organized crime files and computers that could give him access to sensitive cases involving the *milieu*. That officer had been a witness against major crimes investigator Mario Lambert when Lambert was found guilty of funnelling information from police databases to criminals.

If authorities really wanted to stop corruption, they didn't have to study the actions just of Vito and his associates. They would have to take a harder look at themselves.

CHAPTER 47

Business of death

I f you must live in exile, there are far worse places than the resorts and warm sands of Acapulco, Mexico. For Moreno Gallo, there was also the comforting presence of many of his contacts in the Canadian mob. Most of the Ontario *camera di controllo* maintained businesses or vacation homes in Acapluco. Despite the resort town's warm charms and familiar faces, though, the millionaire baker still missed Montreal, and talked of plans to move north to rejoin his wife and sons. His desire to return raised eyebrows, as back home men considered disloyal to Vito were falling at a steady pace.

In Mexico, Gallo took frequent trips to the Forza Italia pizzeria in a tourist area near the beach on the Costera Miguel Alemán. The food and the coffee were to the baker's liking, and the owner was a friend. So it wasn't surprising that the exiled Mafioso was there on the evening of Sunday, November 10, 2013, looking casual in white pants and a pink polo shirt with white stripes. Forza Italia is an often-bustling place, although Sunday nights are calmer. No one paid much attention when a thin man in black entered around 9:40 p.m. Perhaps customers and staff thought he was reaching for his wallet when his hand moved towards his waistband.

Gallo sat near the entrance, so it took only a few strides before the thin man was directly behind him. He pumped nine shots from his nine-millimetre pistol into Gallo's back and head, ignoring the pan-icked customers and staff. Then the stranger disappeared quietly into the warm evening. There's no doubt that, back in Montreal, Vito was thinking of his father as Gallo lay freshly dead on the floor. It was three years minus a day since Nicolò was shot dead in front of Vito's sister and mother.

Vito's enemies kept dying as the Christmas season of 2013 approached. On the afternoon of Wednesday, December 18, someone took a break from the season's festivities to shoot Roger Valiquette to death beside his black Mercedes SUV, in the parking lot of a St-Hubert restaurant in the Chomedey district of Laval.

He was less than three kilometres from the office of his mortgage brokerage. Despite a criminal record for cocaine trafficking and active mob associations, Valiquette somehow still had a permit from the Office of Consumer Protection to loan money as an "alternative" lender. He also owned ATMs and was involved with Desjardins in the soil decontamination business.

At the time of his murder, Valiquette faced charges for death threats and assault with a firearm. He must have known he was in danger of not living to his trial date. His partner in real estate development was convicted cocaine trafficker Tonino Callocchia, who had survived five bullets in a similar murder attempt in another Laval restaurant parking lot on February 1. Valiquette had also been close to Joe Di Maulo and Moreno Gallo. All three men were enemies of Vito, and all three assas-sinations remained unsolved.

Just because Vito likely had reason to want Valiquette dead didn't mean that he ordered the hit. Valiquette had plenty of other enemies in the *milieu*. At the time of his murder, he was vying for control of the Rivière des Prairies territory in Montreal, which had previously been controlled by Ponytail De Vito. Remants of Ponytail's old group opposed Valiquette's push into their territory. The surest way to keep him out was to fill him with bullets.

Ponytail's name was back in the news that December, after the coroner's office finally completed its investigation into his death. That work had been delayed as coroner's office resources had been diverted to the fiery train derailment that took forty-seven lives in Lac-Mégantic in July. Ponytail's autopsy showed that he died from cyanide poisoning. How the lethal drug was smuggled into maximum-security Donnacona Institution remained a mystery, although Ponytail had orchestrated plots to smuggle drugs and cellphones into the Rivière des Prairies detention centre when he was an inmate there. It also wasn't clear if Ponytail's death was a murder or suicide.

It wouldn't have been the first time the mob turned to cyanide. Prolific New Jersey mob hit man Richard (The Iceman) Kuklinski claimed to have taken more than one hundred lives, sometimes with cyanide. Men like Kuklinski knew that the chemical compound quickly dissipated from a body and required an experienced and alert pathologist to detect it. A cup of coffee spiked with cyanide had been used to murder imprisoned financier Michele Sindona in 1986 in Italy. He was believed to be on the verge of exposing government ties to the Mafia and the Masonic Lodge, and exposing details of the murder of bank director Roberto Calvi under a London bridge, at the time he sipped from the fatal cup.

In the fourteen months since his return to Canada, Vito had clearly put revenge ahead of business. One man who met Vito in the Toronto area during the second half of 2013 remarked that he had the bullet eyes of a stone-cold killer. His work was far from over, as at least a half-dozen of his enemies were still believed to be targeted for death. This all-consuming lust for vengeance upset many of Vito's former associates, including influential people in the construction industry. The continuing scrutiny of the Charbonneau Commission meant that the mob had to scramble to regain contacts in industry and government. It was a job Vito could have handled, had he not been preoccupied with bloodletting on an epic scale. The *milieu* had never needed a clear mind for industry more than it did now, but the undisputed CEO of the Canadian underworld was suddenly bad for business.

CHAPTER 48

Home for Christmas

Surveillance officers trailed Vito at a discreet distance in the weeks leading up to Christmas 2013. He looked happy and younger than his sixty-seven years as he bounced from bar to restaurant to bar wishing old contacts the best of the season. Perhaps he had some special holiday surprise planned for his mother, wife, children and grandchildren. Maybe he was just happy to be alive.

Vito routinely returned home at 2 a.m. This was just as it had been in his younger days, when he held court in corner tables of the city's best bars and restaurants, accepting drinks as tributes until he was tipsy by the wee hours of the morning. All appeared well through the evening of Saturday, December 21, until Giovanna found him unconscious on the floor of their new home after midnight.

Vito was confused and feverish when rushed by his family to Sacré-Coeur hospital in the Cartierville district suffering from what appeared to be lung complications. It was the same hospital where his father had been treated just a few years ago while a prisoner at the Bordeaux Prison. The hospital was overbooked that night, but Vito was admitted without debate. Despite the hour, friends and family gathered to wish him well and there was a collective sigh of relief with news that Vito's health appeared to be improving. Then, just an hour later, as he lay in bed surrounded by family, Vito's heart stopped for good.

Hospital officials attributed death to natural causes, then refused to elaborate. Reports surfaced that he'd had aggressive lung cancer, most likely brought on by years of smoking, and that he had contracted pneumonia. Stories followed that he'd chosen to delay cancer treatments so that he could spend the holidays with his family.

Such was Vito's world that it was more puzzling that he died of reportedly natural causes than if he had been the victim of an assassin. There had been no rumours or signs of his declining health, as would be expected from cancer. If anything, he appeared robust, closing down restaurants and bars like a man decades younger. He also appeared to have gained weight when he returned from the Dominican Republic a month earlier.

Since Vito hadn't taken out a government health card, it was tough to chart his medical history. He did complain of a lung ailment when he was sentenced in New York back in 2007, but his medical checkup on his way back into Canada in 2012 didn't show any serious medical problems. It wouldn't have been too difficult to slip something into one of his many drinks, like the cyanide that ended Ponytail De Vito's life. But Vito's death would remain a mystery: within hours of his passing, it was announced that there would be no autopsy.

There were no tears in some quarters of southern Ontario. Believing that Vito had a list of at least another half-dozen enemies marked for death, one Woodbridge cannoli maker was said to have donned a bulletproof vest immediately after Vito's release from prison and then started taking extended vacations.

No obituary was written for the website of the Rizzuto-owned Complexe Funéraire Loreto in Saint-Léonard, but none was necessary. Hundreds lined up in the cold for his visitation, while others drove directly into the underground parking of the ultra-modern funeral facility. This convenience was appreciated by visitors who preferred to stay away from police and press cameras. Some guests arrived after regular visitation hours.

Greeting them all, and appearing very much the man in charge, was Rocco (Sauce) Sollecito. He had visited Ontario at least a half-dozen times in the months before Vito's death, so he was familiar with many of the out-of-province guests. Some respected him for his muscle, others for his business sense. Some of the mourners he welcomed arrived in a chartered bus, like the one used for Paolo Cuntrera's wedding anniversary in 2011.

Among those paying their respects was Rock Machine founder Salvatore Cazzetta, who was on parole for a massive cigarette-smuggling operation through the Kahnawake reserve. Cazzetta was now wearing a Hells Angels patch and was considered by many to be the top member of *les Hells* who wasn't behind bars. At fifty-six years of age, he looked every inch the old-school biker, with his mane of grey hair and arms full of tattoos. Also paying their respects were street-gang member Gregory Wooley, representatives from the New York mob and a group of men who arrived in a van with a Mohawk Warriors flag.

Other visitors included members of the old Cotroni family and the Ontario 'Ndrangheta. There was an impressive number of floral bouquets, including at least one bearing the word *Nonno* and another with *Farewell my friend*, but none was larger than the one sent by the Ontario Hells Angels.

The funeral was set for Église Notre-Dâme-de-la-Défense in Little Italy, the same historic church in which Vito's family held ceremonies for Nick Jr. and Nicolò, and which had been the site of so many funerals in the *milieu* before, including for the Violi brothers.

At the church doors, mourners in long black overcoats and furs were asked by security guards if they were friends of the family before they were allowed inside. Vito's ceremony was simple, with an organist, violinist, trumpet player and small operatic choir. Mass was conducted entirely in Italian, but there was no eulogy. Vito didn't feel the need to explain himself in life and no one from his inner circle felt the need to justify him now that he lay at the front of the room in a coffin. When there was doubt about what to say, silence had always remained the best option.

Among those standing outside, braving the bitterly cold, minus-twenty-five temperature and sharp wind, was a Montreal waiter who remembered Vito as a polite, if careful, customer. The waiter had known Vito for two decades and recalled how Vito had told him to watch that no one poisoned his food when dining out. Who could say if another waiter from another restaurant knew why Vito's health had suddenly spiralled in the final hours of his life? If one did, he stood to gain nothing by talking about it.

An hour later, bells tolled as they had for the Violis and so many others. Vito's body, Libertina and the remnants of his family were led from the church by greying men in matching black fedoras, a tribute to Vito's beloved father. Vito was escorted slowly to the St. Francis of Assisi cemetery, in a convoy of a dozen black limousines that had been parked on Dante Street.

POSTSCRIPT

There's a term in Italian—*staffetta*—that translates roughly to "passing the baton." It is natural to wonder if Vito had made plans to pass the baton to another or others in his group before his death. Even if he wasn't dying of cancer, he must have contemplated the possibility of his own murder.

Revenge was an all-consuming and sacred pursuit in the final year of his life. A short list of his next murder victims is believed to have included a long-time member of a street gang, a developer and an Ontario mobster with a long history of drug problems. Vito's death meant the new leadership of his group had the choice of picking up the baton and continuing the slaughter or moving on to rebuild after the damage done by Project Colisée and the Charbonneau Commission. Or would they choose a Canadian compromise, killing a few of his enemies as a nod to the old guard in the family and then turning to business?

Police surveillance officers were startled in early 2014 to see Vito's last *consigliere* Rocco Sollecito making the rounds with a fresh face in the *milieu*. This man has a clean criminal record but enjoyed a tight, affectionate tie to Vito. Sollecito seemed bent on introducing him to everyone who was anyone in his world. As he made the rounds with Sollecito, the man carried himself with the utmost seriousness, as one might expect from the new boss of a major crime family.

The quick decision not to hold an autopsy on Vito's body means the cause of his death will be forever a mystery. If Vito did indeed die of cancer, it was an odd strain of the disease as in recent weeks he looked as though he had put on a little weight and seemed full of energy. If he was murdered, it was likely poison dropped in a glass from a smiling well-wisher. If Ponytail De Vito could be poisoned in maximum-security

Donnacona penitentiary, then Vito could be drugged in a bustling public nightspot. Perhaps the killer even liked Vito, but chose business over blood. Perhaps the new boss already knows the answer to this riddle.

There were good reasons to fear Vito's revenge, even months after his death. In April 2014, Carmine Verduci of the Toronto 'Ndrangheta was shot dead in mid-afternoon outside a café in Vaughan. Verduci had been host of the *camera di controllo* meeting in his yellow brick home in Woodbridge on October 7, 2009, while Vito was in prison and his family was under siege in Montreal. "To me it's a huge message," a police officer specializing in organized crime said. "It's not over just because Vito's dead. . . . Certain people have to die before business gets done." On the evening of August 2, 2014, the body of gang leader Ducarme Joseph was found in the middle of a St. Michel district street. Someone had pumped multiple gunshots into the prime suspect in the murder of Vito's son, Nick Jr.

As this book goes to press, a half-dozen other men on Vito's hit list have not yet been murdered. They do not need this book to know they are fortunate to be alive.

CAST OF CHARACTERS

VITO RIZZUTO'S MONTREAL GROUP

Francesco (*Compare* Frank) Arcadi. Underboss in Rizzuto crime family.

Agostino (The Seigneur of Saint-Léonard) Cuntrera. Member of wealthy international money-laundering family.

Federico (Freddy) Del Peschio. Family friend of Rizzuto crime family.

Lorenzo (Skunk) Giordano. Tough senior member in Rizzuto crime family.

Mike Lapolla. Enforcer for Rizzuto crime family who was murdered March 10, 2005.

Domenico Macri. Murdered soldier in Rizzuto crime family and nephew of lieutenant Francesco Arcadi.

Paolo Renda. Trusted *consigliere*, cousin and brother-in-law of Vito Rizzuto.

Nicolò (Nick) Rizzuto Jr. Murdered eldest son of Vito Rizzuto.

Nicolò (Zio Cola, Uncle Nick) Rizzuto Sr. For decades he was the top Mafioso in Canada, before passing control to his only son, Vito.

Vito Rizzuto. Son of Nicolò Rizzuto and top figure in Canadian Mafia.

Rocco (Sauce) Sollecito. Member of Vito's inner circle. His son Stefano was part of Vito's expansion into Ontario in the early 2000s.

MONTREAL PLOTTERS AND ENEMIES OF VITO RIZZUTO

Giovanni (Johnny) Bertolo. Close associate of Raynald Desjardins, and murder victim.

Raynald Desjardins. One-time ally of Vito Rizzuto who broke ranks after serving a lengthy sentence for drug trafficking and sparked a bloody underworld war.

Giuseppe (Joe) Di Maulo. Brother-in-law of Raynald Desjardins and senior underworld figure.

Paolo Gervasi. Montreal strip club owner who was murdered on January 19, 2004. Vito Rizzuto was blamed for his killing.

Moreno Gallo. A millionaire baker who was once a member of Vito's group. He backed Salvatore Montagna of New York in his push to run the Montreal mob.

Lorenzo (Larry) Lo Presti. Neighbour of Vito Rizzuto and son of murdered Mafia lieutenant.

Vittorio (Victor) Mirarchi. Suspect in murder of New York City Mafia boss Salvatore Montagna.

Paolo Violi. Former head of the Cotroni crime family of Montreal, which for a time included Vito and Nicolò Rizzuto.

VITO RIZZUTO'S TORONTO GROUP

Juan Ramon (Joe Bravo) Fernandez. Former Toronto lieutenant for Vito Rizzuto.

Gaetano (Guy) Panepinto. Toronto lieutenant for Vito Rizzuto.

TORONTO 'NDRANGHETA

Antonio Coluccio. Brother of 'Ndrangheta members Giuseppe and Salvatore Coluccio. Told by federal government he is inadmissible to live in Canada.

Giuseppe Coluccio. Former Toronto resident said to be top member of international 'Ndrangheta crime family.

Salvatore Coluccio. Former Toronto resident said to be high-level 'Ndrangheta member.

SICILIAN MAFIA

Andrea Fortunato Carbone. Sicilian bodyguard for Michele Modica in Canada.

Pietro Scaduto. Sicilian companion of Michele Modica in Canada. Deported from Canada after 2004 shooting that paralyzed Louis Russo.

NEW YORKERS

Joe (Big Joey) Massino. Former head of the informer-infested Bonanno crime family of New York City.

Salvatore (Sal the Ironworker, The Bambino Boss) Montagna. Head of New York–based Bonanno crime family.

George (George from Canada) Sciascia. Associate of Vito Rizzuto who was murdered in New York City at behest of Big Joey Massino.

ASSORTED BIKERS

Maurice (Mom) Boucher. One-time leader of the Hells Angels' Nomads chapter in Montreal, he was serving two life terms for murder by the time Vito Rizzuto was extradited to the USA.

Salvatore Cazzetta. Founder of the Rock Machine, which warred with the Hells Angels in the late 1990s and early 2000s. He was close to Boucher in the early 1980s, when they both were members of the SS gang.

ENDNOTES

CHAPTER 1: BLOW TO THE HEART

An American prison source told of Vito's moods when getting the news of his son's death.

Sicilian Mafia boss Tommaso Buscetta spoke with the RCMP in 1987 about his time in Canada. We were able to obtain a copy of this report, which provided his assessment of why Nicolò was admitted to the Mafia.

Vito's top spot in Canadian organized crime was outlined in a secret report to the Minister of Justice and Solicitor General of Canada dated February 1996 and entitled *Présentation au Ministre de la Justice et au Solliciteur Général du Canada*.

An excellent overview of Vito's financial situation was: Tax Court of Canada, Invoice number: A-238-2003, February 12, 2003, Tax Court of Canada, Appellant: Vito Rizzuto.

Financially, there's also *Cour Canadienne de L'Impôt, entre M. Vito Rizzuto et Sa Majesté La Reine*, September 14, 1998.

One of the few times Vito testified in court was at the 1995 trial of Valentino Morielli, in which he said he played more than one hundred times a year. Vito also spoke of playing in charity golf tournaments with other mobsters, including Vincenzo Di Maulo. Morielli was an old school chum of Vito's involved in major-league drug importing and money laundering. He died of natural causes in January 2014.

CHAPTER 2: NICK JR. AND NICOLÒ

"Records show Mob boss worked on Expo 67, city parks," by Linda Gyulai, Montreal *Gazette* civic affairs reporter, January 30, 2014, gives an excellent look at Nicolò's early business interests. Gyulai went through the city archives to write a series of stories that also appeared on January 31, 2014. She led the way in reporting on Rizzuto ties to city works in the 1950s, 1960s and 1970s especially.

Oreste Pagano's voluminous statements to Canadian police told us of the wedding of Nick Rizzuto Jr. They include: "Transcripts, Project Omerta, July 8, September 21, November 18, 1999"; Emanuele Ragusa's parole files helped explain his situation.

Confidential police sources helped as well.

For Project Colisée, Annexe C2, 2002-UMECO-3438 helped with financial records and key conversations from transcripts.

A particularly useful report is Tom Blickman's *The Rothschilds of the Mafia on Aruba*, published by Transnational Institute (http://www.tni.org), Transnational Organized Crime, vol. 3, no. 2, summer 1997. It deals with the complicated rise of the Cuntrera–Caruanas and the importance of *Rapporto giudiziario a carico di Bono Giuseppe + 159*, issued by the Questura di Roma on February 7, 1983.

The Scotto trial was spared prosecution because of the statute of limitations.

CHAPTER 3: EL PADRINO

Buscetta's 1987 interview with the RCMP helped again here.

A police report states that Antonino Manno emigrated to Canada with the help of a federal politician, but it does not identify who that politician was.

CHAPTER 4: GOING TO WAR

Like Vito and Violi, Mammoliti betrayed no shame about his lifestyle. He lived openly after breaking out of prison in 1972, to the point that he married his fourteen-year-old girlfriend at the Santa Maria Assunta church in Castellace di Oppido Mamertina on August 23, 1975. The church was a short walk from a police station, but that didn't deter Mammoliti, who needed the church's large hall for his many guests. The wedding was celebrated by the priest and Violi's relative, Don Serafino Violi.

Aruba called "Mafia Island" by *Corriere della Sera* on March 4, 1993, and "the first state to be bought by the bosses of Cosa Nostra."

Again, we were aided by insights from Linda Gyulai, Montreal *Gazette* civic affairs reporter. In works cited in chapter 2 endnotes, Nicolò Rizzuto's daughter, Maria Renda, represented the brothers Paolo and Gaspare Cuntrera in 1983, when the brothers lived in Caracas, Venezuela, and the city wanted to expropriate 9,040 square feet of land they and their brother Pasquale owned in Rivière des Prairies. City officials had lost touch with the Cuntreras, and so ads were taken out in the Montreal *Gazette* and *Le Devoir* to inform them of the city's intentions. It was an odd dance, as Italian authorities sought to locate the Cuntrera brothers to extradite them on drug and money-laundering charges, while Venezuelan officials said they didn't know where to find them, even though they were living in the South American country. Meanwhile, Montreal city officials negotiated with them on the expropriation through Maria Renda.

The *Quebec Official Gazette* for Saturday, December 7, 1968, notes: "Notice is hereby given that under the first part of the Companies Act, the Lieutenant Governor dc province granted islands letters patent, dated 17th day of October 1968 to incorporate: Robert Papalia, Antonio Papalia, both businessmen, 7347 Papineau Avenue, and Vincenzo Messina, tailor, 750, Iberville Street, all three of Montreal, for the following purposes: Operate and administer nightclubs, restaurants, bars, night clubs, record companies and other entertainment and shopping as well as performances and musical and dramatic performances, under the name 'The New Cheetah Club 69 Ltd.' With a total capital of $40,000, divided into 1,000 ordinary shares of a par value of $10 each and 3,000 preferred shares of a par value of $10 each. The registered office of the company is Montreal, judicial district of Montreal. The Deputy Minister of Financial Institutions, companies and cooperatives, Ls- Philippe Bouchard. 27067 4838-68."

CHAPTER 5: INVISIBLE ENEMY
Moreno Gallo's parole records were particularly useful. They are: Immigration and Refugee Board of Canada, Immigration Division, N° *de dossier de la* SI / ID File No.: 0018-A8-01482, Record of Proceedings,

The Minister of Public Safety and Emergency Preparedness and Moreno Gallo, February 12, 2009, Montreal.

CHAPTER 6: DANGEROUS NEW ASSOCIATES

Confidential police reports were of great use.

Radio-Canada's *Enquête* team broke the story of the 1000 de la Commune residents. Their investigative work on corruption in the construction industry was truly excellent. The tape of Vito's conversation with Tony Magi was played at the Charbonneau Commission in March 2014.

CHAPTER 7: GANGS

Richard Ogilvie's deportation file was useful.

CHAPTER 8: BLOOD TRAIL

Police and parole files on Giovanni Cazzetta were of great help.

There's also: *R. v. Cazzetta*, 2003 CanLII 39827 (QC CA).

Few people understand the complicated world of Quebec outlaw bikers better than Paul Cherry, author of *The Biker Trials: Bringing Down the Hells Angels*, ECW Press, Toronto, 2005.

CHAPTER 9: UNRAVELLING

Police sources told of Vito's reaction.

Michele Modica's was dealt with in the cases against Peter Scarcella et al. in the Louise Russo shooting.

Sources helped put Salvatore Calautti's background into perspective, as did confidential police files.

Parole hearing records for Annie Arbic and Sharon Simon helped.

As this book goes to press, Sergio Piccirilli and his co-accused Antal Babos have been granted a new trial by the Supreme Court of Canada on twenty-two offences related to firearms and the production and trafficking of methamphetamines.

CHAPTER 10: UNDECLARED WAR

Author Peter Edwards toured the Streit plant north of Toronto.

CHAPTER 11: PONYTAIL'S NIGHTMARE

Former Rock Machine member Normand Brisebois told of how Nicolò and Vito Rizzuto would visit Cabaret Castel Tina.

CHAPTER 12: WHO'S NEXT?

Italian prosecutor Nicola Gratteri helped with perspective.

Police sources helped with Vittorio Mirarchi.

For Vito's case in the Three Captains Murders, there was: United States District Court Eastern District of New York, United States of America against Vito Rizzuto, CR 03-1382(S-1), May 4, 2007, before the Honorable Nicholas G. Garaufis, United States District Judge.

CHAPTER 13: FOREIGN SHORE

We have copies of Vito Rizzuto Sr.'s citizenship papers from November 5, 1931, and Calogero Renda's travel papers from Palermo, Sicily.

We also drew from Vito Rizzuto Sr.'s immigration files, obtained from the US Department of Homeland Security.

Carmine Galante's FBI file helped with his Montreal connection.

Paterson, NJ, is the birthplace of Joe Pistone, the FBI agent who infiltrated the Bonanno crime family and rocked the world of Vito Sr.'s grandson, Vito Jr.

There were a couple of explanations of why town fathers added a *t* to their community's name. One theory was that a founding member of the community simply didn't care about spelling. The other possibility is that the extra *t* was added to avoid confusion with their larger, better-known counterpart. Whatever the case, it was a tiny, out-of-the-way place, perfect for lying low.

The history of the New York City Mafia is dealt with exhaustively by Selwyn Raab in *Five Families: The Rise, Decline, and Resurgence of America's Most Powerful Mafia Empires*, Thomas Dunne Books, St. Martin's Press, New York, 2005.

Italian sources and archives helped with the Rizzuto family history.

The *Binghamton Press, Brooklyn Daily Eagle, Pawling Chronicle, Pawling-Patterson News, Putnam County Courier* and *Rome Daily Sentinel* helped with Vito Sr.'s murder and the fate of his killers, as did "Supreme Court:

Putnam County, November 4, 1933, The People of the State of New York Against Stephano Spinello, Rosario Arcuro and Max L. Simon. Indictment for Murder, first degree."

Author Antonio Nicaso interviewed Liborio Spagnolo in Sicily about Nicolò Rizzuto

CHAPTER 14: ADMINISTRATIVE MEETING

Vito Rizzuto's May 2007 sentencing report was useful here.

A confidential police report helped with the wedding of Giuseppe Bono.

Vito's extradition for the Three Captains Murders is dealt with in "United States v. Vito Rizzuto, Criminal No. 03-1382 (NGG), Legal Statement in Support of Request for Extradition of Vito Rizzuto, Nicholas Bourtin, Assistant United States Attorney, Eastern District of New York."

CHAPTER 15: NORTHERN AIM

Police sources helped us with the movements of Salvatore Montagna in Canada.

CHAPTER 16: FRIENDS LIKE THESE

Police sources told us of Salvatore Montagna's time in Canada.

Giacomo Luppino died of natural causes in Hamilton, Ontario, in July 1983.

The video for "Blue Magic" from Jay-Z's 2007 album *American Gangster* featured a drug dealer opening up a suitcase full of €500 bills.

Various confidential police sources told of the 'Ndrangheta in Canada.

In 1998, Oreste Pagano, an informer from the Cuntrera–Caruana group, described a myriad of relationships in the underworld for Ontario authorities. He left no doubt about whom he considered the most powerful Canadian Mafioso. "Vito Rizzuto is the head of the Mafia in Canada," he told authorities after becoming a police agent. Then he added: "When you enter the Mafia, you get out in two ways. Either the way I'm doing it . . . or in a casket."

CHAPTER 17: CLEARING SPACE

Author Peter Edwards spoke with hit man Kenneth Murdock.

Police sources told of Salvatore (Sam) Calautti's troubles and relationship with Gaetano (Guy) Panepinto.

CHAPTER 18: MAN IN THE SHADOWS

Police reports and sources told of Vito Rizzuto's time in Toronto.

Stefano (Steve) Sollecito's parole records also noted his Ontario connection.

Carmelo Bruzzese's deportation hearings in Toronto in 2013 and 2014 gave background on the 'Ndrangheta in Canada and Italy.

Italian court records dealt with Bruzzese's relationship with Vito Rizzuto. They are: Immigration and Refugee Board, Immigration Division, Record of a Detention Review held under the Immigration and Refugee Protection Act, concerning, Carmelo Bruzzese, hearing: Public, September 16, 2013 before Kiris Kohler, Presiding Member.

From Italy, there's: "Procura Generale Della Repubblica, presso la Corte d'Appello di Roma Oggetto: BRUZZESE, Carmelo, 14 AGO 2008."

Also from Italy, there's: "Repubblica Italiana, Tribunale di Roma, Il Giudice dell'udienza preliminare, 19-12-2008, Sentenza a carico di Mariano Turrisi, Carmelo Bruzzese, Felice Italiano."

At a meeting in the early 2000s, Vito's men and local mobsters talked of how crystal meth was a scourge in Vancouver and Toronto. Vito and the others wanted nothing to do with the drug. It wasn't because it was devastating for users, quickly creating physical and psychological dependency. The problem was a purely business one: crystal meth dragged down the price of cocaine on the streets, as it retailed for half the price.

CHAPTER 19: STEEL BRACELETS

Author Peter Edwards attended Juan Ramon Fernandez's court case in Newmarket, Ontario.

Confidential police reports dealt with the Coluccio brothers' time in Canada.

CHAPTER 20: *LUPARA BIANCA*

Paolo Renda's parole records were useful here.

An American prison source told of Vito Rizzuto's reaction to the death.

CHAPTER 21: HOME FIRE

Nicolò's tax records were of great use here.

Libertina Rizzuto's troubles in Lugano, Switzerland, are dealt with in a Swiss justice department report entitled *Il Procuratore Pubblico della Repubblica e Cantone del Ticino aux autorités judiciaires compétentes du Canada,* dated December 16, 1994.

An RCMP investigation that was launched in 2006 led to the firing of nine employees from the Montreal office. Criminal charges were laid against six of them, amidst allegations of kickbacks, bribes and other unsavoury links to the Rizzuto crime family.

CHAPTER 22: RELUCTANT MOB BOSS

Author Peter Edwards visited Vic (The Egg) Cotroni's old home in Lavaltrie, Quebec.

Police reports and sources dealt with Alfonso Caruana's wedding in Toronto in April 1995.

Normand (Casper) Ouimet was originally charged with twenty-two counts of murder but pleaded guilty in March 2014 to the lesser charge of conspiracy to commit murder.

CHAPTER 23: HOME FRONT

Author Peter Edwards visited Antoine-Berthelet Avenue.

A prison source told of Vito's reaction to his father's death.

Sources and reports dealt with Nick Cortese's arrest. His parole records were also of use.

A police source told of the box left outside the church before the funeral.

CHAPTER 24: TALE OF BETRAYAL

A police report and sources told of the funeral of Cosimo Stalteri and the Cuntrera anniversary celebrations.

CHAPTER 25: OUTLAW IN-LAWS

Author Peter Edwards interviewed mobster Joe Di Maulo.

Police reports told of Di Maulo's golfing relationship with Vito Rizzuto.

Raynald Desjardins's parole records also helped us.

CHAPTER 26: FAULT LINES

Police reports and sources told of Giuseppe (Joe) Lo Presti.

CHAPTER 27: TIME FOR TIMS

Sources who cannot be named were of great help here.

In the days after the failed shooting of Desjardins, one of Arcuri's relatives had phoned to taunt him. The relative said he knew Arcuri's group was behind the failed attack on Desjardins and he was going to miss him. To make things worse, the verbal jab was on the phone, which was much easier to intercept than an encrypted text message. Was Arcuri's relative so cruel he wanted police to listen in?

CHAPTER 28: THE HUNT FOR MICKEY MOUSE

Again, sources who cannot be named were of great help here.

Moreno Gallo's parole records were also of use.

When Gallo had spoken of the Angelo Facchino murder to the parole board, he had tried to package as a public service of sorts shooting the Dubois clan associate three times on Saint-Denis Street. They didn't buy it. "The victim was apparently a drug dealer dealing drugs in your younger sister's school," a parole board detention review hearing stated. "You had warned the person to stop but he had continued. You say that it was self-defense. . . . However, you had a Beretta .9 mm pistol and an accomplice."

CHAPTER 29: MICKEY'S BAD DAY

Again, sources who cannot be named were of great help here.

CHAPTER 30: SOMEONE'S WATCHING

Yet again, sources who cannot be named were of great help here.

CHAPTER 31: HOMEWARD BOUND

Moreno Gallo's deportation hearing records helped us here.

CHAPTER 32: VITO'S RETURN

Author Antonio Nicaso interviewed Giuseppe Spagnolo's son, Liborio, in Sicily.

Author Peter Edwards was part of the media horde awaiting Vito Rizzuto's return to Toronto on October 5, 2012, at Pearson International Airport.

Vito Rizzuto was related to his wife, Giovanna, by blood as well as by marriage, since his mother and wife are first cousins. Vito Rizzuto was also related to his father-in-law, the late Leonardo Cammalleri, by blood and marriage. Leonardo Cammalleri was the brother of Vito's maternal grandmother, Giuseppa Cammalleri Manno, making him also Vito's great-uncle.

CHAPTER 33: OLD HAUNTS

Police sources and Peter Scarcella's parole records were of use here.

CHAPTER 34: THE OTHER MEDIATOR

Police sources and Daniel Renaud's work in La Presse helped us. Renaud is consistently one of the top reporters covering organized crime in Quebec and he graciously recounted his interview with Di Maulo. The interview was not for publication at the time and Renaud wrote of it after Di Maulo's death.

Thanks to Linda Gyulai of the Montreal *Gazette* for the report from the Broward Sheriff's Office.

CHAPTER 35: FRIENDS IN HIGH PLACES

Hot Freeze by Martin Brett helped here.

CHAPTER 36: GREASY POCKETS

The Montreal *Gazette* report cited in chapter 2 was of use again. Since the Charbonneau Commission only goes back fifteen years, this investigative report is particularly important for anyone hoping to understand the roots of the current corruption problem in Quebec construction.

CHAPTER 37: TRUSTED FEW

Rapporto giudiziario a carico di Bono Giuseppe + 159, issued by the Questura di Roma on February 7, 1983, states that Antonino (Don Nino) Manno was forced by police to leave Cattolica Eraclea and lived in another part of Italy for a time because he was considered to be in the Mafia and dangerous, in a process known as *soggiorno obbligato,* or internal banishment.

Domenico Manno's court and immigration files helped here.

There was: "United States Court of Appeals for the Eleventh circuit, June 23, 205, Thomas K. Kahn clerk, Domenico Manno versus United States of America, Appeal from the United States District Court for the Southern District of Florida"; "United States Court of Appeals, Eleventh Circuit, Atlanta, Georgia, August 15, 2005, Clarence Maddox, clerk, Appeal Number: 04-16329-DD, Case Style: Domenico Manno v. USA, District Court Number: 04-60424 CV-JAG."

For Divito, there's: "U.S. District Court, Middle District of Florida (Tampa), Criminal Docket for Case #: 8:94-cr-00169-RAL-4, Case title: USA v. Dubois, et al, Date Filed: 08/12/1994; Date Terminated: 03/13/2006, Judge Richard A Lazzara, Defendant, Pierino Divito."

CHAPTER 38: BFF

Police files and sources told of Vito's 2005 trip to Casa de Campo. There's some debate about why those tapes were never used in court. One theory is that the quality was poor. Another theory is that they were simply forgotten somewhere in storage. Odd as it sounds, the tapes made by Robert Menard of Paolo Violi's old ice cream shop were forgotten for years before they were properly analyzed.

CHAPTER 39: PUBLIC SPOTLIGHT

La Presse and the Montreal *Gazette* were our best sources here.

CHAPTER 40: NON-STOP HITS

Moreno Gallo's immigration file and parole files helped us here.

A police source told of Gallo's difficulties in Ontario with mob gambling operations.

In March 2013, former RCMP translator Angelo Cecere pleaded guilty to breach of trust and disclosing private communications. The plea was for removing sensitive RCMP documents from the force's C Division headquarters, on Dorchester Boulevard, to his home and then passing them on to Nicolas Di Marco, who had helped run an illegal casino in Saint-Léonard for Nick (The Ritz) Rizzuto Jr. The documents were removed between 1993 and 2007, until the force was finally tipped off by an undisclosed source that they had a security leak among their employees.

When sentencing Cecere to jail for a year, Court of Quebec judge Gilles Cadieux didn't accept a defence argument that jail would be unduly harsh as it meant Cecere would lose the services of his guide dog. Prosecutor Lyne Décarie wasn't so sure it was a real guide dog anyway, noting that it hadn't been trained by a recognized association for the blind.

In July, the blind mole applied for parole. He told the Quebec parole board that he helped out the mob at a time when half of his salary had been swallowed up by his divorce and he was under the influence of antidepressants. He had hoped to get at least $250,000 from the Mafia for the information. Commissioners Celine Chamberland and John Dugré also heard that he had been held in the jail infirmary after bullying from other inmates who wanted him to help with their legal forms and correspondence. The commissioners praised his candour and then turned down his bid for parole. Justice might often be blind, but crime could be too.

CHAPTER 41: TRIANGLE OF DEATH

Italian court and police records helped here.

The hit man who detonated the explosives that killed Giovanni Falcone was Giovanni (U Verru, The Pig) Brusca (born May 20, 1957, in San Giuseppe Jato), the son of Bernardo Brusca. Both men committed multiple homicides. Nicolò Rizzuto appeared in a Rome police report called *Rapporto giudiziario a carico di Bono Giuseppe + 159*, issued by the Questura di Roma on February 7, 1983. The report dealt with suspects believed to be involved in the "French Connection" heroin network, in which heroin was refined in Marseilles, France, and then smuggled to North America. Vito Rizzuto was on the list of 160 suspects, along with his friend Gerlando (George from Canada) Sciascia.

Another man on the list, Tommaso Buscetta (1928–2000), later became widely known as the first important member of the Sicilian Mafia to co-operate with authorities and break the code of silence, or *omertà*.

Yet another member of the list was Vittorio Mangano. He was a member of the Sicilian Mafia as well as the stable keeper at Silvio Berlusconi's villa in the 1970s. Berlusconi went on to become Italian prime minister while Mangano became known as *lo stalliere di Arcore*, "the stable keeper of Arcore."

In the 1959 investigation, Nicolò Rizzuto is portrayed by police as taking part in a revitalization of the old French Connection network. The network also includes Michele Zaza and his smuggling associates in the Camorra crime group of Naples. Later it would be concluded that the Cuntrera–Caruanas were also involved, washing money with hotels and other related businesses in Caracas, Venezuela, and Valencia, Spain.

CHAPTER 42: MAN IN THE MIDDLE
Italian court and police records formed the basis for this chapter.

CHAPTER 43: SEVERAL CHURCHES
Italian court and police records again guided us.

CHAPTER 44: HIT MAN GETS HIT
Police sources told of Vito's movements.

CHAPTER 45: UNHOLY TRINITY
Author Peter Edwards checked out the exterior of the King City home where Vito Rizzuto often stayed.

CHAPTER 46: CIRCLE OF CORRUPTION

A source with knowledge of the Montreal police told of their security problems, including in the IT department.

Paul Cherry's January 29, 2014, story in the Montreal *Gazette* entitled ORGANIZED CRIME OFFICER UNDER INVESTIGATION IS ASSIGNED TO LESS IMPORTANT DUTIES was useful. Cherry is consistently one of Quebec's top organized crime reporters, for both the Mafia and outlaw bikers.

On March 13, 2014, Benoit Roberge, fifty, pleaded guilty in court to participating in the activities of a criminal organization and breach of trust before Court of Quebec judge Robert Marchi. Court heard he made some $115,000 selling information to René (Balloune) Charlebois of the Hells Angels. Charlebois had been convicted of killing a police informant in 2000. Charlebois escaped from prison in September 2013. Just before his escape, he telephoned Roberge and told him he had made recordings of previous conversations between them. At that point, Roberge had retired from police work and was working for Revenu Québec. Charlebois had initially hoped to blackmail his way into regaining his old drug-trafficking network. Instead, he killed himself in a chalet on Île Guèvremont in Sorel on September 25, 2013. One of his associates helped police in their sting operation against Roberge, who was arrested trying to buy back the recordings. In court, Roberge portrayed himself as the victim of a deadly threat from Charlebois. "Your Honour, my life has been destroyed," Roberge said. "The fight begins today for the good of my family, which has suffered enormously. And I want to offer my apologies to the society I served for twenty-eight years at the risk and peril of my life and that of my family. I take the entire responsibility for my acts which were done under the influence of a threat toward [a relative whose name cannot be published because of a court-ordered ban] by René Charlebois.

"[My] message to other police officers is that if you find yourself in the torment and the constraints, ask for help and advice to find the best solution."

CHAPTER 47: BUSINESS OF DEATH

Police sources told of Gallo's troubles with gambling operations.

Tonino Callocchia was sentenced in 1998 to ten years in prison for importing cocaine through Toronto's Pearson International Airport.

There's a plaque in the basement of the Loreto Funeral Home with a sign "Dal 01 novembre 2012 al 31 ottobre 2013" to commemorate people who had funerals out of the home between those dates. In the third column, four names from the top, is an intriguing entry; "De Vito Giuseppe." Did Ponytail make some kind of peace with Vito's family at the very end of his life? Or did the Rizzuto family make some sort of peace with De Vito's family?

CHAPTER 48: HOME FOR CHRISTMAS

Police and government sources told of Vito Rizzuto's movements and health.

POSTSCRIPT

Among the mourners at Verduci's funeral was a GTA construction company owner who's also a major new mob boss. He came to York Region from Iran via Italy, and seems connected to most of the key players in Vito's old world.

ACKNOWLEDGEMENTS

As always, there are plenty of people to thank.

Elizabeth Kribs came up with the original idea. Agent Daphne Hart of the Helen Heller Agency found it a good home with Craig Pyette and Anne Collins of Random House Canada, who provided their usual intelligent and positive editing and support.

From Italy, there were Carabinieri colonels Fabio Bottino and Sergio Schiavone, and prosecutor Nicola Gratteri.

Other thanks must go to Mike Amato, Luciano Bentenuto, Denis Castelli, Tony Cianciotta, Calogero Giuffrida, Emmanuel Marchand, Donato Santeramo and Antonio Vitti.

Also, there was unselfish and cheerful support from Daniel Renaud of *La Presse* and Linda Gyulai of the Montreal *Gazette*.

There are also some valued sources who should know we appreciate them but who cannot be thanked publicly for professional or personal reasons.

INDEX

P eter Edwards has written for the *Toronto Star* for over twenty-five years, specializing in organized crime and justice issues. He is the author of twelve non-fiction books, including *The Bandido Massacre: A True Story of Bikers, Brotherhood and Betrayal*; *One Dead Indian: The Premier, the Police and the Ipperwash Crisis*; *A Mother's Story: The Fight to Free My Son David* (with Joyce Milgaard); and *Unrepentant: The Strange and (sometimes) Terrible Life of Lorne Campbell, Satan's Choice and Hells Angel Biker*. Edwards has been awarded an eagle feather from the Union of Ontario Indians and a gold medal from the Centre for Human Rights.

A ntonio Nicaso is a bestselling author of twenty-seven books on organized crime, a regular consultant to governments and law-enforcement agencies, a keynote speaker at symposia around the world and a lecturer at several universities. He teaches post-graduate courses on the history of organized crime at the Italian School of Middlebury College at Mills (California). In Italy, Nicaso has co-authored nine bestselling books.